THE WILD HORSES OF THE CHILCOTIN

These two wild stallions from the Highland Valley–Logan Lake area are descendants of the horses introduced to the BC interior by Indigenous people in the early to mid-1600s. Of the tens of thousands of wild horses that once flourished here, only about 3,000 survive today. *Image courtesy of Prescott Patterson.*

THE WILD HORSES OF THE CHILCOTIN

THEIR HISTORY AND FUTURE

Wayne McCrory

HARBOUR PUBLISHING

1 2 3 4 5—27 26 25 24 23

HARBOUR PUBLISHING CO. LTD.
P.O. Box 219, Madeira Park, BC, V0N 2H0
www.harbourpublishing.com

EDITED by Maggie Paquet and Lynne Van Luven
TŜILHQOT'IN EDITOR: Alice William
INDEXED by Colleen Bidner
TEXT AND JACKET DESIGN by Libris Simas Ferraz/Onça Publishing
PRINTED AND BOUND in Canada

Canada | Canada Council for the Arts | Conseil des arts du Canada | British Columbia Arts Council | British Columbia

HARBOUR PUBLISHING acknowledges the support of the Canada Council for the Arts, the Government of Canada, and the Province of British Columbia through the BC Arts Council.

LIBRARY AND ARCHIVES CANADA CATALOGUING IN PUBLICATION
Title: The wild horses of the Chilcotin : their history and future / Wayne McCrory.
Names: McCrory, Wayne, author.
Description: Includes bibliographical references and index.
Identifiers: Canadiana (print) 20230509738 | Canadiana (ebook) 20230509762 | ISBN 9781990776366 (hardcover) | ISBN 9781990776373 (EPUB)
Subjects: LCSH: Wild horses—British Columbia—Chilcotin Plateau Region. | LCSH: Wild horses—British Columbia—Chilcotin Plateau Region—History. | LCSH: Wild horses—Ecology—British Columbia—Chilcotin Plateau Region. | LCSH: Wild horses—Conservation—British Columbia—Chilcotin Plateau Region. | LCSH: Wildlife management—British Columbia—Chilcotin Plateau Region.
Classification: LCC SF360.3.C3 M33 2023 | DDC 599.665/50971175—dc23

THIS BOOK IS DEDICATED to the Xeni Gwet'in Tŝilhqot'in Nation, whose members taught me about their wild horses and showed me the way, for their protection of the wild horse in creating western Canada's first wild-horse preserve, the first of its kind in North America.

In addition, I dedicate this book to Lorna Visser, my wife and long-time fellow conservation activist. Without her love, support, patience and good-natured forbearance of my many quirks, this book never would have been born or finished. I know she often felt like a "wild-horse widow" when I was lost in reviewing a seemingly endless stream of background documents, books, explorer journals, and scientific publications on wild horses. I was often lost to her, lost in my mind, calcifying memories that I wanted to capture; lost in front of my computer, writing sections of this book; or literally lost in the field on my numerous trips to the Chilcotin wild-horse country. After surviving cranky grizzly bears, crossing raging rivers and creeks, fleeing from forest fires, being charged by a band of wild horses, getting a severe burn, and camping in life-threatening cold, it was always a joy and a relief to come home to my lovely wife and our safe, warm, beautiful home.

TABLE OF CONTENTS

PROFESSIONAL QUALIFIER

The author is a consulting wildlife biologist and registered professional biologist in the province of British Columbia with over fifty years of research experience in wildlife and ecology, and twenty years of research experience in the field of wild horses. He has produced over eighty scientific reports, including some published in peer-reviewed journals. This includes participation in several papers published on wild horses. In writing this book, the author has gone to great lengths to fact-check information from published and unpublished reports, historical documents, anecdotal accounts, books, interviews, and Tŝilhqot'in published and oral history and cultural heritage related to the horse. He has drawn upon his extensive notes of field surveys and interviews. He also consulted a number of knowledgeable Tŝilhqot'in, including working closely with Tŝilhqot'in elders, wildlife researchers and knowledge keepers to assist with research and fact-checking. Fact-checking has also been conducted by another practising biologist. In some cases, the author has had to rely on his own professional judgement where factual or anecdotal information was confusing or contradictory. Any errors and omissions in the materials in this book are the responsibility of the author. While this book is an accurate and authoritative treatment of the subject matter, no liability is assumed with respect to the use and application by others of the information it contains.

FOREWORD

The magnificent and sacred wild horse/qiyus (cayuse) is an important part of our lives as Tŝilhqot'in people of the Xeni/Tŝilhqot'in Nation. To protect our existence, we must also protect our wild horses and our rights to work with them. To protect them means never to break the spirit of the wild heart.

As recognized in the BC Supreme Court's William case, the Tŝilhqot'in Aboriginal Right to capture and use the wild horse for work or transportation was a first-ever Aboriginal Right recognized. To protect the horse, its habitat must also be protected in order to ensure its healthy survival into the future. This is part of our obligation to, and intricate connection with, Mother Earth and future generations.

It was not a difficult path over these past decades to work with world-renowned and highly respected Canadian biologist Wayne McCrory and cooperate in his research of wild horses, grizzly bears and their habitats throughout Xeni Gwet'in territory.

In this book, Wayne takes you into the secret world of our Tŝilhqot'in people's wild horses, what we call qiyus or cayuse. Wayne first came into our sacred ancestral homeland in 2001 to study grizzly bears to help our people stop an invasion of our territory by massive clear-cut logging. He found himself in a wild-horse ecosystem for the first time. Initially conflicted by his anti–feral horse sentiments, through science, dreams, talking to our elders, and direct experiences of the wilderness and beauty of qiyus, Wayne was able to discover they are not terrible alien animals overgrazing and overpopulating our native grasslands.

Based on his scientific report, our People established North America's largest wild-horse preserve. We have continued to keep out logging and mining. Through our successful Supreme Court of BC and

Marilyn Baptiste. *Image courtesy of Goldman Environmental Prize.*

Canada Rights & Title case, we have won recognized Aboriginal Title to some of our wild-horse preserve. Working with our People and Friends of Nemaiah Valley, Wayne was able to guide genetics research that unlocked the unique hidden ancestry of our horses.

Using these efforts and exposing the century-long history of government wild-horse bounty hunts and other research, including our People's traditional oral knowledge, Wayne's book builds a strong case for the protection of all wild horses left in western Canada. This includes his plea for fully legislated national and provincial protection that recognizes Aboriginal rights and laws that should serve as an inspiration for all Canadians to help preserve this legacy forever. The world is watching.

— **Marilyn Baptiste**, former Nits'il?In (Chief) of the Xeni Gwet'in First Nation and third daughter of the late Marvin Baptiste, former chief before Marilyn was born. She is also the 2015 winner of the prestigious Goldman Environmental Prize.

PREFACE

In the remote Chilcotin wild-horse country of west-central British Columbia, where the vast Interior Plateau backs into the high ranges of the Coast Mountains, there still survive about 2,800 wild horses. They still run free where, for centuries, they learned to survive with grizzly and black bears, predatory packs of wolves, stealthy mountain lions, winter snows up to their bellies, and winter deep-freezes the equivalent of Siberia, with ice over their winter forage. They also faced constant threats of government roundups and culls and raging wildfires. It remains a mystery how the qiyus first thrived before the coming of the colonial white settler culture, trailing its large herds of cattle, and then miraculously managed to survive a century and a half of persecution and bounty hunts by that cattle culture (acts orchestrated and approved by successive colonial governments' wild-horse eradication laws). But survive the horses do today, as handsome, beautiful, near-perfect wild-horse qiyus.

What has also survived in the wild Chilcotin population is the original Spanish Iberian ancestry—the bloodlines of the horses of the conquistadores, which were introduced to the Americas in the early 1500s. Additionally, the wild qiyus in the more isolated Brittany Triangle have a different and unique ancestry: that of the Canadian horse and possibly the Yakut horse from East Russia, with a bit of Spanish thrown in. About twenty per cent of the 2,800 free-roaming qiyus population of this vast Chilcotin Plateau are protected today by the large Eagle Lake Henry ?Elegesi Qiyus (Cayuse) Wild Horse Preserve, established in 2002 by the Xeni Gwet'in. The preserve is part of a dynamic, ancient predator-prey ecosystem not found elsewhere on the continent; it also protects qiyus from the blight of clear-cut logging. Here in the preserve, qiyus are the centrepiece, both ecologically and culturally. Today, government range managers with university degrees in agriculture, whose job it is to preserve most of the free grass on public lands for 30,000 or more cattle ranging in the Chilcotin, still scheme to have wild horses outside of the preserve periodically culled or, if the secret truth were ever revealed, eradicated altogether. The fate of the last qiyus thus remains uncertain; they are caught in a vortex of scientific spin-doctoring based on false claims of overgrazing and overpopulation, combined with an economics-first backwoods political system inherited from British colonial times.

Qiyus, or cayuse, both used in this book, generally refers to any Tŝilhqot'in (Chilcotin) wild horse or Tŝilhqot'in-owned domestic horse. The term was likely adopted historically by the Tŝilhqot'in from the Cayuse (Liksiyu) Tribe, a Columbia Plateau culture living today in Oregon and Washington, with whom the Tŝilhqot'in may have traded for their first horses. The Cayuse (Liksiyu) were well-known Indigenous horse breeders. Apparently, the word cayuse came from the name the French gave their horse. The Cayuse (Liksiyu) traffic in horses led to an extension of the tribal name to Indian ponies in general.[1 2]

According to some authorities, the Cayuse are said to have acquired Spanish-type horses in the first half of the 1700s. However, a more recent comprehensive study indicates that the Spanish horse from the south had been spread to the northern Rockies and central plains by Indigenous trade networks much earlier than thought: by the first half of the 1600s.[3] The fact that the Tŝilhqot'in adopted the same name for the horse used by the Cayuse and other Plateau cultures is evidence that the foundation breeds of horses were funnelled into the remote Chilcotin grasslands along intertribal trade corridors that had been in use for centuries.

The Tŝilhqot'in also have older words in their mother tongue for the horse, *naŝlhiny* or *nazlhis*, but there is also an ancient term, *nizexlhin*.[4] Today, they also call a young wild horse a "slick" when it is not branded or halter-broken and is of an age suitable to capture for domestic purposes. The Tŝilhqot'in had to go to the BC Supreme Court to legally win back their ancestral rights to capture qiyus for domestic purposes, and to the Supreme Court of Canada to obtain recognition of Aboriginal title to some of their ancestral lands, including a good portion of the Wild Horse Preserve.

This book is the story of qiyus and the battle by the Xeni Gwet'in Tŝilhqot'in and others to save them. It also explores the efforts of others to save the last wild horses in the Alberta foothills, for the future benefit of humanity and wild horses to come.

INTRODUCTION

When I was about midway through this twenty-year-long wild-horse book project, I was contacted out of the blue by a group called the Long Riders' Guild, whom I had never heard of before. I discovered they were an international organization dedicated to equestrian explorers who have taken rides of over a thousand miles. The organization provides a forum for "horse people" to share and discuss their mutual love of horses and long-distance equestrian travel. They were fascinated by the Chilcotin wild-horse genetic research I was doing in some of the northernmost fringes of the continental grasslands, in the remote interior of British Columbia. They were also supportive of western Canada's first large wild-horse preserve, established by the Xeni Gwet'in First Nation, who have been an Indigenous "horse culture" for a very long time. They had established the preserve in collaboration with a dedicated conservation organization called Friends of Nemaiah Valley. The Long Riders' Guild had appreciated my 2001 baseline report on this unique, remote wild-horse ecosystem, which recommended just such a sanctuary be established.

This book has been its own long ride! What began two decades ago as a one-year grizzly bear and biological inventory in a mysterious (to me) wilderness in the remote Chilcotin area of British Columbia threatened by massive clear-cut logging, ended up being my own long—and unexpected—love affair with the mysterious world of wild horses.

On my first Chilcotin field trip, I wrestled with my own negative feelings about any type of feral animal, including wild horses. But then I had a strange dream about a magic stone horse. In my Technicolor dream world, I was on a solo journey, hiking along wild-horse trails through a vast bunchgrass prairie to reach a legendary Indigenous spiritual mountain called Ts'ilʔos, the "Man Who Turned to Stone." In the local Indigenous belief system, he was a guardian and protector of the Tŝilhqot'in Horse Nation. Along the way, I encountered a beautiful stone horse blocking my path. That strange dream launched me into my own long ride into the wild horses' history and survival.

As a young biologist, I had seen the huge habitat destruction wrought by feral goats and other alien animals in the Galapagos Islands. Little did I realize that my life would involve two decades of wild-horse research, with residents of the Tŝilhqot'in Horse Nation as my teachers. Nor did I think I would become one of a legion of spokespersons working for horse preservation in Canada.

During my long ride, I continued to experience the horses' wild spirit and beauty by studying and photographing qiyus. I assembled a large library of popular publications on the horse and read at least fifty background research papers and management plans to enhance my scientific understanding. My work was spearheaded in concert with the Xeni Gwet'in Tŝilhqot'in Nation and two conservation organizations (Friends of Nemaiah Valley and Valhalla Wilderness Society), resulting in the first genetic studies of wild horses in western Canada. I worked with two of the world's expert labs on horse genetics, researched numerous historical documents on the century-long BC wild-horse bounty hunts, including some never-before-released internal government documents, and interviewed Tŝilhqot'in elders and knowledge keepers. I reviewed all available historic documents, including early explorer and fur-trade journals, as well as Tŝilhqot'in traditional knowledge and anthropological studies, to establish the approximate time period before colonialism when the Tŝilhqot'in first brought in the horses.

Along the way, I helped start and supervise biologist Sadie Parr's wolf-diet study in the Brittany Triangle wild-horse ecosystem and helped with its publication as a co-author. I also assisted Ph.D. candidate Jonaki Bhattacharyya in starting on her range ecology study. I completed a scientific review of the past and current management of the Alberta foothills wild horses. I helped with the first Xeni Gwet'in management plan for wild horses and carried out six wildlife studies in their traditional territory, including on grizzly bears. I also authored two mining-impact studies on grizzly bears that contributed to the Xeni Gwet'in's herculean effort to stop Canada's largest proposed open-pit mine in the heart of their Aboriginal and wild-horse preserve.

To say it's been a long ride is an understatement. I became extremely discouraged at times during some of the historic and genetic research on qiyus. I felt like I was swimming in a sea of uncertainty. In the end, I agreed with one of my favourite authors, J. Frank Dobie, who wrote in his 1952 book *The Mustangs*, "to try to distinguish all the strains in the bloodstreams of nations, whether men or horses, is like trying to trace to their geographical origins the component drops in a bucket of the ocean's water."[1]

Dreams came and went. A wild stallion thundered past my tent one moonlit night. Hundreds of wild horses ran in and out of my field of vision and past my camera lens. Wolves in dark woods across a frozen lake howled to the full moon. I dodged female grizzly bears and wildfires. I helped, along with volunteer friends, to put out peat fires to protect meadows that were key wild-horse habitats. My wife got so tired of me locking myself in my office for days on end that she began calling herself the "Wild-Horse Widow." She suggested, sarcastically, that I should also be saving wild cows. Many people, some who are angels in my opinion, have helped me along this long ride.

Throughout, it appeared that Ts'il?os, the Stone Man Mountain and protector of the Tŝilhqot'in people and their ancestral ecosystem, must also have been watching over me and our work, bringing safe passage.

Now, with the end of this long ride in sight, comes the challenge of how to develop a blueprint that I hope will reset Canadians on a better path of understanding our last wild horses, a path to protect them before they are all gone.

In 1952, long before the age of computers and Google Scholar, or genetics labs that could reveal the bloodlines of wild horses, Frank Dobie concluded: "No naturalist ever went out to study the habits of wild horses as many naturalists have studied possums, muskrats,

The author in camp on one of his many wild-horse research trips in the West Chilcotin. *Image courtesy of Jonaki Bhattacharyya.*

rabbits, sparrows, mice, ants, fever ticks, cockroaches, fruit flies, and other lesser creatures. The best I have been able to do on the biology and habits of the most picturesque wild species of the land is not enough. Much else on the side of fact I wanted to know I could not learn."[2]

There would be no qiyus left today in BC's West Chilcotin if it were not for the Tŝilhqot'in and their deep cultural connection to their wild-horse and its preservation under the protection of their guardian, Mount Ts'il?os. May their good work continue and inspire the rest of Canada to do the same.

I only hope that Ts'il?os, "the Man Who Turned to Stone," will continue to guide the way to a better future for Canada's last wild horses.

— **Wayne McCrory**, March 2023

New Denver, British Columbia

Sacred Mount Ts'il?os (pronounced "sigh-loss") is the highest peak in the region and presides over the Tŝilhqot'in people in the Nemiah Valley. Legend has it that in the time of their ancestors, Ts'il?os and ?Eniyud were a Tŝilhqot'in husband and wife living with their family in the mountainous area around the Nemiah Valley, where Mount Ts'il?os towers today. When the two decided to separate, ?Eniyud left and Ts'il?os turned into a stone mountain. ?Eniyud returned to the northwest and also turned into a stone mountain, known today as Mount Niut. Both are responsible for protecting and watching over the Tŝilhqot'in people forever. *Image courtesy of Wayne McCrory.*

CHAPTER 1

THE STONE HORSE

It is part of the sense, caught up in our celebration of wild horses, that spiritually as well as materially, psychologically as well as physically, we need horses. They run free, and become our friends, in our field of dreams.

—J. Edward Chamberlin[1]

Biologist's Field Journal. Dawn, June 1, 2001

My dream:

I'm hiking knee-deep in bluebunch wheatgrass as it undulates in the wind, stretching far away towards my destination: the snow-clad Mount Ts'il?os, an important Xeni Gwet'in spiritual site.

The wind at my back pushes me forward through the tall grasses that bend towards the distant mountains. I feel like I'm floating in a prairie sea, walking through waves of grass instead of water. Some of this grass sea has narrow pathways made by herds of wild horses heading towards the same mountain. Following their trail makes my journey so much easier.

Suddenly, a large sandstone cliff looms up before me, blocking my way. Carved by the last glaciers as they ground their way across the

A band of free-roaming horses enjoy a spring evening in the Nemiah Valley. *Image courtesy of Wayne McCrory.*

landscape over 10,000 years ago, the cliff is now smoothed and rounded by centuries of water and wind erosion during a time when the last Yukon Horse likely went extinct. Its rock face is striated with horizontal layers of alternating white and light cerulean sandstone, as if lit from within. The cliff rises 20 or so metres out of the prairie and has a domed top, looking strangely like something from another planet has landed here.

I stand in a carpet of yellow-green bunchgrass and gaze upwards, marvelling at the extreme beauty of the radiant blue-and-white stone layers, knowing this is something I have never seen before. The surface of the cliff glows like a jewel in the late afternoon sun. Reality suddenly returns as I see that in order to continue on my journey across this prairie to sacred Mount Ts'il?os, I must climb up the cliff face and over the dome. Carefully, with a terror of falling, I start working my way up the cliff, using foot- and handholds, progressing with unexpected ease. I remind myself, as the fear of falling infuses me, of what a mountain-climber friend once told me: always keep three of your four appendages on hand- and footholds; use the fourth appendage, the free hand or foot, for finding the next hold.

Partway up, the cliff above me suddenly reveals a perfectly shaped life-sized stone head and body of a horse, formed of ocean-blue and white striations. I am stunned by such beauty. Bracing myself, I reach over to touch the horse's head; it comes alive and responds to my caress of its cheek. I detect that unmistakable sweet, wild scent of a horse. As I grab on to one of the magic horse's legs just above me so I can climb up further, the leg suddenly comes loose and turns back to stone.

Nearly losing my balance, I carefully put the stone leg back in place on the stone horse. I decide I must climb up higher yet in order to mount the stone horse; if it comes alive again, I could ride it down the other side of the cliff, where it would take me across the bunchgrass prairie to the sacred mountain.

As I start to climb, I am suddenly faced with an impassable rock projection. There are few cracks or hand- and footholds. Since I'm not a rock climber, if I cannot scale the cliff, I will never complete my journey. If I try and fall, I will die and never reach the sacred mountain.

The terror of falling overwhelmed me, and I woke from the dream, startled and confused, my adventure unfinished. As I opened my eyes, still hovering in that weird gloaming between the dream world and wakefulness, I saw only the darkness of the cabin walls, with shafts of dim moonlight illuminating the window next to me. I felt the warmth of Lucy, my faithful bear-research dog, curled up on my sleeping bag at my feet.

I realized I was at Far Meadow, a log cabin owned by retired professor David Williams, where I'd been for the last ten days. I was researching grizzly bears and other wildlife in the Brittany Triangle Plateau in the interior of British Columbia's last wild-horse country, the Chilcotin.

David's log cabin, situated at an abandoned stump ranch, was well suited for the research we were doing. It is located in the middle of a new BC provincial park named Nuntsi. The park was created to protect moose habitat; the plateau boasts a rich mosaic of wetlands, dry meadows, lakes and ponds. Interspersed with vast pine forests, the ecosystem is favoured by bands of wild horses, moose, wolves, grizzly bears and a whole variety of waterfowl and other birds.

I had gone to bed the previous evening, exhausted from hiking 20 kilometres of wild-horse trails through the vast lodgepole pine flatlands, meadows and wetlands. We were mapping grizzly habitat and documenting wildlife signs for an organization based in Victoria, BC, called Friends of Nemaiah Valley (FONV), run by David, his wife, Pat Swift, and a small board of directors. David was helping me and bear biologist Marty Williams, a good friend from Michigan, conduct the field research.

Our job was to try to help the Xeni Gwet'in First Nation stop or modify the logging planned for their 770,000-hectare Aboriginal Preserve. Their Nits'il?in (Chief), Roger William, told me they established the preserve in 1989 and no industrial logging, mining or hydroelectric dams were to be allowed. He said neither the provincial nor federal government cared about protecting Xeni Gwet'in land. The province just wanted to log it to feed the hungry sawmills in Williams Lake, which were running low on timber.

The Xeni Gwet'in are one of six Indigenous nations of the Tŝilhqot'in (Chilcotin) Nation, so named after the Chilcotin River that defines their homeland. The six nations are Tŝideldel (Redstone), Yuneŝit'in (Stone), Xeni Gwet'in (Nemiah), ?Esdilagh (Alexandria), Tl'esqox (Toosey) and Tl'etinqox (Anaham). The Tŝilhqot'in territory stretches over a vast plateau from the Fraser River to the Coast Mountains. The nation has about 450 people and is traditionally Dene (Athabascan) speaking, a commonality shared with the Navajo far to the southeast.

The name Chilcotin comes from Tŝilhqot'in, which has a number of different interpretations, including "People of the River," "Ochre River People" (ochre refers to the orange-red mineral used by Tŝilhqot'in and other Indigenous communities as a base for paint or dye), or "People of the Blue Water," referring to the Chilcotin River's colour, caused by glacial silt.

Much of the Chilcotin Plateau was already criss-crossed with thousands of kilometres of new logging roads and massive clear-cutting of the expansive lodgepole pine forests, threatening the fragile balance of a once intact productive wildlife ecosystem. Cattle ranchers' predator-control programs had already taken care of most of the grizzly bears and wolves that used to wander down from the mountains and out into the grassland prairies and canyonlands. Clear-cut logging was now delivering a double whammy to the once vibrant Chilcotin ecosystem.

Unlike the areas of the five other Tŝilhqot'in nations, the Xeni Gwet'in's traditional territory was still largely an intact wilderness because of its remoteness. They had fought hard to keep it that way.

After ten days of wildlife research in the Brittany Triangle, I saw that it was a precious intact plateau wilderness with what appeared to be healthy grizzly bear and wolf populations. It was one of the last refuges from human development in the Chilcotin; it offered a final enclave for the grassland grizzly bear ecotype now extirpated from most of the BC interior grasslands towards the Fraser River. As I lay awake pondering all of this, I wondered if my dream of the stone horse was a symbolic message related to the conflict I was feeling after finding, to my surprise, that the Brittany Triangle had a healthy population of fine-looking wild horses that appeared to have integrated into the natural ecosystem. I also wondered if my dream had been triggered the previous day by the stallion that had suddenly burst out of the woods, galloped across our field of vision and then vanished in a wink, leaving only its thundering hoof-beats in our ears.

A wild stallion of the Brittany Triangle. *Image courtesy of Wayne McCrory.*

In 1966, just after graduating from the University of British Columbia with an honours degree in zoology, specializing in wildlife, I had the opportunity to work in the Galapagos Islands as an assistant on wildlife studies and on a film documentary. There, I witnessed the destruction that feral goats, cattle, pigs and other introduced species had inflicted on the fragile native island habitats that sheltered many species found nowhere else in the world. When I returned home, I started a small letter-writing campaign to UNESCO, the agency that had just cooperated with the Ecuadorian government to protect the Galapagos as a World Heritage Site and National Park. I felt that the area would not be protected until the most destructive of the introduced species, including the feral goats, were eradicated.

During our first days of field surveys in the Brittany Triangle (called Tach'elach'ed by the Xeni Gwet'in, meaning high plateau with many meadows), we had encountered small numbers of wild-horse bands. I found them beautiful but felt angry that such an introduced feral species had not been eradicated in order to save the natural habitat.

However, as our wildlife surveys went on, and as I continued to see the wild spirits of the free-ranging horses we encountered daily, I also realized that they were not the runty hammer-headed "Indian" horses I'd read about in cowboy books as a boy. These horses were generally quite large and as handsome as some of the domestic breeds I had once ridden in Mexico and South America, and on wildlife patrols with park wardens in Canada's Yoho and Jasper parks. I saw none of the grassland range degradation I had expected from these horses.

I tried to force myself back to sleep so I could finish my dream and better understand it. Despite the outdoors quiet, indoors the snoring was too loud: David up in his loft and his pit bull, Alligator, stretched out on the cabin floor 5 metres from my head. Their only competition was the distant night call of an owl hunting over the marsh. I plugged my ears with rolled-up pieces of toilet paper to block out the snoring so I could drift off.

I awoke to sunlight streaming into the log cabin window. The dogs stirred restlessly, and a red-winged blackbird sang down by the marsh. I was disappointed that I hadn't returned to my magic horse dream.

Still, I felt there was a parallel between my dream of following the wild-horse trails across the bunchgrass prairie and the way, during the day, we hiked the real horse pathways that took us far out into the plateau's pine forests and meadows before circling back by a different route. Some days we veered, worried that we wouldn't get back to the Far Meadow cabin before dark. But I was also learning that good adventures, life lessons and stories often go in circles.

I took a deep breath and arose from my log bunk bed. Lucy tried to lick my face to remind me it was her breakfast time. At fifty-nine, a maverick wildlife biologist, I had another field day ahead.

From where the flatlands merge with the front ranges of the Coast Mountains, the vast Chilcotin Plateau and wild-horse country that forms the Brittany Triangle stretches across the landscape as far as the eye can see. Here is author Wayne McCrory with Xeni Gwet'in knowledge keeper and wild-horse researcher Norman William and Lucy the Bear Dog. *Image courtesy of Wayne McCrory.*

CHAPTER 2

THE BRITTANY TRIANGLE

A WILDERNESS UNDER SIEGE

We experience a spiritual longing to be out on the land. My worldview, the holistic way I view the world, and the cumulative grief I have inherited and experienced during my extensive research, make it very challenging for me to remain positive in the present time with all that is happening. Our past is embedded within the clearcuts; the broken landscapes hold our most cherished memories. But, it is the disfigured land we see first, it is the emotional pain we experience first, and this anguish overshadows what was there before. Now, we must build upon these layers, and create new visions on the land. But, it is impossible to obliterate the horror on the landscapes and see past this, to the purity and the cultural wealth that was there before. How can a Tŝilhqot'in create new life and new memories upon what was butchered, and bring new life upon what appears to be dying?

In my mind, everything is connected. We are Nenqayni, and Tŝilhqot'in have been connected to their lands for many generations, and Tŝilhqot'in elders would say this connection has been there since time began. The land is what makes us complete; it is an extension of our body and our soul; it is what gives us joy; it is what gives us security; it protects us; it feeds us; it comforts us; it heals us; it is Our Mother. We love our land and its life forms. Like an infant away from its mother, most Tŝilhqot'in feel lost elsewhere, and we miss our landscapes.[1]

— **Linda R. Smith**, Nabas oral literature documentation

Biologist's Field Journal. June 10, 2001
Far Meadow Log Cabin

In the mellowness of the spring morning, satisfied by ten productive days of wildlife research, David and I sat on his cabin porch with coffee and our two dogs. In the sun's warming rays, we listened to the different mating trills and eerie squawks emanating from the marsh, now full of spring life. I raised my field glasses towards the small herd of wild horses grazing on the other side of the marsh: a bay stallion and four mares with two newborn foals. They looked like a vital part of the plateau landscape. A lone black horse, probably an outcast bachelor stallion, grazed in a lush meadow on their opposite side. I puzzled over how long wild horses had been out here and what their fate would be, given that many had already been exterminated from most of BC's interior grasslands.

David said this band of healthy and good-looking wild horses and some bachelor stallions occasionally showed up to graze on the swamp grass and the adjacent pocket grasslands that surround his cabin.

I had not discussed my dream of the magic stone horse because I was still mulling it over. Could it have been a reminder of the beauty of wild horses? Did it have something to do with the Xeni Gwet'in legend of Ts'il?os, the Man Who Turned to Stone, who guarded the land against the century-long threats of government bounty hunts to eradicate all of the wild horses? Maybe learning more about the horses in the Chilcotin wilds would help me interpret my dream?

Retired from Simon Fraser University, David is a congenial, helpful host, knowledgeable about wildlife and local history. David's surname descends from his great-great-grandfather John Williams, a martyred South Seas missionary. He also descends from another great-great-grandfather, St'at'imc Chief Joseph, or Tsil.Husalst, of Xaxli'p in Lillooet, a town over the mountain ranges to the south. This Indigenous ancestry helps to explain the passionate commitment he, wife Pat Swift, and the Friends of Nemaiah Valley devote to help the Xeni Gwet'in stop the Brittany Triangle from being logged.

History haunts us all. A year later, a Xeni elder recalled that Deer Creek Ranch near Hanceville used to be McCrory Ranch. A Don McCrory, my possible distant Irish relative, shot some people at the ranch that bore his name and then committed suicide by jumping into the Chilko River. The person who found his body on an island near the ranch was paid a $10,000 reward. The elder claimed you can still see the markings of the bullets on the wall beside the ranch-house door.[2] Deer Creek was once owned by Chilko Ranch. Prior to the Chilcotin study, another man with a family name similar to mine, claiming we were distant Irish cousins, wrote me to tell me of his efforts to save Newfoundland pit ponies. Eventually, the Chilcotin horses would bring me around to helping save the ponies too.

The Brittany Triangle is a vast wilderness ecosystem. Lodgepole pine forests stretch to the far horizons in every direction, intermixed with hundreds of sloughs, ponds, lakes and meadows. These waterbodies were formed as a result of depressions and small basins that remained after the glaciers of the last Ice Age receded. The Brittany Plateau is underlain by a bedrock plain of lava from ancient volcanic outflows. It gets little rainfall, as it is in the rain shadow of the towering Coast Mountain Ranges just to the west. The abundant rains carried by the large storms that blow in off the Pacific drop most of their precipitation on the coastal side once they reach that high barrier. As the coastal storm-winds rise up and dry out over the mountains, they sometimes create warm Chinook winds in the middle of winter. These winds may cause ice and snow-crust conditions that make it difficult for wild horses and other wildlife to move about and forage for food.

Reviewing the logging plans and related documents David had assembled, I realized the Brittany Triangle was a vibrant plateau ecosystem and held a rich Indigenous cultural heritage. There are numerous ancient Xeni Gwet'in villages, burial sites and networks of trails all across the area. A large spiderwork of ancient pathways links all these sites.[3]

Today, however, due to smallpox and other colonial decimations, this area is essentially uninhabited except for Far Meadow and a few small cattle ranches and lodges to the west along the blue Chilko River. Most Xeni Gwet'in survivors reside in the pastoral Nemiah Valley, just over the mountain range, at the south end of the triangle.

Still well-used in the triangle is the trapline home of trapper Lester Pierce and Rosie Quilt at Upper Place, some 10 kilometres to the east of David's place. Their log cabin overlooks a large willow meadow frequented by moose and wild horses, near where the old wagon road drops down for half a kilometre through lava formations and forests of giant Douglas fir and bunchgrass into the deep valley of Elkin Creek.

On one of our wildlife surveys, we stopped in to visit Lester and Rosie, to get to know them and obtain some wildlife information. We found Rosie very shy: she disappeared quickly into the cabin when we arrived. David said she was born and raised on the plateau. Her father, Eddie Quilt, had run a trapline and built the Upper Place cabin.

A formal green government "Tourist Accommodation" sign was nailed to the front of the cabin near the door—one of Lester's jokes. The cabin's back wall was covered with rusted leghold traps of different sizes. A large sign duct-taped to the outhouse door warned: NEVER MIND THE DOG, BEWARE OF OWNER. The sign included a sketch of the barrel of a six-shooter pointing straight at us, with a hand around the pistol grip and a finger on the trigger.

Despite this warning, we found Lester happy to have a visit. In his raspy voice, with an American twang, he told us that Rosie's Xeni Gwet'in father had lived here before them and had killed off all the wolves in the Brittany. Now the wolves were coming back. Lester catches a few on his trapline each year.

When we asked him how long the horses had been here, he did not know. He said that in 1988 he had been hired by the BC Forest Service to kill off all the wild horses in Elkin Creek.

Later, David told me that when he first came to look at buying the Far Meadow property, he ran into Lester on the access road, cutting firewood and getting their Upper Place trapline cabin ready for winter. When David explained that he was interested in the purchase of Far Meadow, Lester immediately laughed and told David and his friends they were crazy.

"That bunch of hairdressers trying to unload it on you city folks have never been there! The wind blows twenty-four hours a day in that Godforsaken place," Lester had said. "Anything you build there will blow away. The mosquitoes are the worst in the Chilcotin, and there are a thousand blowdowns between there and here, another 6 kilometres. That old wagon road is impassable now. You'll never get through."[4]

Nevertheless, David, a strong outdoorsman, did chainsaw his way through; he fell in love with the place and bought it with some friends. Now we were using it for our research headquarters.

Far Meadow, David said, had been homesteaded by a famous local Xeni Gwet'in rancher and wild-horse bounty hunter called Eagle Lake Henry. He pointed to an old log cabin, now with an overgrown sod roof, where Henry and others had survived many hard winters. It was a hard-knock land, where making a living running a trapline and raising a few cattle and horses was always a challenge; but this was nothing new for the Xeni Gwet'in. They had lived here for thousands of years and had adopted some of the white-settler culture ways while maintaining their freedom to live on and protect the land.

The European name Brittany Triangle bothered me when I first heard it; I could see no resemblance between Brittany in France and the wilderness plateau. I could not locate the source of the European name, but I did find out that the Xeni Gwet'in name for the area is Tachelach'ed, which has several Xeni Gwet'in interpretations, including "Place Between the Waters," because it is bounded by two large glacier-fed rivers. According to Elder Alice William, it is an ancient name. According to Chief Roger William, it is "the whole plateau between the rivers and the mountain . . . it's fairly high and fairly flat with many meadows."[5] However, because everyone I met referred to it as the Brittany Triangle, we continued to use the term.

The geographic descriptor "triangle" refers to the near-perfect triangular configuration of two large, widely separated, glacial-fed salmon-bearing rivers—the Chilko and the Dasiqox-Taseko—that eventually join at the north end of the plateau in the apex of the triangle. On the south, the plateau merges into the alpine-topped bighorn sheep ranges of the Konni and Nemiah mountains.

David's logging maps suggested there would be 130 kilometres of new logging roads built from the northern tip of the Brittany Triangle to the mountain range at the south end. Numerous branch roads would spread their tentacles east and west, into the plateau's pine forests.

Up to 62,500 logging truckloads of the Brittany's pine forests might be carted off to sawmills in the cow- and mill-town of Williams Lake. I found staggering the scale of planned logging in such a pristine landscape.

According to documents in David's library, when the Xeni Gwet'in first heard about the logging plans they applied to the BC government for a large wilderness designation for all of their traditional lands. They received a letter of refusal from district manager R.J. Reeves. Written on his typewriter in the Alexis Creek Forest Service office, Reeves's letter stated that the Xeni Gwet'in's territory did not fit the government's definition of wilderness as an "uninhabited region" because the Xeni Gwet'in still lived there on the land. This was incredibly ironic since nearly all of the "wilderness" in British Columbia had been occupied by a great number and diversity of Indigenous people and cultures before many had been forced—by government—to move on to small "Indian" reserves.

Documents showed that, by 1989, the BC government had approved large-scale logging of the Brittany by Riverside Forest Products, which had a big sawmill in Williams Lake. One other company had also been given logging rights. The Xeni Gwet'in were not consulted, and their previous concerns were ignored.

One of the government's excuses for logging was that clear-cutting was needed to control the outbreak of the mountain pine beetle (*Dendroctonus ponderosae*), which was killing large areas of mature pine forests in the BC interior. Some independent foresters and scientists maintained that logging would not control the beetle epidemic. Many said it was a natural occurrence; others said the sawmills had already drastically overcut their quota.

We had observed small sites of these beetle-killed pine trees on our surveys in the Brittany Triangle, but the beetles did not appear to be threatening the ecosystem. Cold winters typical of the Chilcotin were known to kill off the larvae laid inside the tree bark by the adult beetles. At some sites, the latticework of the blowdowns of beetle-killed trees was causing the wild horses and wildlife to establish new detour trails, a slight inconvenience within the grand scheme of things. We witnessed nothing on the scale that the Forest Service claimed to justify carting off most of the healthy pine forests of the Brittany Triangle.

When, in 1989, the government refused the Xeni Gwet'in's request to create a large protected wilderness area, the Xeni leaders reacted to the rising threat of logging by declaring that their whole 770,000-hectare ancestral Caretaker Area (about the size of Yellowstone National Park and which includes the Brittany Triangle), as the Nemiah Aboriginal Wilderness Preserve (Nenduwh Jid Guzitin). With the help of the Western Canada Wilderness Committee, the widely circulated Indigenous protection poster, one of which was hanging on David's cabin wall, included a statement from the elders that there would be no commercial logging, mining or hydroelectric development. This political manoeuvre appeared to make the logging companies go away for a while—but not for long.

Unfortunately, in true Canadian colonial fashion, neither provincial nor federal governments in Canada recognized Indigenous protected areas (nor do they today). This left the potential for massive clear-cutting of the Brittany and the Aboriginal Preserve as a stark political reality. David told me that Friends of Nemaiah Valley (FONV) was formed to help the Xeni Gwet'in promote and protect their Aboriginal Wilderness Preserve from such a man-made ecological disaster. He said they were hoping that if I documented the potential impacts on grizzly bears, it might help their cause. First, I said, we would have to see what we found: as a professional biologist, my research had to be independent and unbiased.

Documents show that in 1989 the Xeni Gwet'in also ramped up their efforts to stop the logging by hiring a law firm, Woodward & Company, well known for representing Aboriginal Rights and Title cases. The goal was for the firm to file a claim with the BC Supreme Court, under section 35 of the Constitution, for recognition of Aboriginal Rights and Title to their group trapline area, which included part of the Brittany Triangle. The Xeni Gwet'in had never ceded their lands to the colonial government.

During an aerial survey of the Brittany Triangle in that tense time, Xeni Gwet'in leaders discovered that Riverside Forest Products had logging equipment parked in the heart of their claim area. The cache of equipment included a Caterpillar tractor, a tree de-limber and two grapple-yarders. That kind of heavy-duty equipment could eat up dozens of hectares of pine forest in a day. In 1991, the Xeni were able to obtain an injunction to temporarily stop the logging.

However, in May 1992, the BC Ministry of Forests issued a permit to another company, Carrier Lumber, to log the Brittany. "So much for the Aboriginal Wilderness Preserve," David said. "The province has no respect for First Nations rights and title to land that has never been ceded to the colonial government."

The logging company moved quickly: it decided the best way to start logging the Brittany was to fix the rustic bridge into the Brittany Triangle where it crossed over the Chilko River at Henry's Crossing. Eagle Lake Henry, who homesteaded David's Far Meadow, had also owned a ranch at Mountain House, where he used to herd his cattle and horses at the river crossing now named in his memory.

The Xeni Gwet'in reacted swiftly to Carrier Lumber's imminent logging activities by calling on the other five Tŝilhqot'in groups to help with a blockade at the Henry's Crossing bridge. Local ranchers, tourism lodge owners and a few feral environmentalists joined the Xeni Gwet'in, led by their youthful chief, Roger William. They lined up on the bridge in protest, with drums and singing, and successfully prevented Carrier Lumber loggers from repairing the bridge that would have opened the door to heavy equipment in the triangle's pine forests.

This protest action forced the BC government to pull the 1992 permit; then-Premier Mike Harcourt promised that logging would not be allowed without the consent of the Xeni Gwet'in. Each year at Henry's Crossing, the Xeni Gwet'in and local communities still celebrate the blockade with singing, dancing, speeches and other traditional events.

After the protest, there followed several years of negotiations between the Xeni Gwet'in and BC to develop a suitable forest management plan. However, this reached an impasse, as the First Nations community resisted any industrial development.[6]

Meanwhile, the provincial government had gone ahead with implementing the 1994 Cariboo–Chilcotin Land Use Plan,[7] completed two years after the blockade at Henry's Crossing. The Xeni Gwet'in were one of a number of Tŝilhqot'in communities keen to learn what the government was planning to do in their caretaker areas. As with many similar land-use plans initiated by the province in contentious areas where citizen groups and Indigenous tribes were rising up against clear-cutting and demanding wilderness protection, Indigenous conservation areas, as proposed by the Xeni Gwet'in, were seldom recognized by government; many legitimate and long-standing new park

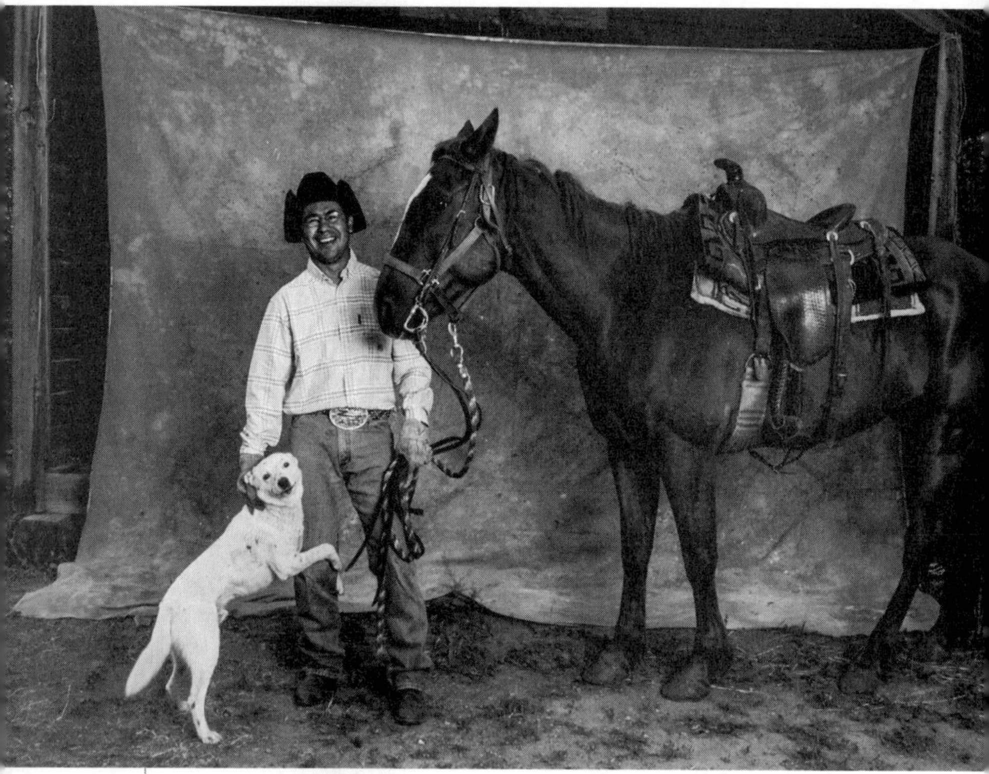

Chief Roger poses with his horse and dog in the Nemiah Valley. *Image © Patrice Halley,* Canadian Geographic.

proposal areas were being clear-cut. For the land-use plans, the province also placed an arbitrary ceiling of only *twelve per cent* protection of the total area of the province's land to be saved in parks, in order to parcel out most of the wilderness to logging companies.

The twelve per cent limit included a number of already protected provincial parks. This politically motivated "divide the pie" ceiling was not science-based and was done despite a growing body of international scientific studies which showed that up to *forty-four to fifty* per cent of a landscape needed to be fully protected if large, wide-ranging species such as grizzly bears were to be preserved. A

Despite the BC government's completion in 1994 of an intensive land-use plan that promised to improve logging as well as wilderness and wildlife protection, massive clear-cuts and extensive logging road networks continue to march inexorably across the Chilcotin Plateau towards the Brittany Triangle and Nemiah Aboriginal Wilderness Preserve today. *Image courtesy of Jeremy Williams.*

conservation area design for the BC coastal rainforest recommended fifty-one per cent.[8] A seventeen-person blue-ribbon science team for the BC government and industry looked at habitat needs for six focal species and recommended forty-four to fifty per cent of the land be protected.[9] This was the conservation yardstick we had been applying to the protection initiatives on the BC coast, such as in the Great Bear Rainforest, where I was working with the Valhalla Wilderness Society. This yardstick was also the measure used by a number of other conservation groups and First Nations as a means to protect large coastal areas for the white spirit bear and grizzly bear.

Not surprisingly, after years of exhaustive meetings in different Cariboo–Chilcotin communities, and a vicious hate campaign orchestrated by loggers and the timber industry against environmental and citizen's groups advocating more land protection, the government's final 1994 land-use plan for the Cariboo–Chilcotin set aside only twelve per cent of the region as parks. This left the majority of intact wilderness to the usual provincial free-for-all by the logging and mining companies.

Very little Chilcotin grassland was given protection; what was to be set aside would still allow cattle-grazing, so it was not fully protected despite the amount of damage to grassland species-at-risk that cattle-grazing had already caused. Consideration for any protection of the wild horses, which were a main concern of the Xeni Gwet'in, who regarded them as a special being, or *nun*, was never part of the discussion. David told me this was because the government considered them feral and alien: they didn't belong to the ecosystem, and the government had every intention of getting rid of all of them.

The government was also unwilling to agree to protect the Xeni Gwet'in's entire Nemiah Aboriginal Wilderness Preserve, though it did approve the large Ts'il?os Provincial Park (also called Chilko Provincial Park), which included only a small portion of the Brittany Triangle.

David noted that the province had also approved another provincial park in the Brittany, called Nuntsi. It surrounded the Far Meadow land so that only about fifteen per cent of the Brittany Triangle was protected. The balance of the Brittany, taking in its vast expanse of lodgepole pine forests, was declared a "Resource Development Zone." That decision would open the door to clear-cutting under the empty promise of "better" logging guidelines.

Still, by some miracle, between the political pressure of the Xeni Gwet'in's 1992 Henry's Crossing blockade and the ongoing BC Supreme Court Xeni Gwet'in Rights and Title case, logging still had not happened in the Brittany by the time I arrived in 2001. However, on the paved highway from Williams Lake across the Chilcotin Plateau, I passed at least a hundred large trucks filled with pine logs heading for the mills in Williams Lake.

For decades the Tŝilhqot'in people have witnessed the logging devastation of the West Chilcotin with very little protection by the BC government. Hundreds of logging trucks cart off the pine forests daily to feed the hungry mills in Williams Lake. *Image courtesy of Gary Fiegehen.*

David said government still had not developed the promised better-logging guidelines for the Special Resource Management Zone in the Brittany, so the logging could happen at any time. Chainsaws and feller-bunchers—giant machines with automated arms that cut and felled large amounts of pine forest daily—loomed like a dark cloud over the Brittany wilderness.

It looked like my grizzly bear and other wildlife inventory and review of the potential impacts of the logging companies' plans could prove crucial. Since some of our research was in Nuntsi Provincial Park, David had a permit from BC Parks, as well as permission from Xeni Gwet'in Chief Roger William and their law firm. David and FONV were working closely with the Xeni Gwet'in and young "Chief Roger," as he was called, who had initially asked David to do the study I had been commissioned to do. And this is where, for me, this all began.

Wayne McCrory and David Williams look at a 2001 map of clear-cuts and roads approved by the BC government for massive logging of the Brittany Triangle. *Image © Patrice Halley*, Canadian Geographic.

CHAPTER 3

THE CHARGE OF THE BLACK STALLION BAND

Biologist's Field Journal. June 10, 2001

On that June morning, after my lengthy logging history lesson from David at the Far Meadow cabin, he, Marty Williams and I headed out with the dogs for another field day. We were armed with notebooks, packs, binoculars, compasses, bear spray and maps, including those showing the logging plans.

Our initial surveys already revealed a healthy ecosystem, including the thrilling sighting of a grizzly bear family and plenty of bear sign by way of droppings, tracks and mark trees where the bears had stood up to scratch their backs and mark their territories. We collected bear hair from their mark trees for genetic analysis and put their droppings in plastic bags to examine later. We set up remote wildlife cameras in key locations, including along wild-horse trails. We had already found evidence of a pack of wolves, a cougar, a Canada lynx and other species. I was impressed with the wildlife values.

Working in grizzly country was not without its dangers. One afternoon, while on my own with Lucy, we saw three large animals grazing far across a meadow, partially hidden by some trees. Horses, I

The Brittany Triangle provides rich grassland foraging habitats for wild horses, plateau grizzly bears, and other wildlife. Major salmon spawning areas are a bonus for bears to fatten up in the fall. This plateau mother grizzly with one of her two teenagers in tow shares a meadow with wild horses. Grizzlies have been nearly extirpated from BC grasslands except for the remote West Chilcotin. *Image courtesy of Wayne McCrory.*

thought, without first training my binoculars on them. Getting out my camera and long lens, I stealthily detoured a distance, through the pine forest surrounding the meadow, heading towards the "horses" to try to get some good photos. When I stepped into the open where I felt the horses should be: Surprise! Not three wild horses but a family group of huge Chilcotin grizzly bears—a large mama silvertip with two nearly grown subadults—all busy grazing on dandelion flowers. Knowing from past experience that the mother could charge without hesitation to defend her young, I quickly got out my bear spray. Lucy (who was well-behaved) did not bark at the bears; I slunk away to a safer location to take photographs. I was amazed to see the mother roll over onto her back and nurse her offspring, who were nearly as large as her. Wild motherhood at its natural best, I thought.

A mother grizzly takes a break from eating dandelion flowers to nurse her two teenagers. *Image courtesy of Wayne McCrory.*

Although wild horses had not been a priority of our research, we decided to document their numbers and map their locations and trails. We had already learned that there were two distinct horse groups that mainly kept to separate territories in the Nuntsi Park portion of our study area. The Bay Stallion Band included about fifteen mares, subadults and foals. The bay stallion was handsome, large, well-muscled and proportioned; he was a delight to my eyes. It was difficult to determine which was the lead mare.

The other band, which we called the Black Stallion Band, had about twelve horses and was led by both a smaller-sized jet-black stallion and a larger bay lead mare, a matriarch with a star on her forehead.

We also found a few ancient-looking weathered horse skulls half-buried in peat bogs; the remains had yellowish and grey lichens growing on them, which supported the Xeni Gwet'in accounts of the horses' long presence. We learned that you can tell the stallion skulls from the mare skulls because the males have an extra eyetooth just behind the front upper incisors. By contrast, moose skulls have only front teeth on their lower jaw and no teeth on the upper jaw because

This handsome bay stallion had a large family group and mostly stayed separate from the adjoining Black Stallion Band. *Image courtesy of Wayne McCrory.*

they have a hard pad there for chomping off stems of the buds of coarse shrubs such as willows. Horses, being largely grazers of grasses and sedges, have incisors on both their upper and lower jaws. This fact enabled us to distinguish the skulls of wild horses from those of moose, which, in adults, are about the same size and outward appearance.

Of course, not finding the expected overgrazing and overpopulation, despite horses' long, dominant presence in the landscape, further piqued my interest in the ecology and population dynamics of these wild horses.

One June evening, on our hike back to the cabin, we swung by the home meadow of the Black Stallion Band to see if any new foals had been born and to try to get some photographs for my report. We crept stealthily along a horse trail, emerging slowly from the shade of the pine forest to the edge of the Black Stallion Band's secluded meadow, into the warmth of the late afternoon sunlight. It was a magical evening, with the first subtle shades of green-up just starting to show in the

This spotted (Appaloosa) colour variation is rare in the Chilcotin.
Image courtesy of David Williams.

buds on the aspen trees. New grasses were poking through the faded gold of winter-dried and horse-cropped vegetation that blanketed the meadow. Dark brown clumps of horse droppings littered the ground.

As we were looking straight into the evening sun, we did not notice the Black Stallion Band about a quarter of a kilometre away until a sharp warning snort from the stallion alerted us. The band already had us pegged; the black stallion paced back and forth some distance from the family group with his tail straight up in the air, blowing and snorting to warn the rest of the herd. We could feel their wild-horse energy radiating across the open meadow.

We froze, then slowly crouched down near the edge of the woods. Excited, we got our cameras ready, not knowing what to expect. David had a good hold on the collar of Alligator, his untrained, city-raised pit bull, while I grabbed Lucy. We'd be okay unless the dogs acted up and scared off the horses.

The evening breeze came from the horses to us. I hoped this gave us some opportunity to observe them for a while without their usual

The wild horses in the Brittany Triangle come in many different colours, with most being black, as above, or bay. *Image courtesy of Wayne McCrory.*

flight at the first scent of us. I was crouched right next to a large pile of fresh, stinking stallion dung, the kind we had seen in various places in the Brittany where the male horses marked their territory.

The soft glow of the evening sun backlit the horses, and their coats shone, contrasting with the fresh spring greenness of the meadow. The breeze caught their long manes and tails. One foal was bedded beside its mother, another was nursing, but they all came to attention as the stallion accelerated the volume of his snorting and blowing. Although not as large as the bay stallion, he was an incredibly beautiful animal with a shiny black coat and a long scruffy mane.

The sight magnified my growing realization that these "feral" animals, which I had considered alien to this ecosystem, were just as at home in the plateau wilderness as the resident bears, wolves, deer and moose.

Our little group of humans and dogs and the band of horses remained suspended in space and time until, suddenly, the black stallion let out a much louder snort-blow. With the large mare at his side, he erupted into a full-on charge straight across the meadow towards us, with all of the herd following. Other wild horses we'd encountered just ran off, either immediately after they became aware of us or after watching us for a short while. I did not know what to expect as the distance between us and the herd closed rapidly, with the thundering of their hooves getting increasingly louder.

I wondered, with a tinge of panic, whether this herd runs people down and tramples them when they feel threatened. Or was this a defensive reaction because we had a black dog the size of a wolf? During my career as a wildlife biologist, I had been charged by my fair share of grizzly and black bears, and rutting bull moose, but never by a herd of wild horses.

I readied my canister of red pepper bear spray, remembering that the inventor of the counter-assault product told me that he once used it to repel an aggressive wild stallion in Montana. We had the option to move back into the safety of the woods, but with our cameras ready and the two dogs under control, we decided to hold our ground and see what would happen.

I thought the herd was bluffing and would not come close, but after disappearing into a hollow they quickly galloped over a rise, closing the space between us more rapidly than we liked. In milliseconds, the wall of undulating brown and black bodies descended upon us from about 100 metres away. Chunks of turf flew into the air as if flocks of little black cowbirds were flitting out of the way. The foals kept pace alongside, as close to their mothers as they could get. At the last minute, about 20 metres away, the herd veered off in amazing unison, as one sees in flocks of birds when they turn. They passed so close we saw the whites of their eyes and the pink insides of their flared nostrils. Sweet, distinctive horse scent lingered as the commotion of rumps and hooves raced back to the far end of the meadow. They came to a standstill while we looked at each other in amazement and relief.

The herd stared at us for a minute, with the black stallion stomping and blowing alongside the prancing, agitated lead mare. Suddenly, they repeated the charge, this time veering off even closer to us in a wild run that equalled any of the greatest horse events on Earth. This time, they galloped back to the far end of the meadow, but they did not stop. They broke their charge formation into single file as if on cue, so that the stallion was no longer leading. He'd fallen behind to let the lead mare, her foal by her side, take the herd at a gallop onto a horse trail in the pine woods. The black stallion's rump, tail flying high, was the last image we saw before the forest swallowed them up.

We remained huddled and stunned for a while, listening to the breaking of branches and the distant thuds of their hooves as they circled around us through the bush. We looked at each other excitedly but with relief.

"Wow! That was something else," I said. "The power of that almost beats my first sighting of a white spirit bear on the BC coast! Have you ever seen this before, Dave?"

He said he had encountered lots of wild horses in the Brittany Triangle over the years and some had rushed at him for a short distance, but he had never been charged so close. Marty avowed that this experience was more awesome than his own first white bear sighting on the BC coast. The pit bull was whining and squirming to get loose from David's grip so she could go after the horses. Lucy simply sat, looking bored. Trained to tune into bears, she had little interest in wild horses, having been around my son's logging horses at home.

We debated whether the horses had charged so close to try to trample our dogs in order to protect the two new foals, especially since Lucy could easily be mistaken for a black wolf. These horses had obviously lived with wolves out in the Chilcotin for a long time. Who knows what all of their defence strategies were? Possibly they were also just curious and knew they had strength in numbers and the ability to flee at top speed if they needed. I wondered: was it similar to the bluff-threat behaviour I had experienced in some charges by grizzly bears?

We tramped contemplatively back on wild-horse trail networks to David's cabin, a welcome sight in the dwindling evening light after our long, long day on sore, badly blistered feet. As we teamed up to prepare a supper of salad and meatloaf, I ruminated on my stone horse dream and this new experience of horse energy. Was the universe nudging me to look more closely at these wild qiyus?

It was a perfect evening to sit on the porch and devour delicious pre-made meatloaf sent on the expedition by David's wife, Pat Swift. Although the dish had been stored unfrozen for a week in David's root cellar under the cabin floor, it went down well with a glass of merlot. We reclined in lawn chairs overlooking the marsh and horse meadows. It was a joy to just sit there listening to the spring chorus of wetland birds: red-winged blackbirds, coots, mallards and the strange jungle cackle of sora rails. The rapid whirring of a male snipe's mating flight also caught my ear.

I went into the cabin and leafed through the faded pages of the only book on wild horses I had chucked into my travelling library at the last minute. It was a tattered 1978 edition of *Mustangs: A Return to the Wild*, written by Hope Ryden,[1] an NBC journalist and film-documentary producer. I bought the book when it was first published, at the recommendation of James Dean Feist, an American hippie-cowboy biologist colleague with whom I had done surveys of the summer migrations of the Porcupine caribou herd in the Yukon. Dean had obtained his master's degree studying wild-horse behaviour in Wyoming's Pryor Mountains horse refuge. He was passionate about the beauty, ecology and protection of wild horses. We had argued a lot about whether the horses should be protected or were alien, feral animals to be eradicated.

For fun, I began reading Ryden's book out loud to Marty and David. Ryden had written about mustangs after she had a foundational experience with wild horses similar to ours while she was filming them. In Wyoming, the horses were considered descendants of the Spanish horses brought to the Americas in the early 1500s. Ryden was adamant that they were a heritage icon that needed to be protected rather than persecuted to extinction in the lower forty-eight states. We were interested by her reports that wild horse bands had both a lead stallion and a lead mare, which confirmed our own observations.

Following our brush with the Black Stallion Band that afternoon, Ryden's words became exciting new material for us. Maybe the horses in the Chilcotin had also come from Spanish mustangs and been brought in from the south by the Tŝilhqot'in, we mused, and not by the early European gold-seekers and ranchers in the 1860s, as was the common Chilcotin rancher precept.

Ryden's work and that of other American horse lovers, such as Wild Horse Annie and my late biologist friend Dean Feist, had led the US federal government to protect their wild horses with the establishment of wild-horse sanctuaries such as that in the Pryor Mountains. I found it interesting that Ryden's book mentioned that Feist had been part of that campaign and had appeared before a US federal panel reviewing the protection of wild horses. I wished he were still around to provide me with more background, but he was killed in a plane crash while continuing caribou surveys in the northern Yukon, after I left.

"Hey, Dave," I half-joked, "I think we are studying the wrong species of charismatic megafauna, even though the grizzlies may be impacted by opening up the Brittany Plateau to logging . . . maybe we should seriously include more information on these wild horses in our biological inventory, both the negative and positive aspects."

David mulled it over and agreed I should include more information on qiyus, since they were such a prevalent part of the ecosystem and of such high cultural and heritage importance to the Xeni Gwet'in. I suggested we continue to look for evidence of wild-horse overpopulation, overgrazing and other negative impacts.

That evening's exploration and discussion, aided by the bottle of merlot and the lingering memory of the black stallion's charge, as well as the strange power of my magic stone horse dream, actually became a turning point for me and the FONV research project on grizzly bears in the Brittany Triangle.

As a wise friend once said to me: "Sometimes it's best to follow, other times to lead." We decided to let the wild horses lead and show us their world and the path forward.

CHAPTER 4

THUNDERING WILD HOOVES ON A MOONLIT NIGHT

On a mellow late-September morning, when the willow leaves had turned many shades of gold and yellow, I, David Williams and graduate student Jonaki Bhattacharyya backpacked with the two dogs to Blue Lake. It was apparently the only one of hundreds of lakes on the Brittany Plateau that still carried suspended glacial silt from the last Ice Age, which reflected in a blue-turquoise colour. We pitched our tents next to a horse trail on a grassy knoll overlooking this serene hidden lake.

After hanging our food in a tree to keep it safe from bears, we set out to look for wild horse and wildlife sign. We found the well-rutted qiyus travel trails along one side of the lake, where they navigated through a maze of grassland pocked with rounded boulders deposited as an esker from the last Ice Age. Besides plenty of fresh wild-horse tracks, we saw wolf and grizzly tracks. We also found an old wolf den in one of the sidehills along Blue Lake. More evidence of a vibrant wild-horse ecosystem was beginning to take shape in my scientific review.

When Lucy and I went for a walk in the evening to explore the lakeshore, she kept pointing with great agitation in the direction of the adjacent thick pine forest. At first, I thought she might have detected a grizzly bear or a wolf; finally, my eyes focused on the outline of a lone roan horse, likely a bachelor stallion, motionless behind a wall of brown pine-tree trunks, like some secretive ghost. Suddenly aware that it had been spotted, the stallion stomped and snorted, then dashed off into a clearing before disappearing into the forest, branches cracking as it went. We arrived back at camp just as the full moon rose over the far hills, casting its silver light across the still waters of the lake.

The lone stallion that ran through our Blue Lake camp on a moonlit night. *Image courtesy of Wayne McCrory.*

After an evening around the campfire with wine, stories and camaraderie, I crawled into my tent and wrapped myself in my sleeping bag while Lucy curled up at my feet. Despite the pale light of the moon, I fell into a deep sleep. Just before I dozed off, I thought we were in the perfect setting for the kind of dream that awakens one's relationship to things. Instead, somewhere towards midnight, I was awakened by a loud thundering of hooves: the ground shook as a horse ran right past the edge of my tent.

At first, I thought I had been dreaming or that it had been one of the ghost horses I had heard the Xeni mention. Lucy's growling and the fading sound of hoof-beats convinced me otherwise. I suspected our visitor had been the roan bachelor stallion we had observed earlier, but I had no idea why it chose to race right past my tent in the light of a full moon.

When I got up in the morning, although not given much to poetry, I tried to capture the emotions of this experience in my field notebook:

> So that . . .
> In your wildest dreams
> On the deepest night of a full moon
> A wild, wild horse will come
> Thundering by
> Will rear up to
> Fill your entire vision
> And then vanish again
> Over the wide, dark plains.
> Vanish.

When I later relayed this experience to a Xeni Gwet'in knowledge keeper, he did not seem surprised; he told me that his people told a story of a ghost warhorse that ran through camp one night.

Our field observations and remote camera images helped me understand why I was not seeing the wild-horse overpopulation and depleted habitats that I had expected to find. I began to accept that the qiyus were an important part of a vibrant predator-prey ecosystem and belonged on this land. It was likely that predation by wolves and cougars, along with severe winters, helped keep the horses in check and contributed to the portrait of a vital ecosystem, with the horse as the centrepiece.

Wild horses were apparently coexisting with the other grazers and browsers—the moose and the mule deer—all prey for the large carnivores. I understood we were exploring a real-life tapestry woven by the threads of the Tŝilhqot'in Indigenous culture, whose ancient trails and villages we encountered in our fieldwork. Nature's balance was remembered in storylines by Xeni we had talked to. Perhaps this tapestry from the Tŝilhqot'in storylines, combined with my stone horse dream, the charge of the Black Stallion Band and the bachelor stallion running past my tent, confirmed that Tŝilhqot'in qiyus were special animals, living exactly where and how they should.

The winter habitat surveys and species inventory were challenging but rewarding. The wild horses were nearly impossible to approach and document, as their sharp ears could detect our footsteps crunching in the snow, and we most often saw them in the distance as they raced into the pine forests. *Image courtesy of Sharon MacDonnell.*

CHAPTER 5

GHOST HORSES OF WINTER

In December 2001, armed with a growing but still incomplete perspective on the ecology and history of the wild horses in the Brittany Triangle, David Williams and I developed a strong itch to go back out to Far Meadow to see how the wild horses, moose and other wildlife were surviving the long, intensely cold Chilcotin winter. What winter habitats did the horses use, and how did they interact with moose and predators such as wolves?

My previous winter research on the Chilcotin military block had been an intensely chilling experience at −35° to −40° C. It got so cold that trees cracked, and ice on the frozen lakes zinged at night; one of my Indigenous co-researchers told me he'd seen cows freeze to death standing up. Just how hardy were the wild horses on the Chilcotin Plateau?

In the early onset of winter, as the days grew shorter and the nights brought below-freezing temperatures, David and I, accompanied by Lucy and Alligator, prepared for another expedition to Far Meadow. We had to be ready for anything; an accident or vehicle breakdown in such harsh conditions, far from the nearest town, could have dire consequences. We were grateful to have a satellite phone that worked at least part of the time, in case something went sideways.

Fortunately, there was not much snow, so we were able to drive the 4×4 on the 25-kilometre bush road to David's Far Meadow cabin.

The winter surveys covered vast areas of the Brittany Triangle Plateau, where we used cross-country skis or snowshoes. Here, David Williams is snowshoeing on patrol deep in Plateau wild-horse country under the watchful eye of Mount Ts'il?os. *Image courtesy of Sharon MacDonnell.*

We were loaded: snowshoes, cross-country skis, parkas, winter survival gear (in case we had to overnight), boxes of groceries, rum for hot toddies, and ample dog food.

Now that the Chilcotin grizzly bears, fattened on wild salmon and whitebark pine nuts, had migrated to their mountain winter dens, we were excited to travel the wild-horse trails without fear of an encounter with a mother grizzly defending her young, or an adult bear on a moose or wild-horse kill. We yearned to photograph winter scenes with wild horses, wolves, coyotes and other denizens.

On the drive into Far Meadow, we spooked a bevy of trumpeter swans feeding on pondweed in the open waters near where we forded Elkin Creek. The area was on a major late-fall migration route, but these were probably birds that stayed behind to overwinter at spring-fed bodies of water.

A herd of wild horses digging for grasses and sedges in a snow-covered meadow. *Image courtesy of Alice William.*

After the long drive, plowing through snowdrifts and chainsawing through beetle-killed trees that had fallen across the road, we rejoiced at the sight of David's log cabin perched on the hillside overlooking the frozen marsh. We could hardly wait to get settled around the warmth of the woodstove.

But when David unlocked the cabin door, we were dismayed: inside was a mess that smelled of bushy-tailed wood rat (packrat). The varmint had scattered droppings over everything, including the kitchen table. The rat appeared to have left the same way it had broken in: via a small entrance it had chewed through wood and pink insulation. In our cleaning, we sterilized the kitchen with bleach. Sharing log cabins with *Rodentia* can have fatal consequences. The risk of hantavirus, a potentially deadly lung condition spread by rodents, is a reality in the Chilcotin.

We spent our days of sub-zero weather hiking dozens of kilometres, following a network of packed wild-horse trails. After a big snowstorm, we strapped on our snowshoes and created a packed trail for the dogs to follow. By reading extensive track and feeding signs, we found that qiyus were surviving on a variety of grasses and sedges in both forested and non-forested habitats. Their favoured feeding sites were the frozen and snow-covered wet meadows, where they used their front hooves to scrape away snow to feed on the sedges. They also

Once nearly extinct, a group of wintering trumpeter swans take flight from an open pond. *Image courtesy of Wayne McCrory.*

Many Xeni Gwet'in still have a subsistence lifestyle, using their horses for hunting and bringing home their meat, as they have for centuries. *Image courtesy of Gary Fiegehen.*

cropped grasses that had been cured by the autumn sun in the numerous drier meadows that dotted the plateau. Surprisingly, the horses also grazed on the dried pinegrass that grew in the lodgepole pine habitat, especially where the snow was shallow under the trees, and bluebunch wheatgrass on windswept hillsides. The horses appeared to move from one area to another instead of staying in one location and overgrazing it.

In mature pine and spruce forests around the edges of meadows, numerous tracks and stallion piles showed us where wild horses sheltered during blizzard conditions and frigid winter nights. Favoured sites were around older spruce trees with thick overhanging branches, in hollows where there would be more shelter and less wind-chill. We found clumps and strands of horsehair on the overhanging branches. (Years later, we would use this knowledge to locate such winter bedding sites to collect wild-horse hair for our genetics study.)

A herd of mule deer swimming in the Dasiqox-Taseko Lake outlet as part of their annual fall migration to their wintering grounds along the Fraser River. Only a few overwinter in the Brittany Triangle. *Image courtesy of Alice William.*

To a lesser extent, the horses browsed on the buds of willow and poplar shrubs, the favoured food items of overwintering moose, whose sign was everywhere. We observed only a small amount of competition between horses and moose; in fact, the tendency of horses to travel in groups meant that they kept the large network of horse trails open through deep snow, making it easier for moose and other wildlife to travel between favoured habitats. These observations confirmed for me the results of a previous academic study done in the Chilcotin in 1977, which showed wild horses had little impact on moose in the winter.[1] Besides moose being an important prey species for wolves and mountain lions, the Xeni Gwet'in told us they were an important food source for their own community. Aside from moose, the only other hooved wildlife overwintering on the plateau were a few mule deer that had remained behind rather than join the extensive 500-kilometre trek across the plateau to the deer overwintering grounds at

A coyote sunning itself near the wild-horse research cabin at Far Meadow. *Image courtesy of Wayne McCrory.*

lower elevations along the Fraser River. This mule deer migration left a lowered ungulate population for the larger predators, wolves and cougars, during the winter. However, we found no signs of predation, perhaps because it was still early winter.

Late one night, I was wakened by the dogs stirring and growling in response to a pack of wolves howling mournfully across the frozen lake. The full moon cast pale light through the windows onto the cabin floor, adding to the moment's magic. I imagined what it would be like to sit silently under a tree near a bunch of resting wild horses, listening to wolves howling in the distance. I also wondered how the wild horses in a distant hollow were reacting to the wolves' howls. I considered how qiyus, as prey animals in the wild, seem to have adapted to survive with the large predators in the Brittany ecosystem; as yet, we had no idea how much the larger predators preyed on wild horses, especially their young.

The next day at Far Meadow, the mercury plummeted to −25°C. With a blizzard starting, I took a cabin day to catch up on my field

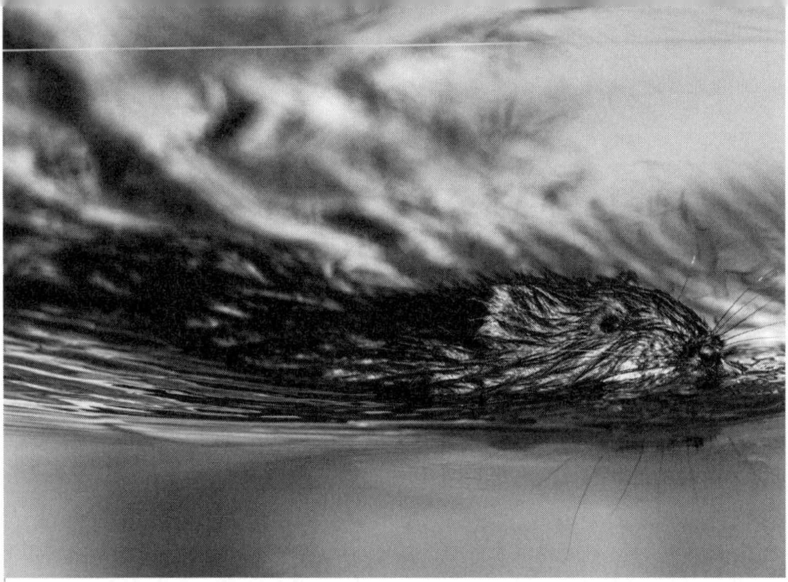

The muskrat is an aquatic rodent well adapted to living in water all year round. *Image © Wolfgang Kruk/Adobe Stock.*

notes and map the different winter horse habitats. By late afternoon, as the all-out blizzard abated, we were treated to the sight of three hunting wolves, most likely the ones that had howled the previous night, braving the wind-chill to trot single-file across the frozen lake in front of David's cabin.

The day after the wolves left, a coyote showed up; it stood on a wooden fence frozen into the lake below, sunning itself. Later, it walked across the frozen lake and entertained us by stalking muskrats at their "push-ups" through the ice. In winter, the small aquatic rodents build "push-ups," feeding stations of frozen vegetation that act as insulation by covering a hole to keep it from freezing. Muskrats use these open holes to bring up underwater vegetation for food.

At one push-up, the coyote pricked up its ears: it had detected the movement of a muskrat inside the mound of vegetation. It quickly leapt high into the air, pivoted 90 degrees and nose-dived straight onto the snow-covered push-up. It emerged with a muskrat clamped in its jaws. The next day, a warming Chinook wind melted the upper layers of snow. Later, the top crust froze hard and iced up some of the qiyus

A coyote stalking a muskrat in its "push-up." *Image courtesy of Wayne McCrory.*

An airborne coyote does a somersault dive to catch a muskrat in its home. *Image courtesy of Wayne McCrory.*

meadows. This would make it much more difficult for the horses to travel between the numerous meadows; now they had to work hard to paw through the deep snow to get enough forage.

Late one afternoon on one of our winter forays, we picked up the fresh track of a large cougar tracking a lone adult horse. The crust allowed the big cat to walk on top of the snow while the heavier horse broke through up to its knees. Wanting to see the outcome, we followed the pursuit on our snowshoes for about an hour. Unfortunately, just as the tracks showed that the cougar had worked the struggling horse into a tangle of fallen timber, nightfall descended. Since we were some kilometres from the Far Meadow cabin, we had to race home as fast as we could, fearing we could end up lost in the dark.

By now, my notebook was filled with observations of the winter forage and habitat of the wild horses and moose, invaluable data for my final assessment. I had also wanted to get winter photos of the wild horses for my report. Only a few times were we able to get close enough. In these instances, the horses, well aware of our presence, appeared to want to stay around and satisfy their curiosity about us.

The crunch of footsteps in snow warns wild horses of an approaching photographer. *Image courtesy of Wayne McCrory.*

We found that the Black Stallion Band still used the same home meadows within a 10-kilometre radius around Far Meadow. The Bay Stallion Band kept fairly separate, ranging more to the east. Some smaller unknown bands also ranged throughout the area. We found that we were only able to view them from a distance through binoculars before they ran off. We also noticed that they had thickened winter coats and rounded rumps from stored-up fat. Like bears, wild horses store body fat in fall to get them through winter.

Most often, when we located a band of qiyus in a meadow, their sharp ears and gazes would point our way, telling us they had already detected the crunch of our boots; they would gallop off in clouds of snow. Many times, they vanished before we even got close enough to see them. We'd hear the distant thundering of their hooves and the crashing of branches when they hit the dense timber. The odour of their urine and dung piles lingered, suspended in the winter air. As one globe-trotting photographer put it: "It is easier to photograph the wind than to get close-ups of these horses in winter."

We were beginning to feel that these so-elusive equids were spirits of the wilderness, what the Xeni called *tsin*, or spirit horses. *Tsin*

Winter horses running off in a snowstorm. *Image courtesy of Wayne McCrory.*

was not a surprising concept, since the Xeni had, over many centuries as a horse culture, developed a deep affinity with the qiyus, embedded in storylines and legends.

The following examples from Terry Glavin's book on Nemiah[2] are a reminder of how qiyus had become a legendary spirit animal to the Xeni Gwet'in:

THE HORSE'S SPIRIT
(As told by Francis Sam)

A while back our grandmother Annie William, Francis's mother, told him about a time when they were going to go up Mount Tatlow to pick beartooth and dry meat. This is around July and August. There was three families going up Mount Tatlow with pack horses and saddle horses. Grandmother had to leave one horse behind because he was sick. He was a really good horse. So they left one person there to watch the horse and Francis said he couldn't remember the person's name. Anyway, Grandma and the other families headed up the mountains. They got quite a ways near Tatlow when all of a sudden the horse that was sick caught up with them and he was just running. Some of them were trying to stop this horse but couldn't. Anyways, this horse ran ahead of them towards the beartooth (avalanche lily) picking. They tried to catch up to the horse but couldn't. The next day the person that was watching the horse caught up with them and told them the horse died. So that horse that ran by them was his spirit. It must have wanted to go up the mountain. The horse died somewhere in Danny William's field.

THE HORSE THAT WENT TO HEAVEN
(As told by Danny Sammy)

Over at Mountain House, he was saying, Eagle Lake Henry had his horse in his pasture. Eagle Lake Henry must've come back from hunting or fishing or something and he noticed his horse wasn't in the pasture. He looked all over but all he saw was tracks in the pasture, not outside the pasture. It was weird, he was saying. He figures the horse must have gone to heaven.

CHAPTER 6

1988

THE LAST (?) CHILCOTIN WILD-HORSE BOUNTY HUNT

Bouncing out from Far Meadow in my beat-up 4×4 Ford Explorer, we stopped to visit local trappers Lester Pearce and Rosie Quilt at their log house at Twin Lakes. They had recently moved down from their trapline cabin at Upper Place on the plateau. They found it easier here to access the Nemiah community and the outside. They also took advantage of a good micro-climate and soil suitable for growing a big vegetable garden.

Now that I was keen on learning more about the wild horses, I was curious to find out more about the 1988 bounty hunt that Lester had mentioned earlier. We saw horse sign all over the plateau, but once we dropped into the deep lava-cliff-lined valley of Elkin Creek, we saw no horses, in spite of some sidehill meadows flaunting healthy ankle-deep bunchgrass. In the open grasslands on the west side of Vedan Lake, we saw well-rutted trails that appeared to have been made by wild horses, as well as centuries of ancient travel by the Xeni Gwet'in into the Brittany Triangle Plateau area that they considered one of their key breadbaskets.

Lester and Rosie were puttering in their yard when we drove into their driveway. Once again, ever-shy Rosie quickly vanished into the cabin, her traditional long dress and moccasins just visible in the shadow as she closed the door. After friendly greetings, Lester explained that his trapline area in Nuntsi Provincial Park, on the Brittany Plateau, was not only a prime place for wild horses and moose, but an excellent area for the fisher, which always brought a good price in the fur markets.

Lester told us proudly that he had once live-trapped a bunch of fishers for the US Fish and Wildlife Service. The animals were transported to an area in the US for re-introduction as part of a recovery plan. The fisher is a dark-coated medium-sized member of the mustelid, or weasel, family. It's a larger cousin of the pine marten and a much smaller cousin of the wolverine. These three animals are among the eight species of mustelids found in the Brittany. All are keystone ecosystem predators at different trophic levels, proof of the wonderful biodiversity of the plateau ecosystem. Many of these small predators, especially the wolverine, would benefit from scavenging the occasional dead horse.

Since the fisher's fur was so valuable and because they were so easy to trap—a few trappers I met called them "trap happy"—they had been extirpated from much of the West, including in Canadian Rocky Mountain national parks. I had documented only one when I did a mammal inventory for Parks Canada in Yoho National Park.

"What about the wild horses?" I asked Lester. "What happened to the ones I heard used to range along Elkin Creek? You can see their old trails and scattered bones."

"I shot them all out for the Forest Service, who said they had overgrazed Elkin Creek!" Lester said. "This Forest Service guy drove into my yard here one day in 1988 and offered me $40 per scalp for each set of ears and the skin in between.

"When I said I was not sure I wanted to go out and shoot the Elkin Creek wild horses, he said, 'Well I'll just hire someone else.' So, what else was I to do? I needed the money. If I had not done it, someone else would have."

We could tell Lester was not happy with this story as he shuffled from one foot to the other. We had seen a number of meadows up on the plateau above Elkin Creek where he had put out salt blocks in wooden cradles for the wild horses and other wildlife, so we knew he liked to take care of the wild qiyus.

"Oh, those wild horses were awfully hard to put down," Lester said. "Once you aimed and started firing, you could see in the distance when the bullets hit their bodies with a thump, but they were slow to go down. I just had to keep pumping the lead!"

As he stood in his yard, Lester pointed a weathered finger to a grassy ridge on the far side of Elkin Creek. "That spot up there by the old tree on the knoll, that's where I shot the last one, an old lone white mare. She was hard to put down, too. Later, I set a trap on her carcass and caught a fine dark fisher."

Lester could not recall exactly how many horses he'd had to shoot but guessed somewhere between sixty and eighty. So far, we had only a rough estimate of 150 to 200 wild horses still living in the area, but if Lester's guesstimate was accurate, the Forest Service had sanctioned killing a considerable portion of the overall Brittany population. Lester told me he had once worked for the US Forest Service in Oregon and had found a cave with a pictograph showing Indigenous people mounted on horses. (He later gave me a photo he took.)

"Those wild horses on my Brittany Plateau trapline, they have been there a long time," he said, "but I heard that the ones that used to be in Elkin Creek before I shot them all were mostly escapees from Purjue's ranch—that's what the Elkin Creek Guest Ranch used to be called. That's what they told me at the time, anyhow, escapees."

Lester's account intrigued me. I had never met anyone who had been a wild-horse bounty hunter. I was also curious about the 1988 claims of wild horses overgrazing Elkin Creek, the excuse the BC Forest Service gave to eradicate all of the horses there. I had taken range ecology as part of my wildlife studies at the University of British Columbia and worked on habitat surveys of mule deer and bighorn sheep ranges overgrazed by cattle along the Fraser–Chilcotin Canyon and elsewhere. The open bunchgrass hillsides along Elkin Creek were some of the healthiest I had seen in a long time. If the wild horses that had been shot in Elkin Creek thirteen years before our 2001 surveys had caused so much overgrazing as to justify their eradication, there would still have been considerable evidence of long-term damage. Replacement of bluebunch wheatgrass by cheatgrass and other invasive plants, common in so much of the interior grasslands, was caused by cattle, not wild horses. However, there was no overgrazing in Elkin Creek that I could see, just as we had observed very little range damage up on the plateau, where the wild horses had not been part of the 1988 slaughter. The only serious damage we observed in Elkin Creek was on the Captain Georgetown private land, where heavy grazing by range cows had damaged part of the bluegrass bottomland meadows so severely that weed species, including knapweed, had taken over.

Dr. Bert Brink, my UBC range-ecology instructor (and one of my favourite professors), was, according to the Canadian Wild Horse Society, one of the supporters of a number of wild-horse preserves proposed for BC's grasslands.[1] Dr. Brink was well respected for both his range research and grassland conservation efforts, so the impetus for the bounty hunt did not make sense.

I was now becoming more aware of an entrenched political agenda by the Cattlemen's Association and their supportive grazing managers and biologists within government: to eradicate these last few Chilcotin wild qiyus, perhaps even those left in the Brittany Triangle. Having done wildlife research in the Cariboo and the East Chilcotin grasslands, where I was told wild horses used to roam, I wondered about their history there. This and Lester's bounty-hunt story also awakened in me a desire to do more in-depth research on how nearly all of BC's wild horses had been eradicated, with no protection whatsoever. My journey of understanding qiyus had only just begun.

CHAPTER 7

BRITTANY PLATEAU

UNIQUE WILD-HORSE ECOSYSTEM

Grizzly bears, wolverines, wolves, cougars, and other large carnivores are the essence of wild landscapes . . . They are one of the defining elements in the landscape, adding mystery and fascination and, with regard to bears, wolves and cougars, an element of challenge. For conservation-oriented scientists and land-use planners, large carnivores help to define ecological integrity and the challenge of maintaining complex natural systems.

— **Dr. Stephen Herrero**, *A Sense of Place*[1]

After the winter research expedition with David Williams and chasing ghost horses, I had to rush to complete my final report for Friends of Nemaiah Valley and the Xeni Gwet'in. The threat of clear-cut logging of the Brittany Triangle still loomed. My results and recommendations had to be presented to the Xeni Gwet'in community meeting in the spring. No pressure here, I said to myself when I got home.

I found this task somewhat challenging: I was primarily a professional bear biologist, wildlife generalist and cumulative effects analyst. For me, the qiyus was totally uncharted territory. However, having had nearly a year to carry out the off-and-on seasonal field inventory of wildlife and wild horses, read numerous background reports and books, and learn about the Tŝilhqot'in relationship to the horse, I found writing the final report fascinating.

I also had to remind myself that it is frequently a challenge for wildlife biologists who have a passion for research in wilderness or park settings to be fully objective. It can be difficult to separate science and conservation from personal experiences of creature subjects and other issues related to the animals and their wilderness homelands.

When I attended the University of British Columbia, I was blessed with great teachers, including famous BC zoologist Dr. Ian McTaggart-Cowan, geneticist Dr. David Suzuki and range ecologist Dr. Bert Brink. They were both scientists and teachers esteemed for their research and objectivity. I especially admired Dr. Cowan's ability to balance research with conservation activism and his passion for speaking up for wildlife and habitat protection. McTaggart-Cowan, interviewed for a documentary on his work, once said science had to leave room for mavericks. Dr. Brink was equally passionate about grassland conservation.

The wildlife section of my report for Friends of Nemaiah Valley in 2002 did not yield the results I had first anticipated. For example, when my bear-biologist friend Marty Williams and I first drove to Far Meadow in autumn 2001, we passed through miles and miles of mature lodgepole pine forest stretching in every direction as far as our eyes could see. Consequently, I was initially unimpressed with the biodiversity values of the Brittany Plateau, even though the large expanses of pine forests were unlogged.

Also, I had done previous wildlife research in the Chilcotin grasslands to the east, near Riske Creek, in what I considered a cattle-ranch "zone of grizzly bear and carnivore extirpation," where any grizzly bear or wolf that happened to wander down from the mountains had its life curtailed by lead bullets, traps or strychnine-poisoned baits. Therefore, I assumed there would be very few North American symbols of wilderness left in the Brittany.

How wrong I was, on all counts.

The Brittany Plateau proved to be biologically rich in diverse wildlife species because of its mix of lodgepole pine forests and hundreds of large and small meadows, wetlands and lakes. Large salmon runs on the Chilko River and small Chinook runs in Elkin Creek provided nutrient-rich food for all residents. Mountain ranges at the south end provided alpine habitats for mountain-dwelling wildlife. The Brittany had never been clear-cut, had limited road access and had only a few small cattle ranches.

Our field surveys and remote camera images showed that all of the larger carnivore species were present: grizzly bears, black bears, several packs of wolves, mountain lions, coyotes, wolverines and Canada lynx. The fisher appeared abundant. Although we found grizzly bears to be of low density on the plateau, up to eighty grizzly bears congregated in the fall along the upper Chilko River to fatten up on salmon for winter hibernation. Although we never saw it, Xeni Gwet'in BC Parks ranger Harry Setah told us that in spring grizzlies also prey on winter-weakened or newborn wild horses, moose and deer. Mule deer and moose were common and are additional prey for these top predators. California bighorn sheep, which are found in the mountains at the south end of the Brittany, add to the wildlife biodiversity. Here they reach their northernmost distribution in North America, just as do the wild horses.

From a conservation perspective, since grizzly bears were my initial impetus for doing the research in the Brittany Triangle, their presence was a good indicator of the health and well-being of the ecosystem. Grizzlies and wolves had already been mostly extirpated from the eastern Chilcotin and BC interior mixed-grassland ecosystem with the influx of cattle ranching, poaching, over-hunting, and the inexorable march of roads and clear-cuts across the vast pine forests. Clear-cut logging now threatened the Brittany, which my research showed was a last major refuge for a viable core population of the dryland, or grassland, ecotype of interior grizzly bear. These bears used to extend all the way down the eastern fringes of coastal mountains to

Members from a pack of eleven wolves on the hunt in the Brittany Triangle. *Image courtesy of Wayne McCrory.*

California and even Mexico, where they are now extinct. In southern BC, only small numbers of the dryland grizzly survive under threat.

Close examination of the logging plans for the Brittany showed that the road densities would be higher than the threshold known to have minimal effects on grizzly bears. Roads would also open up the area to poaching and mortality from hunter-bear conflicts. Some habitat values would be compromised, while cut-blocks might improve some of the berry production.

Although trophy hunting for grizzlies in Brittany Triangle and West Chilcotin has been closed for some years due to concerns over low numbers, locals we talked to said that some grizzlies were still killed in apparent conflicts with cattle ranchers. Some bears are killed by First Nations when they raid salmon smokehouses and curing racks on the Chilko River. However, I was impressed—given that most of the grassland-type grizzly bears (and wolves) had been eliminated by cattle ranchers from the interior BC grasslands—that the Xeni Gwet'in appeared to have worked out a reasonable coexistence.

This is not your typical grassland or sagebrush wild-horse habitat in North America. Wild horses thrive in the Brittany Triangle pine forests and mixed open habitats, with a rich assemblage of wildlife as far as the eye can see, to the coastal mountains in the distance. *Image courtesy of Jeremy Williams.*

The common presence of the gray wolf was another positive indicator of the conservation value of keeping the Brittany Triangle intact. The wolf plays a keystone role in multi-level predator-prey relationships; packs demonstrate complex social behaviour over wide-ranging territories. Our remote camera detected a family pack of eleven wolves, including six young, along the road near our Far Meadow research base. Although we never found a wolf kill of a wild horse, the presence of horsehair in quite a number of their droppings suggested a strong relationship between this top predator and the large qiyus species.

One of the most exciting things I had learned from my research was that both the wolf and horse have evolved similar complex pack/herd behaviour, which includes an alpha male and female sharing the leadership of their family group. The grizzly bear, on the other hand, is mainly solitary, except during the mating season and when the mothers raise their young at heel. The advanced social evolution of the horse and wolf has allowed humans, historically, to domesticate both of these species, our dogs evolving from wolves. Individual horses

A large aggregation of wild horses in the Brittany Triangle. Typically, the horses keep to small families and bachelor groups. However, sometimes family groups combine in large numbers to better protect their foals and yearlings from predation by wolves and mountain lions. *Image courtesy of Alice William.*

and dogs, separated from their herds and packs, learn to bond with humans instead.

Unfortunately, several keystone wild species, such as the woodland caribou and elk, had already vanished from the Brittany, apparently in the early to mid-1800s, for unexplained reasons. The book *History and Legends of the Chilcotin* recounts that the first white cattle ranchers still observed large numbers of elk roaming the East Chilcotin grasslands near Riske Creek before the bad winter of 1886–87. Afterwards, one settler observed the carcasses of elk "by the thousands" in 1888; another recounted turning up many elk bones when plowing his field.[2]

But what about the wild qiyus? Where did they fit in, since they are neither classified as wildlife nor true domestic livestock? Under

Moose, such as this cow feeding on aquatic vegetation in a small pond in the Brittany Triangle, thrive here alongside wild horses and deer. *Image courtesy of Wayne McCrory.*

BC's current laws, they have no protection. Should they be protected as well? This was a complex question. I hired Robert A. Ruttan, a part-Mohawk biologist with previous research experience of Alberta foothills' wild horses, to provide me with background information for my report on the ecology, history and conservation of North American wild horses.

Based on the preliminary findings of the Brittany wild-horse surveys and Tŝilhqot'in oral knowledge, we both agreed that the horses had been in the area long before colonization and had become part of the ecosystem. As well, they appeared to have existed without overpopulating and damaging the grassland and wetland habitats, except for a few small sites.

Robert estimated there were approximately 5,000 wild horses left in Canada, where there once had been tens of thousands. He found that although wild horses on US federal lands are protected and there were numerous federal and state horse preserves, in Canada only the wild horses on Sable Island, off the coast of Nova Scotia, were protected.

Based on these compelling biological factors, my final report recommended that the Brittany Triangle be fully protected as western Canada's first wild-horse preserve.[3]

The Brittany Triangle was indeed a vibrant, intact ecosystem with free-roaming bands of qiyus as the unique animal centrepiece, overlain with a rich tapestry of the Xeni Gwet'in Nation's history of traditional use, ancestral legends and storylines tied to the land. Why not protect all of these values instead of ravaging such a unique wild-horse ecosystem with D-9 bulldozers, logging skidders and feller-bunchers?

CHAPTER 8

CANADA'S FIRST WILD-HORSE PRESERVE

The Road to Nemiah Wild-horse Country, a Hidden Paradise

Consider the implications of a dead-end road. It is, in the modern world, a metaphor for hopelessness, literally shorthand for the place you don't want to be—a blind alley. Take the same road, call it a cul-de-sac and you get a completely different impression: a vague suggestion of prestige in fact. No longer a place you don't want to go, it becomes a haven, a refuge, a cloistered retreat for the privileged. Make this haven a valley, bordered by water, coddled by mountains—raw, wild and mostly unspoiled—and you have found Nemiah . . . The name carries a ring of romance, and if it falls gently on the ear, it is still easier on the eyes. The valley is beautiful in every direction. Icy blue Chilko Lake lies to the west; north and east, a low range of mountains gives way to rolling hills and rocky pine forests of Chilcotin country. Turn south and you will be awed by Ts'il?os, the overwhelming stone presence of a spirit that was once man.

— **Richard Littlemore**, Nemiah: Home of the Xeni Gwet'in[1]

Biologist's Field Journal. June 6, 2002
Nemiah Valley Community Hall

I had spent a long winter glued to my computer screen, analyzing data and finalizing my Brittany Triangle report. After it was carefully reviewed by Xeni Gwet'in Nits'il?in (Chief) Roger William and lawyer Jack Woodward in spring 2002, they invited me to present my recommendations to the Xeni Gwet'in community at their hall in the Nemiah Valley.

Shaking the cobwebs out of my brain, I realized I was eager to get out into the wilds again. Looking out my office window, I saw that the first green buds had appeared on the birch trees. When I received the Xeni's invitation, I was relieved to be able to spend some time in the Nemiah Valley and Brittany Triangle with my wife, Lorna. I'd felt some trepidation when I accepted the invitation, because the Xeni people were so knowledgeable, while I was only beginning to learn about wild horses. Since I was recommending that the Brittany Triangle be protected as western Canada's first wild-horse preserve, I was nervous; some of the non-Native ranchers in the area hated both wolves and wild horses. I was glad Lorna was coming with me to lend support.

From my experience in 1987—in association with Friends of Ecological Reserves, the Valhalla Wilderness Society, World Wildlife Fund Canada, and a number of other conservation organizations—using research to form the underpinnings that helped save the Khutzeymateen Valley as Canada's first grizzly bear sanctuary, I knew that a lot more baseline research would be necessary in order to build a strong case to make the Brittany Triangle a wild-horse preserve.

The cattle ranchers and government range department's misinformation and eradication campaign against wild horses in BC had cemented a century of political momentum that had nearly reached its goal of extirpation of the last Chilcotin wild horses. The thousand or more estimated to be left in the West Chilcotin in 2002 had only

A Xeni Gwet'in rancher drives cattle across the Dasiqox-Taseko River. *Image courtesy of the Estate of the Jimmy Bulyan Family.*

survived because of the Tŝilhqot'in's deep relationship to qiyus, established well before the coming of the white man.

It was a lovely early spring afternoon as Lorna, I and Lucy drove into the parking lot of the Nemiah Valley community hall. As we stepped from our vehicle, the sweet scent of cottonwood buds greeted us. Distant vistas showed mountains, including the sacred Xeni Gwet'in guardian, Mount Ts'il?os, which rose to snow-clad peaks shimmering high against the western sky. We could have been in Nepal, in the Himalayas. Strangely, I felt like I was coming to a home place, a feeling that grew as I returned year after year to do more research.

The parking lot was already packed with a mix of mud- and dust-splattered new and old Ford F150s and GMC 4×4s. Some rusty older model pickup trucks sported fenders held together with binder twine. I reminded myself that the motor vehicle had replaced horse-drawn wagons to connect the community to the outside world only after 1973, when the Canadian Army Corps of Engineers completed the 100-kilometre dirt road across the plateau into Nemiah, with a bridge spanning the Dasiqox-Taseko River. Prior to that, the Nemiah people and their wild horses were isolated from the outside world.

A wagon fording the fast-flowing Dasiqox-Taseko River before the 1973 road and a bridge here were built. *Image courtesy of the Estate of the Jimmy Bulyan Family.*

The horse and wagon trips to Williams Lake took more than a week and included dangerous crossings at a ford on the milky Dasiqox-Taseko River or at Henry's Crossing on the Chilko. These were also treacherous river crossings for Xeni ranchers driving their cattle to market.

Old horse and wagon means of travel persisted for the Xeni Gwet'in until the road to Nemiah was built in 1973. *Image courtesy of David Williams.*

Since we were late for the meeting, we were greeted by an anxious Friends of Nemaiah Valley (FONV) contingent comprised of David Williams, his wife Pat Swift, and Garth Woodworth, another director. It was already crowded inside the hall. I could see that the women had prepared a feast: steaming moose stew, roasted mule deer, smoked salmon, jerky, fry bread and all kinds of other sumptuous foods. While most people had already eaten, stage fright subdued my appetite. I rushed to set up my slide projector, but quickly discovered there was no screen. I would have to project the images on the opposite white wall of the hall.

As I was setting up, I met Jack Woodward and other lawyers from his firm, who were going to give a community update on the Xeni's legal Aboriginal Rights and Title case that was before the BC Supreme Court. Xeni elders had been bused in from outlying homes and ranchsteads all over the Nemiah Valley. I felt I was in an ancient time in another land when I saw the Xeni women in their long, colourful dresses, flowered kerchiefs and moccasins. The elder men, many with weather-worn faces, were dressed in faded jeans with large, shiny rodeo-type belt buckles, black Stetsons and cowboy boots.

Also present was a contingent of local non-Native ranchers, a few grizzled unshaven trappers, and a nervous-looking assortment of government officials, including the range manager from Alexis Creek, whose bailiwick included the Brittany wild horses. With the exception of the government people and lawyers, many of these folks, Native and non-Native, were the ones who had united in 1992 at Henry's Crossing to successfully blockade the logging company.

After an opening prayer and community introductions, Chief Roger William introduced Woodward, whom he called *Dlig ya*. The term means "Little Squirrel" and drew chuckles from the audience. (When the community had been fighting to keep logging companies out of the Brittany in the 1990s, Jack had said to Roger, "But what about the little squirrels? They will lose their homes.") Jack, well known for his long involvement in legal cases involving First Nations rights and title, made a compelling presentation.

Eventually, the Xeni Gwet'in Rights and Title case in the BC Supreme Court had some bearing on the wild qiyus and gave the Xeni the right to capture them for domestic use and other rights, but the case did not confer title to their land. It was only years later, in 2014, that the Xeni Gwet'in won recognition of title to a large portion of their Aboriginal preserve as a result of a Supreme Court of Canada ruling.

After Jack, it was my turn. As I nervously started my slide presentation, I remembered my wife's advice to speak clearly. I paused after each slide so Gilbert Solomon, the local Xeni medicine man and knowledge keeper, could translate my narrative into the ancient Tŝilhqot'in language for elders who did not speak English. I hoped that the spirit of the wild horses would infuse my images, as it did when the elders spoke of qiyus. The translations turned out to be complicated for Gilbert since some of the scientific terms did not transfer well to the ancient Tŝilhqot'in tongue. However, the images communicated the meanings.

At one point, pausing to let Gilbert translate my comment that we had not seen any sound evidence of wild horses overgrazing their habitat in the Brittany, I noted the range manager from Alexis Creek lean over to say something to the woman sitting next to her. She did not realize that the newcomer was my wife, who, being a professional journalist, was an astute observer of human nature.

Lorna told me after the meeting that the range manager had whispered that our observations of the wild horses not eating themselves out of house and home in the Brittany Triangle was wrong and that "wild horses were notorious spot grazers." Lorna also told me that before the meeting the wife of one of the outside activist groups present whispered to her that they were "not your normal hippie-type environmentalists" and that raising a firearm to defend nature was not out of the question. Welcome to the wild Chilcotin, I thought.

I ended my presentation with the recommendation that the *entire* Brittany Triangle be protected from logging and become western Canada's first wild-horse preserve. This brought a loud round of applause. After ten minutes of questions, I was relieved to turn off my slide projector and sit down.

I had expected the meeting to draw to a close, but Jack and Roger both stood up. Roger announced that, based on my recommendations, their whole Nemiah Aboriginal Wilderness Preserve was being designated as "Eagle Lake Henry ?Elegesi Qiyus (Cayuse) Wild Horse Preserve" in honour of the now-deceased but revered Xeni rancher and horse breeder. Roger read out the whole *Wild Horse Declaration* and received a large round of applause. I took note of the government range manager and other officials as they squirmed in their seats.

The declaration covered not just the Brittany Triangle but the Xeni's whole Caretaker Area—much larger than what I had recommended. The preserve covered all of the Xeni Gwet'in's traditional lands, some 770,000 hectares (1.9 million acres), including three provincial parks. It would be the largest wild-horse preserve ever established in North America. While wild horses are not found in all of the preserve, such as around the deep-snow headwaters of the pristine Dasiqox-Taseko salmon river or most of Ts'il?os Provincial Park, it covers a complex of ecosystems and different land areas, including much of the Brittany Triangle and Nemiah Valley, as well as large areas of wild-horse country to the north of the Chilko River. Large clear-cuts are slowly encroaching southward in Xeni Gwet'in territory. At Fish Lake (Teztan Biny), a giant Canadian mining company's drilling rigs, with diamond cutters, were probing deep holes into a large low-grade copper-ore body that lay underneath the lake. The company, Taseko Mines, had plans to create Canada's largest open-pit mine in that location. Meanwhile, as Jack Woodward had explained, the Xeni Gwet'in's BC Supreme Court case (which included the area of the proposed mine) was still navigating through the provincial legal system.

I found the creation of the Indigenous wild-horse preserve rewarding. Seldom are a biologist's scientific "conservation" recommendations so quickly implemented. (Some of my previous independent biological reports had been shelved for life as dust-collectors when they did not say what the client group wanted to hear.) So western Canada's first major wild-horse preserve was born, even though both the provincial and federal governments refused to legitimize this new Indigenous Protected Conservation Area—and still have not to this day.

ʔElegesi is the Tŝilhqot'in name for Eagle Lake Henry. Here is a photo of Eagle Lake Henry and his favourite dogs, including Gyp, at the Far Meadow homestead cabin. A respected Tŝilhqot'in forebear of many Xeni Gwet'in, he "enfranchised" (gave up his Aboriginal rights), which enabled him to pre-empt or buy land to raise cattle and horses off of the Indian reserve where he was raised. He pre-empted the land upon which David Williams's Far Meadow wild-horse research cabin now sits, as well as several other meadows. He was a well-known horse breeder and trader. *Image courtesy of June Draney.*

After the community meeting, I attended a follow-up meeting in Williams Lake with FONV president David Williams and BC Parks officials. While the regional authority in charge of provincial parks said he was not officially able to recognize the new preserve, he did agree that it was all right for Harry Setah, the part-time Xeni Gwet'in ranger for provincial parks, to be recognized as a Xeni wild-horse ranger for the new preserve—as long as FONV raised the funds for that. Canada now had its first wild-horse ranger to patrol and conduct horse counts on western Canada's first-ever wild-horse preserve.

Despite my delight, I realized that there was still a long, uncertain road to travel to convince the provincial and federal governments to pass laws to protect these last wild horses and to solidify Xeni Gwet'in and other First Nations' rights and title to their lands. Previously, the only wild-horse laws ever passed in BC had been designed to eradicate

In 2002, Harry Setah became Canada's first wild-horse ranger, combining the work with his official role as a ranger for BC Parks in the area. *Image courtesy of Wayne McCrory.*

them. The Cattlemen's Association supported bounty hunts that either shot wild horses or rounded them up for slaughter. I knew century-old range prejudices against wild horses were not going to disappear easily.

Some positive media coverage followed the Xeni Gwet'in declaration, showing considerable public awareness of the need to protect our last wild horses. However, I was not surprised when one government official in the Biodiversity Branch of the Ministry of Water, Land and Air Protection said, "horses are not considered wildlife in this province; they're feral domestic animals and our ministry does not recognize them as having value. People like the idea of wild horses; it's a very popular idea and it appeals to a lot of people."[2]

Later, as more positive publicity continued, Chilcotin author and former Member of Parliament Paul St. Pierre lamented with a threat in the *Williams Lake Tribune* (October 21, 2003), saying, "Alas, the ecologists have taken up the cause of the wild horses which run on the Dildil Plateau and other parts of the Chilcotin Country and every sensible man will slip the safety catch on his pistol."[3]

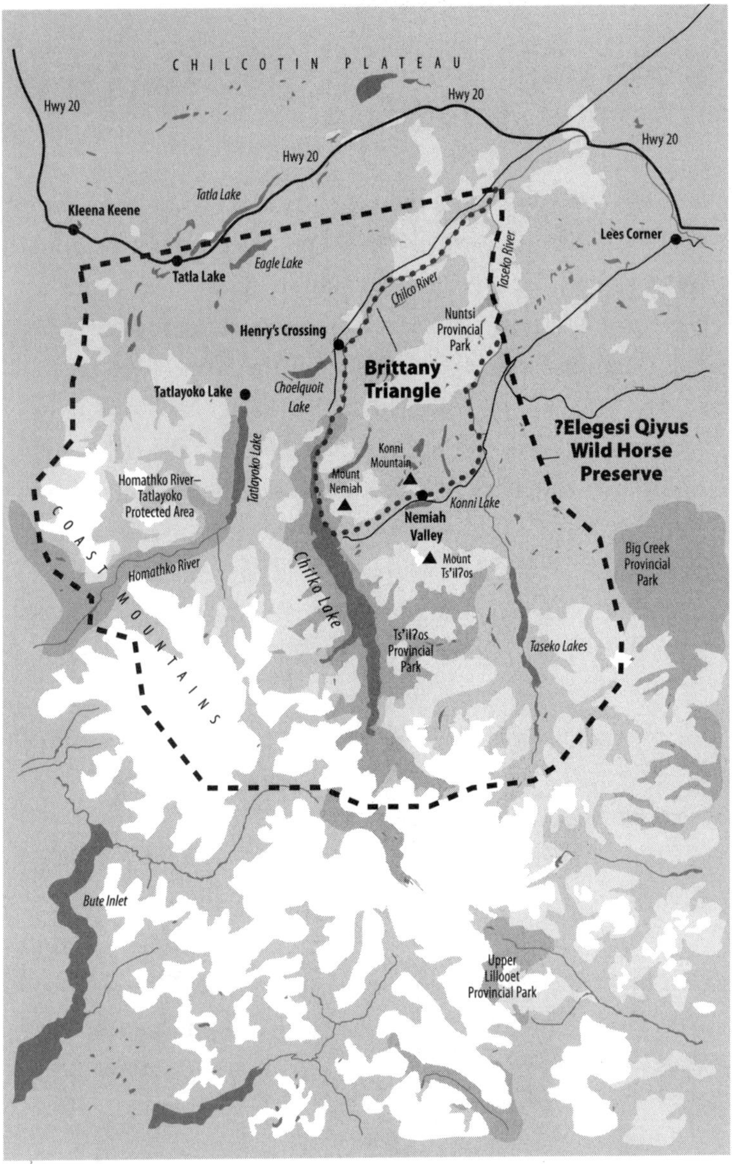

A map of the new ?Elegesi Qiyus (Cayuse) Wild Horse Preserve. At 770,000 hectares (1.9 million acres), it is North America's largest preserve for free-roaming horses, though some of the more mountainous areas in the south are too rugged for wild horses to survive. *Modified image courtesy of* Canadian Geographic.

EAGLE LAKE HENRY ʔELEGESI QIYUS (CAYUSE) WILD HORSE PRESERVE DECLARATION

Let it be known as of June 6th, 2002: We, the Tŝilhqot'in people of Xeni, known as the Xeni Gwet'in First Nations Government, declare the following in accordance with the *Nemiah Aboriginal Wilderness Preserve Declaration:*

The traditional relationship between the Xeni Gwet'in and wild horses shall continue, and the Xeni Gwet'in First Nations Government, while recognizing and affirming the rights and traditional practices of other members of the Tŝilhqot'in Nation, shall be the authority and steward on all matters concerning wild horses within the lands delineated by the *Nemiah Aboriginal Wilderness Preserve Declaration*, which is hereby declared the ʔElegesi Qiyus Wild Horse Preserve.

The ʔElegesi Qiyus Wild Horse Preserve shall, subject to the *Nemiah Aboriginal Wilderness Preserve Declaration* and the exercise of traditional Tŝilhqot'in practices, be protected from human-related disturbance.

Wild horses are sensitive to disruption of the natural environment and their preservation and security requires protection of their habitat; therefore, disruption of the environment, including flora and fauna, in the ʔElegesi Qiyus Wild Horse Preserve is prohibited unless authorized or consented to by the Xeni Gwet'in First Nations Government.

CHAPTER 9

THE XENI GWET'IN DEFEND THEIR HOMELAND

The creation of the wild-horse preserve was one of many ways the Xeni Gwet'in protected their homeland from destructive outside developments. Much had already happened and more was yet to come as we expanded our research on wild horses, work that would help shore up the protective status of the wild-horse preserve and surrounding areas.

Long a nation of warriors, the Tŝilhqot'in had a history of defending their traditional lands from invading outside tribes and white settlers. In 1864, they started the now-famous Chilcotin War that helped stop the construction of a "gold road" across their territory from the Pacific Ocean through to the Cariboo goldfields.[1]

Situated in the remotest area of the West Chilcotin, the Xeni Gwet'in were in a much better strategic position, historically, than the other five communities of the Tŝilhqot'in Nation. The Xeni resisted settler immigrants' attempts to take over their wilderness domain for cattle ranches and get rid of their wild horses. It was not until 1973 that a government dirt road was built into the Nemiah Valley.

When the first settlers tried moving in with their cattle in the 1880s to pre-empt Xeni Gwet'in land, the fiercely independent people put up a strong and mostly successful resistance. They did not want to be forced onto small Indian reserves and have the rest of their best traditional grasslands pre-empted for cattle ranches—as they had seen already happening to the Toosey (Tl'esqox) and others to the east. Writing in 1887 about the Xeni Gwet'in, Indian Reserve Commissioner P. O'Reilly reported that the Tŝilhqot'in "are good hunters and trappers, and living on the confines of a country abounding in game, large and small, they are able to make an easy livelihood." Another reserve commissioner two years later similarly observed, "Seventy Indians winter in the [Nemiah] valley. . . They claim to have 150 horses in the valley but own no cattle, depending altogether for their living on hunting, trapping, and fishing." This reserve commissioner allocated four small reserves totalling 1,257 acres (509 hectares) for the Xeni, noting that "a good deal of this land is entirely worthless."[2]

Many of the Xeni Gwet'in simply ignored the "worthless" small reserves and continued to live across the landscape, as they still do today. At the same time, they were able to drive out most of the first cattle ranchers who had tried to move in and pre-empt their lands.

The following are two classic stories from Xeni elders speaking against cattle ranchers pre-empting their lands during the early colonial days.

TATLOW
(As told by Eugene William)

Long ago a guy named Roy Haines was riding the country to see if he could raise cattle out here. This was when the people around here didn't own any cattle or very many horses. They just moved around. Them days there was no moose at all and very few deer, just fishes is mostly what they lived on and also berries, wild potato, and bearteeth plant. Things like that.

Anyway, this guy Roy Haines rode this country and he figured this was a hell of a place to raise his cattle because he seen all of the grass around stood tall and on the hillsides was at least a foot tall and down low was two feet or more. I guess Sammy William was riding with him and he told Roy the story about Mount Tatlow. He told Roy that this peak called Mount Tatlow was once a man before. Tatlow had a wife named ?Eniyud. Between them they had six kids altogether. I guess they split up. Couldn't get along with each other. Each of them took three kids and separated. Tatlow turned into rock with his kids above Xeni Lake and ?Eniyud turned into rock with her kids over the other side of Tatlayoko Lake. Sammy told Roy when you point at Tatlow he'll make it rain or snow on you. Roy told Sammy he was going to bring his cattle and horses out here because he figured there's lots of hay out here. So Sammy told him that Tatlow didn't like white men.

Roy Haines and his cowboys brought some of his cattle out anyway, then they went back to pick up the rest of the cattle and started to chase them out towards Nemiah. When they got close to Nemiah, where they could stay for a while, he got his men to ride ahead to check the other cattle in the valley. When they got down in the valley they found that all the snow on the mountain slid down about four feet high in the valley. So their cattle were stranded in the slide, plus the horses they left there. Then the boys went back to Roy Haines and told him, so Roy took his cattle back and made a ranch over by Chilko River, other side of Stone, which is now called Chilko Ranch.[3]

By 1940, the Chilko Ranch held exclusive grazing rights between Big Creek and the Taseko River, and controlled a vast empire of 850,000 acres (343,982 hectares) of former Tŝilhqot'in homeland for cattle.[4] This included the controversial usurping of some key meadows that were important to the Tŝilhqot'in ancestral uses, resulting in conflicts.[5]

CHIEF ?ACHIG
(As told by Henry Solomon)

Henry said a long time ago there was a white guy named Elkins. Henry said he didn't know his real full name. Elkins was trying to move into Nemiah. Anyway, he had his camp set up over Lhizbay Lake, just five miles east of Chilko Lake, and a Nemiah chief by the name of ?Achig told Elkins he'll give him a week's time to move out of the valley, or I'll move you out myself.

So ?Achig left Elkins and went home. A week later ?Achig came back to see if Elkins obeyed his command. When he got there at Lhizbay he found out Elkins hadn't moved.

So ?Achig went over to Elkins camp and told him, I gave you one week to move out, and if you didn't I'd do it myself now. Since you didn't obey my orders I'm going to move you out myself. Elkins wasn't scared of ?Achig. He figured ?Achig was just another Indian trying to push him around, and that the Indians didn't own any land as far as he was concerned, as he figured he can just move in. So ?Achig and Elkins started to fight. They fought for quite a while. Elkins is supposed to be a tough person, Henry was saying. Anyway ?Achig finally started to tire Elkins out, then he got a good hold of him and bit his ear, and ripped a big chunk off, then Elkins gave up and found out Chief ?Achig was serious and that he was telling the truth about the land.[6]

The healthy bands of wild qiyus still hiding out in the foothills, the Nemiah Valley and the Brittany Plateau landscapes that back against the Coast Mountains remained largely inaccessible and thus also isolated from many outside colonial government influences. Not until 1988, nearly a century after the start of the first government wild-horse eradication programs, would a representative of the BC range division get around to driving out the long, winding dirt road to Nemiah. He paid trapper Lester Pierce a bounty to shoot all of the wild horses in Elkin Creek in the Brittany Triangle to make way for a non-Native Crown grazing allotment. This appears to be the last government attempt to complete the total eradication of BC's last wild horses through their bounty-hunt system and roundups.

Thanks to the Tŝilhqot'in, the last government inventory of the West Chilcotin wild horses, in 1999, showed that 2,800 wild horses still remained.[7] They are Canada's last large viable population. The 1999 survey also reported no population increase in recent times, refuting cattle ranchers' and range managers' claims of wild-horse overpopulation. The story of the Xeni Gwet'in's protection of their homeland and the wild-horse preserve does not end here. More was yet to come, thanks to the leadership of chiefs Roger William, Marilyn Baptiste and others, often in partnership with lawyer Jack Woodward and his law firm.

For one thing, since the provincial government does not recognize Indigenous protection areas and other such initiatives, dual threats continued from clear-cut logging and, over Fish Lake (Teztan Biny), on the east side of the wild-horse preserve, the simmering proposal for Canada's largest open-pit mine by Taseko Mines Limited.

It turned out that 2014 was a big year of successes for the Xeni Gwet'in. The Supreme Court of Canada confirmed existing Tŝilhqot'in Aboriginal Title over a portion of their traditional territory that included a large area of the wild-horse preserve and the proposed open-pit mine area.[8] This rectified the 2007 Xeni Gwet'in loss, because of a technicality, of their case before the BC Supreme Court (BCSC) to have their existing Aboriginal Title confirmed, even though they had never surrendered their Aboriginal Rights and Title. The BCSC did confirm

The Tŝilhqot'in National Government Nits'il?in (Chief) Joe Alphonse (left), Xeni Gwet'in Nits'il?in (Chief) Roger William (middle), and Yuneŝit'in Nits'il?in (Chief) Russell Myers Ross (right) celebrate the 2014 Canadian Supreme Court ruling recognizing Tŝilhqot'in Aboriginal title. *Image courtesy of the Tsilhqot'in National Government.*

recognition of their Aboriginal Right to continue to hunt, fish and trade furs for their livelihood. For the first time ever, the court confirmed the Tŝilhqot'in Aboriginal Right to capture wild horses for domestic use and transportation.[9]

This confirmation of Indigenous rights to wild horses was a first for North America. It was also ironic since it was the Tŝilhqot'in and other interior BC grassland Horse Nations who had first introduced the horse to the country, long before the white man arrived. The BCSC's denial of confirmation of Aboriginal Title, however, meant that the provincial government, under the BC *Forest Act*, could still issue permits to logging companies to clear-cut the Brittany Triangle and other wilderness areas of the horse preserve.

However, the BSCC also found that the BC government had breached its "duty to consult" by issuing cutting permits to logging companies in areas where the Xeni Gwet'in were claiming Aboriginal Title. This meant that provincial laws such as the *Forest Act*, which allowed logging, no longer applied and that the Xeni Gwet'in would now direct land uses in territory that had been wrongly taken from them by colonial powers. This was a huge victory for the Tŝilhqot'in people and, among numerous benefits, would help secure the ecological integrity of the Brittany Triangle and other areas of the Xeni Gwetin's wild-horse preserve.

Canada's largest proposed open-pit mine, called "New Prosperity," would have drained Fish Lake (Teztan Biny), which has 85,000 rainbow trout. The mine would have had a major adverse impact on fisheries, grizzly bears and other wildlife, as well as the Xeni Gwet'in traditional lifeway. The mine would have harmed the wild-horse preserve, including mine traffic killing Chilcotin wild horses. Two federal environmental impact reviews rejected the mine application. *Image courtesy of Wayne McCrory.*

That same year, 2014, was also a landmark year for the Xeni Gwet'in and their Tŝilhqot'in allies when the Canadian Environmental Assessment Agency (CEAA) panel rejected the Taseko Mines Ltd. proposal at Fish Lake for an unprecedented second time. This was largely thanks to the work of the Xeni Gwet'in leadership, including the outstanding effort of Chief Marilyn Baptiste, who convened a diverse group of tribal chiefs, elders and scientific experts to prepare comprehensive reports and information on Xeni Gwet'in environmental,

Alice and Norman William doing grizzly bear habitat surveys at Fish Lake for the Xeni Gwet'in that showed how the area was a major travel corridor for the threatened dryland grizzly bear. Alice and Norman grew up on a ranch at Little Fish Lake. Their research was one of many background studies that helped stop the proposed mine. *Image courtesy of Wayne McCrory.*

cultural and economic relationships, and potential impacts of the mine to their well-being and future use of their territory.

When the CEAA began its review of the mine proposal in January 2010, my contribution was an independent scientific review that demonstrated that the large scale of the mine and associated high levels of vehicle access would jeopardize the already-at-risk grassland grizzly bear population. It could also cause considerable mortality to wild horses along the main access road.

Canadian Prime Minister Brian Mulroney rejected the mine proposal based on the recommendations of the CEAA panel's 2010 report. In 2011, Taseko, after submitting a revised mine proposal to the BC

International award-winning Nits'il?in (Chief) Marilyn Baptiste helped rally major support and research that helped stop the New Prosperity open-pit mine at Fish Lake and establish a large Indigenous Protection Conservation Area Tribal Park that includes the proposed mine area. It also co-protects a large share of the wild-horse preserve. *Image courtesy of Goldman Environmental Prize.*

government, began moving heavy machinery into Fish Lake under their BC mine exploration permit. Marilyn Baptiste initiated a blockade with her husband, Emery Phillips, and niece Marie William. They stopped a contingent of equipment from moving in to work at the mine site.

The second round of CEAA hearings in 2013–2014 led to the mine's second rejection, but at great cost of time and effort by the Xeni community and their allies, including Friends of Nemaiah Valley. Both times, the panel produced a scathing report, saying that the mine would have adverse environmental impacts to grizzly bears, salmon,

Runs of Pacific wild salmon in the Dasiqox-Taseko River would have been negatively impacted by the proposed Prosperity mine at Fish Lake. Some of the "Super Chinook" salmon are so large that the Xeni Gwet'in have used horses to pull their salmon nets out of the river. *Image courtesy of Alice William.*

rainbow trout and other species. It would also impact the Tŝilhqot'in's existing and future use of the area.

Since Fish Lake and the rejected mine proposal were not in Aboriginal Title land, in fall 2014 the Xeni Gwet'in and Yuneŝit'in declared a large tribal protected area that covered the upper Dasiqox-Taseko watershed, including the proposed Fish Lake mine site. They had already been working on a protected area proposal. This was shored up by a conservation report by me and knowledge keepers and researchers Alice William and Linda Smith; our report helped to substantiate the high wildlife, salmon and other conservation values of the area.[10]

The new tribal-protected area protects much of the wild-horse preserve, as well as a large area of wilderness and Spanish Iberian horse country on the east side of the Dasiqox-Taseko River. In 2015, Chief Marilyn Baptiste won the prestigious international Goldman Environmental Prize for her conservation work, which included her leadership in stopping Canada's largest open-pit mine on behalf of her people. The prize honours grassroots environmental heroines and heroes from around the planet.

The 2003 Chilko wildfire just after it blew up in late July 2003. *Image courtesy of the Ministry of Forests 2003 Chilko wildfire website.*

CHAPTER 10

THE WILD-HORSE PRESERVE BURNS

Going into 2003, some areas . . . in the southern interior were in the middle of their worst drought in one hundred years . . . Evidence of prolonged dryness was everywhere. Near-record low stream flow (10 to 20 per cent of normal in some areas) and deficient ground water raised the concerns of power companies, water utilities and homeowners on wells. The Fraser River peaked near the first of July at one of the lowest stages since record keeping began 90 years ago. Hungry bears roamed the suburbs; hordes of beetles munched on pine trees; salmon suffocated in lethally warm streams; worried utilities imported energy; and water-desperate ranchers culled herds. Just when you thought it couldn't get worse, it did! During most of the summer, a large Pacific high-pressure area anchored near the coast kept weather away from British Columbia. At some weather stations in the Interior, temperatures soared to 40C . . . The forests in the south were tinder-dry and the forest floor volatile—a spark away from igniting. Then came flashes of dry lightning, strong gusty winds and a bit of human carelessness.[1]

—**Weather bulletin**, Environment Canada

July 22, 2003

On the heels of the Xeni Gwet'in's 2002 declaration of protection of the wild-horse preserve, along came BC's largest wildfire. It was called the Chilko wildfire.

Out in the wild-horse preserve on the Brittany plateau, it burned thousands of hectares of pine forests, turning them into black, charred ghost forests. In the end, what appeared catastrophic provided our study team with the opportunity to learn about the relationship between wild horses and wildfires, including wildfire-driven habitat changes.

The big Chilko fire was not surprising: during our fieldwork, we had observed excessive forest-fuel build-up in the Brittany Triangle from decades of wildfire suppression by the BC Forest Service, whose gospel was saving trees for the logging industry. In the early days before wildfire-suppression policies took hold, the inter-montane grasslands of British Columbia evolved in the presence of periodic wildfires such as those caused by lightning. Historically, the BC interior grassland biome and adjacent dry forests had burns every five to twenty years.[2] The Forest Service changed all of that.

Wild-horse and BC Parks ranger Harry Setah had also warned us. He told us that the Forest Service made the Xeni stop their own controlled burns, set at the right time. Two years after the first burn, the Xeni would go back and reburn the tall grass and other plants that had grown back. Harry said that this helped restore things, including making the grasslands better for the cayuses and wildlife. According to Harry, "The Forest Service made us stop this practice to keep the trees for the logging companies and then charged my people with arson when they tried their traditional burning. An old Xeni Gwet'in woman once told me she had a dream that one day a big wildfire would come and destroy everything and that my people needed to be ready for this."

Harry told us this the previous July when he, Chief Roger William and Raphael William, rode their horses 22 kilometres out to Far Meadow to be featured for their role in establishing the wild-horse preserve in the documentary *Wild Horses, Unconquered People* for Canadian Geographic. My wife, Lorna Visser, and I had driven out to be part of this film, along with David Williams.

One afternoon, smoke from a wildfire billowed high into the sky to the west, not too distant from the cabin. Strong westerlies were already blowing the blue smoke our way. In a panic, Lorna and I jogged about a kilometre towards the wildfire to retrieve our wildlife cameras. When we got back to the cabin, the Forest Service fire warden had already showed up to warn us of the wildfire but did not issue an evacuation order. We decided to leave, but the film crew and others stayed to finish their shoot. The Forest Service was able to put out the fire.

On July 22, 2003, David Williams spent part of the day at Far Meadow checking on the wild horses and retrieving film from the wildlife cameras. The whole BC interior was still in an unprecedented heat wave and drought. Many ponds in the Brittany Triangle had dried up; the grasslands were so dry they crunched underfoot. Over on the Chilko River, at the ancient Tŝilhqot'in village of Biny Gwechugh (Canoe Crossing), the first runs of large spring salmon had arrived at their spawning gravels with sadly depleted energy. The warmer river temperatures and lower water levels of the Fraser and Chilcotin rivers that summer left many of these giant salmon spent after their 1,400-kilometre journey from the Pacific Ocean.

The afternoon of July 22, 2003, saw the usual hot outflow winds funneling down the river from the north end of Chilko Lake. There were no lightning-bearing dark clouds on the horizon that day, but everyone in the Chilcotin was on edge, in fear of what could happen.

That afternoon, Karen McLean, owner of Ts'ilʔos Lodge, along the upper Chilko, happened to be working outside when she noticed a cloud of smoke billowing up down-river, near the ancient village of Biny Gwechugh. Realizing it was a fire, Karen raced inside to report it to the Wildfire Call Centre. Firewatch Gail MacIntyre, stationed in the fire tower at Tatla Lake, heard the call come in. By the time the Forest Service swung into action and mustered a waterbomber from Williams Lake to drop a load of retardant on the fire, it was too late. The west winds had already fanned the ground fire into a small firestorm that leapt across the Chilko River and ignited the wild-horse preserve. There was no stopping it.

Later, there was much speculation and rumour as to how the fire had started. A few thought it might have been set deliberately. Others said it was careless fishermen camped at Biny Gwechugh who had left their campfire burning. A year later, when I visited the ancient village site, I found, from the blackened trees and rose-coloured residue of the fire retardant still splattered on the ground, that the wildfire had most likely started somewhere on the hill where stood the Father Nobili Cross.

It took only a day for the wind-driven wildfire to eat up 15 kilometres of pine forest and reach Far Meadow. David Williams, who had seen the fire blow up on July 22, was still hoping to stay and save his log cabin. As he nervously watched the approaching fire from his porch, the fire warden arrived and ordered him to evacuate because the fire had jumped the fireguards in spite of the area having been hit hard by numerous waterbombers. David did not have time to collect the wildlife cameras that lay in the fire's direct path.

Fortunately, just after David left, the fire crew helicoptered in, landed and set up a portable water pump in the lake, connecting to sprinklers positioned around the cabin. They then started the pump and left in their chopper just ahead of the fast approaching fire.

The fire was raging so hot that it jumped the wide lake, but the sprinklers saved the cabin. However, the fire left David's four-wheel-drive vehicle (that we had used for our surveys) a blackened hulk. As well, the fire burned to the ground the old log sod-roof homestead cabin where Raphael Williams had been born. It also cremated corral fences around the property.

The fire continued to blaze east across the plateau, burning up ninety per cent of Nuntsi Provincial Park, the favoured home of the Black and Bay Stallion bands.

Trapper Lester Pierce told me later that when he heard the fire was near his trapper's cabin at Upper Place on the plateau, he hopped on his three-wheeler ATV and raced towards the cabin to pick up his steel traps and other possessions. However, he ran into the Forest Service fire warden coming out and was turned back. Lester said the flames were already shooting 500 metres into the sky on the valley rim. He found out later his cabin and outbuildings had not burned, nor had the outhouse with the warning sign "Never Mind the Dog, Beware of the Owner."

The fire raged so hot that it burned down into the valley bottom of Elkin Creek and right across the half-kilometre expanse of wetlands and willow flats of the old Captain Georgetown ranch. On August 13, the three-week-old Chilko fire had run its course across the 40-kilometre-wide Brittany Plateau. It was finally contained by several fireguards on the eastern side of the plateau. Bulldozed fireguards on the south and north also contained it, preventing it from burning the Nemiah Valley and all of the northern half of the Brittany Triangle.

The combination of the BC Forest Service's fire-suppression policy, widespread beetle-killed trees, climate change, extended drought, and the prohibition of Indigenous controlled burns had allowed the 2003 Chilko wildfire to burn over a much larger area and burn hotter than normally might have happened.

It was BC's largest wildfire that year and burned 29,000 hectares (71,660 acres). The total cost of containing the fire was $8 million. The effort included 200 firefighters, 18 to 20 bulldozers, and numerous helicopters. The once nearly roadless core of the new wild-horse preserve now had 140 kilometres of fireguard roads, 20 kilometres of bulldozer trails and 93 cleared helicopter landing sites.[3 4]

The extensive road network meant our wild-horse study area was no longer remote wilderness. The Forest Service had plans to

The Brittany Triangle with large burned areas and patchworks of unburned pine forests after the 2003 wildfire—part of the renewal cycle of wildfire-driven dry interior ecosystems, with global warming starting to have a greater influence. *Image courtesy of Jeremy Williams.*

deactivate only a few of the new fire roads. Perhaps they hoped that the local First Nations could be persuaded to let the logging companies come in under the government's "fire sale" policy and salvage the burnt—but still marketable—timber.

We feared we'd lost all our wildlife cameras and two months of photo data. Even more unsettling, we wondered what happened to all the wildlife, as well as the Black Stallion and Bay Stallion bands. Their core habitats were squarely in the fire's path.

I was able to do an exploratory field survey in late September 2003. When I returned to the Brittany Triangle, non-Indigenous moose hunters were already camped in the wild-horse preserve and had cut an ATV bypass to detour around the main road blockages made by the Forest Service. The hunters were using motorized access along the extensive fireguard network to search out any moose that had survived the wildfire. When I reported this to the Xeni Gwet'in, we and others wrote letters to government asking them to stop the moose and deer hunt, but officials kept it open. I thought it unfair to hunt the few moose and deer that had survived the inferno after so much of their habitat had been lost.

Bear-dog Lucy and I hiked long-distance transects across the burned plateau to record any dead and live wildlife, wild horses and their sign. At the start, I found the fresh tracks of a lone wild horse going into the burn from the west, as if it had survived outside of the fire zone and was now going back to check out its home territory. I wondered if this might have been the black stallion. I followed the fresh tracks of a large grizzly bear that wandered for a long distance through the burn towards the salmon spawning grounds on the north Chilko River. Maybe it had also been hunting for wild animals injured or killed by the fire.

I also found the white skeleton of a large bull moose that had been trapped by its large antlers inside a dense thicket of small pine trees as it tried to escape. It must have experienced a horrific death. The fire had burned so hot that when I picked up a leg bone, it instantly turned to white dust between my fingers.

I saw large areas where all of the forest was blackened: much of the grass and sedge forage for wild horses and wildlife was gone. In some areas where the fire had slowed and only burned the forest floor, it left patches of green trees with intact shrubs and grasses. In one of those treed islands, I saw a snowshoe hare sitting still beside a log, trying to look inconspicuous. This little hare and the tracks of the wild horse and grizzly reminded me that life would quickly return to the area.

Interestingly, I found no remains of burned horses in and around some of their main meadow habitats, nor did I see either the Black or Bay Stallion band. However, fresh tracks and droppings indicated some horses had returned. Given that most of their grass forage had burned off, it was unlikely they would have enough to eat over the winter. From memory, I was able to locate the remote cameras. All but

Most of the 2003 wildfire had burned out or was stopped by fire-guards, but we found many of the wild horses' favourite Brittany Triangle meadows being consumed by peat fires in the fall. Since we had only observed a few meadows with small exposed glacial till from earlier peat burns, we decided what was happening was unprecedented, and a group of volunteers then put out most of the peat fires in the core area. *Image courtesy of Wayne McCrory.*

two were black charred metal frames dangling from burnt tree trunks. But luckily, I found the slightly scorched but intact camera at the station set up on the horse trail leading from the Black Stallion Meadow. I retrieved another intact camera from a timber frame we had set out in an unburned meadow. Although the plastic edges of the cameras had melted, I was able to remove the undamaged rolls of film and have them developed.

What alarmed me most was that many of the core wild-horse meadows still had smouldering peat fires. These would burn all winter, down to the underlying glacial till from the last Ice Age. I felt this would destroy for a long time the rich meadows for the horses, bears, deer and other wildlife. Not only that, but since peat stored in wetlands is one of the better repositories for carbon sequestration, the

An interesting ecological twist we discovered was that many peat fires in the wild-horse meadows were started by small grass fires that ignited dried horse droppings, which burned like hot coals and then ignited the peat substrate below. *Image courtesy of Wayne McCrory.*

fires would release more carbon into the atmosphere that would also contribute to global warming.

While surveying some of the burning meadows in Nuntsi Provincial Park, I again encountered ranger Harry Setah. He shared my concern; he knew that peat fires left to burn over the winter can ignite new wildfires in the spring. Grass fires sometimes ignited dried horse droppings that burned hot enough to ignite the dried peat.

Up to this point, I had no idea that many of the meadows had, for thousands of years, gradually accumulated rich layers of decaying organic plant matter that formed the deep layers of peat. Many of them were dry meadows in drought years and ponds in wet years. Peat was what my Irish ancestors used to heat their homes; they pronounced it "torf" instead of "turf."

Once I returned home, I continued to be haunted by thoughts of the Black and Bay Stallion meadows slowly being consumed by peat fires. Nowhere had we seen evidence where previous wildfires had burned off the peat underlay of large areas of the meadows. I had difficulty sleeping, troubled by images of starving mares trying to keep their foals alive during winter. My bothersome thoughts would not go away, no matter how hard I tried to corral them. After a week, I reluctantly told my wife that I needed to go back to the Brittany to put out some of the peat fires—if I could find some volunteers.

"Yeah, well, you won't get much sympathy from me right now," Lorna said, "especially as when you left to go up there in September you put a box of wolf scats in the freezer in the basement and then left the lid open. Everything went bad. I had to clean up your stinking mess. You lost a lot of going-away-for-research points on that one!"

A phone call from a tree-planter named John Huizinga, who had read a news article about the horses in the Brittany Triangle possibly starving in the winter, clinched things. He said he knew from some of his firefighting colleagues that you could put out peat fires by digging deep trenches around them. He volunteered to come, bringing one other person. My husky nephew Shea Pownall and another volunteer also joined us.

Upon returning to Far Meadow, we learned from Lester Pierce that the Forest Service had already extinguished some of the peat fires, but many were still smouldering. We set up our base at the Far Meadow cabin. Over the next ten days, the four of us were able to put out numerous peat fires by digging trenches around them. As it was late October (early winter) on the plateau, digging kept us warm. We packed up and left just as a big Chilcotin winter storm blew in. We felt satisfied that we had put out about a hundred peat fires, many of them small but which could have grown larger. We'd saved many productive meadows from reverting to depressions of barren Ice Age glacial till.

A surprise awaited at home when I opened the envelope containing images from the film of our surviving wildlife cameras. What had started as a calamity turned out to be a rare opportunity: we had images of wild horses and wildlife behaviour close to the time of the fire's arrival.

TOP AND ABOVE: Thanks to the hard-working volunteers, many wild-horse meadows in the core Brittany Triangle research area were saved from being burned down to the glacial till. According to wild-horse ranger Harry Setah, this also reduced the risk of peat fires smouldering over the winter and causing new wildfires in the spring. *Images courtesy of Wayne McCrory.*

Despite our wildlife cameras burning up in the 2003 wildfire, one camera near the Black Stallion meadow survived to give us a rare window into the black stallion and wildlife fleeing the wildfire as it approached. The following sequence (opposite) shows the black stallion at the camera, then fleeing, then a black bear and deer fleeing in the same direction. The last two images show the fire approaching and the forest smouldering after the wildfire passed. *Image courtesy of Wayne McCrory.*

One camera showed several horses surrounded by smoke just before the fire reached them; several had cowbirds riding on their backs. Images from the other camera that survived near the Black Stallion Meadow showed a remarkable sequence of the black stallion and a variety of wildlife fleeing from the approaching fire. One of the final images showed the flames burning some of the camera sensor equipment.

In early spring 2004, I was able to return to assess our efforts to put out the peat fires and also to see if any horses had returned to the burn and survived the winter. I also wanted to spend some time with my thirteen-year-old dog, Lucy; given her age, it would probably be our last field-trip together. I called it my "alone dream-time," a reflection of my need for solitude. Sometimes such dream-times work out; sometimes not.

After I'd set up headquarters at the Far Meadow cabin, I took my ATV out to discover that the fireguards we'd dug had extinguished most of the peat fires in the meadows. The same small band of wild horses was using the meadow where one of the surviving cameras had photographed them just before the fire started. They now seemed back home, bedding and rolling in

Images courtesy of Wayne McCrory.

the rust-coloured dust left behind from ashes of the peat fire. Even the cowbirds, which had migrated south for the winter, had returned to ride on the same horses' backs as the previous year.

I continued to search for signs of the Black Stallion and Bay Stallion bands in their normal meadow territories, but they were nowhere to be found. One day I hiked to one of the home meadows where the Bay Stallion Band had overwintered in years past and

This bachelor stallion survived the 2003 wildfire but barely survived the winter as the wildfire burned off most of their dried grass and sedge forage. *Image courtesy of Wayne McCrory.*

came across a sad sight: a small overgrazed meadow was littered with brownish horsehair, skulls and assorted bones of four dead horses. Judging by the large number of horse bones clustered in one area, and the grasses and sedges mowed down to ground level, I guessed this small group of potential wildfire survivors had yarded up here in the deep snow to overwinter.

I used a small saw from my pack to cut an adult femur (leg bone) in half. I found the inside bone marrow was blood-red, meaning the horse had used up its last energy reserves as it gradually starved to death. The lack of winter forage in the burn had sealed the fate of the surviving members of what I assumed to be the Bay Stallion herd trapped in the deep snow. Wolves and mountain lions had either killed them in their weakened state or cleaned up their remains. I felt sad and questioned whether we had made the right decision not to artificially feed the wild horses that survived the big fire.

ABOVE AND OVERLEAF: Bachelor stallions enjoy their home meadow, using the peat-fire ash from the 2003 Chilko wildfire for rolling and bedding the following spring. *Images courtesy of Wayne McCrory.*

Despite this painful discovery, Lucy and I were settling into a pleasant routine. I enjoyed the solitude at Far Meadow and the numerous birds that were returning to the marshes. On Day Five, I laced up my hiking boots to check more peat-fire trenches. I tied my boots so that the top was left a bit open, an old habit that was more comfortable for my creaky ankles. Loading Lucy into the padded box on the back of the ATV, I headed off on another bright day of surveys. Late in the afternoon, I arrived at the meadow where we had dug the deepest trenches last October. I found a section of one trench still smouldering. The peat fire was gradually eating its way underground towards the adjacent unburned forest.

Seeing that it would not take long to deepen the trench, I took up my shovel. Standing on the edge of the smoky trench, I shovelled hot ashes onto a patch of wet bare ground. All of a sudden, my left foot plunged into the trench where the peat fire had undermined its edge. My leg went right down into the smouldering ashes. I quickly backed

out. I felt a searing pain: the coals had gone into the partially open top of my boot. I yanked off the boot, cursing at my carelessness. When I took off my sock, a patch of burned skin over my ankle tore off with it. I hobbled over to my first-aid kit, put some Polysporin over the wide raw wound, then wrapped it with a compression dressing.

I was in deep, deep horseshit—over my head!

The pain was unbearable. I knew the burn would need immediate medical attention, but I was 22 kilometres from my vehicle, then a two-hour drive to the hospital in Williams Lake. My quiet time in the wilds with Lucy and the wild horses was done. I packed as quickly as I could, locked the cabin and headed out with Lucy on the back of the ATV.

Arriving about 9 p.m., near dark, at the main ford over a large creek, I found the river had risen considerably since I had first come in.

I had no choice but to take a run with the ATV, hoping the water hitting the spark plugs would not stall the motor. I barely sputtered across, with the water coming nearly up to my knees. The cold soothed my throbbing ankle, but I was in considerable pain when I checked into the hospital's emergency entrance at about midnight. As staff were busy, I had to wait.

Eventually, a nurse rushed in with a basin and asked me to clean the wound myself. Later, she came back with the doctor, who dressed my ankle. I had a serious second-degree burn, but my cartilage was not damaged. By the next morning, I had a throbbing infection that took several months to heal. Nevertheless, I had gotten off lightly.

The remains of wild horses that starved to death the winter after the 2003 wildfire, after yarding up in deep snow with their herd in a small meadow. We assumed it was the Bay Stallion Band, since they were never observed again. Wolves and other predators had cleaned up the carcasses. *Image courtesy of Wayne McCrory.*

Over the next years, we continued to do what we could to see the large network of fire roads decommissioned, while monitoring how the wildfire had rejuvenated the habitats and how the wild horses had adapted to these changes. The mature and younger classes of the green pine forests, which had survived slow ground "understorey" burns, provided a nice combination of habitats for the horses: tree cover for winter shelter and travel, and lush carpets of nutrient-rich pinegrass. In the more intensively burnt areas, the effect of the fire was more obvious in the great resurgence of new plant growth: lush green pinegrass, thriving flowering forbs, the start of new berry-producing shrubs and pine forests. What had once been a catastrophic event in the world of the qiyus and the wild-horse preserve had turned into horse heaven.

Starting in 2004, we observed a major shift of wild-horse habitat use, from concentration in open meadows to the burned-out forest areas. We speculated that this shift was the result of nutrient recycling caused by the wildfire improving the protein and energy content of the naturally revegetated pine grass. After all, these plateau pine forests were historically wildfire-driven ecosystems; the wild horses over centuries of occupation had learned to adapt to the different successional stages.

We also learned from the 2003 Chilko wildfire that such fire-driven horse heavens are short-lived. Fifteen years after the fire, the intensive regrowth of new pine forests had choked out much of the pinegrass and other forage species needed by the horses and other wildlife. The roots of standing burnt trees also rotted and many blew down, creating large morasses of criss-crossed fallen trees, impeding the horses' travel. After this, we observed that the horses in the Brittany Triangle shifted back to again spend more time in their old home meadows and wetland habitats.

With climate change intensifying, more wildfires followed: in 2009, the Lava Canyon fire—BC's largest that year at 66,719 hectares—burned much of the remaining northern pine forests of the Brittany Triangle.

In 2017, the Hanceville wildfire blew up from lightning near the Tŝilhqot'in Yuneŝit'in (Stone) reserve to the north of the Xeni Gwet'in wild-horse preserve. It burned another large area of the Chilcotin wild-horse country to the east of the Brittany Triangle, creating big firestorms along the way.

Nutrient recycling created by the wildfire caused a resurgence of plant growth, improving the forage abundance and quality for wild horses and wildlife for many years. *Image © Patrice Halley*, Canadian Geographic.

The pine forest wildfire was followed by the nutritious regrowth of pinegrass and other ground plants, opening up previously forested habitat for increased foraging by wild horses in the Brittany Triangle. Here we see horses wintering in the 2003 burn. *Image courtesy of Chris Harris.*

After several decades, the resurgence of the new lodgepole pine forests and blowdowns made many of the burnt areas uninhabitable for wild horses. Heat from wildfires is needed for waxy coated pine cones to release their seeds. *Image courtesy of Wayne McCrory.*

This raging wildfire also provided a harsh illustration of what can happen when a herd of wild horses gets trapped by a firestorm. After the fire, one of the Xeni Gwet'in made a gruesome discovery. She found a herd of eleven dead horses together, including several foals. All of the surrounding burned lodgepole pine trees left standing after the fire were bent over or broken by what appeared to have been a fast-moving firestorm that trapped the horses. Later, some caring people erected a large white cross with eleven horseshoes on it at the edge of the road. Ironically, the wild-horse memorial site was several kilometres away from where a sharpshooter illegally killed five horses in December 2016.

In the spring of 2018, I observed a lone bachelor stallion frequenting the horse memorial. I wondered if he might have been the only one that survived and was mourning his lost family group, as elephants do. Sheer whimsy on my part, of course.

A roadside memorial cross was erected by some Xeni Gwet'in for the eleven horses killed in the fire. The bent trees indicate the direction of the severe firestorm. *Image courtesy of Wayne McCrory.*

In 2018 and afterwards, I observed that several hundred wild horses had moved into the 2017 Hanceville burn area, including sixty horses in one aggregation. This was an unprecedented number compared to the few horses we had observed in the same area prior to the big fire.

A herd of eleven wild horses died after being trapped in a thick pine forest while trying to escape the 2017 Hanceville firestorm. *Image courtesy of Bonnie Myers.*

Severe starvation winters, alternating droughts and high water-table levels, wildfires with nutrient recycling and rejuvenation, large predators constantly searching for prey—all have been part of the natural world of the wild horse

A year after the 2017 Hanceville wildfire, hundreds of wild horses moved in to take advantage of the new growth of nutritious forage. It appears to be an age-old pattern of habitat-shifting by the wild horses that have survived wildfires in the West Chilcotin for four centuries. *Image courtesy of Wayne McCrory.*

Plateau grizzly and black bears also benefit from the improved growth of green plants and berry-producing shrubs created by wildfires. A plateau grizzly, far away from the mountains, is hunting the Hanceville burn, where mares have their newborn foals. *Image courtesy of Wayne McCrory.*

A bachelor stallion, perhaps a survivor of the herd, frequents the boneyard of eleven wild horses killed in the 2017 wildfire. *Image courtesy of Wayne McCrory.*

for centuries. And the horses constantly adapt. Increasing climate change, unless abated, will likely continue to play a greater role in the frequency and intensity of wildfires. Nothing is ever stable in the life and death of the Chilcotin qiyus.

CHAPTER 11

THE ANCIENT RELATIONSHIP BETWEEN WOLVES AND WILD HORSES

The Tŝilhqot'in People of Xeni share Nenqay, which may also be described as a kinetic value system. This value system is holistic and sees all parts of the Earth as relations, in other words "kin." Nenqay and kincentric values direct Xeni Gwet'in to protect all life and ensure the well being of all parts of ecosystems for generations.

—**Xeni Gwet'in interpretive sign**, Nemiah Valley, BC

If it wasn't for those wild horses, you couldn't put a cow out there. The wolves would wipe out the cow herd. They're picking on the horses, is what they're doing; they're saving the cattle.

—**Anonymous Chilcotin rancher**[1]

The Eagle Lake Henry ʔElegesi Qiyus (Cayuse) Wild Horse Preserve is one of the last strongholds for the interior grassland wolf. They have been nearly wiped out through persecution and eradication programs by agriculture, including cattle ranching. Here, a Chilcotin gray wolf fed on the carcass of a wild horse shot by an unknown person near Far Meadow wild-horse research station in September 2019. Sadie Parr's wolf study found that wild horses are a major part of the diet of Chilcotin wolves. *Image courtesy of Sadie Parr.*

After the 2002 declaration of the Eagle Lake Henry ʔElegesi Qiyus (Cayuse) Wild Horse Preserve, we embarked on a more detailed research program, in part with the Xeni Gwet'in. These studies over the next two decades included knowledge keeper Alice William and other Tŝilhqot'in, biologist Robert Ruttan, and others. Several background studies were done by university-sponsored graduate students Katherine Card and Jonaki Bhattacharyya. Sadie Parr did a wolf-diet study. Dr. Gus Cothran directed our research of the wild-horse genetics, while Dr. Ludovic Orlando carried out horse genome sequencing.

A pack of gray wolves taking down an Ice Age Yukon Horse from a distant time. The wolf survived the late Pleistocene extinctions in North America, but the Yukon Horse and many other mammals did not. *Image courtesy of the Government of Yukon and artist Julius Csotonyi.*

This research generated much more information on wild-horse population size, genetics, origins, bounty hunts, range ecology, viewpoints on horse management by local ranchers and First Nations, Indigenous cultural and heritage values related to qiyus, wolf diet and more. In the end, most of this research broke new ground about the Chilcotin wild horse. (This body of wild-horse ecosystem research and Tŝilhqot'in traditional knowledge is integrated in later chapters and is

A dead cow baited with Compound 1080, part of a government program to kill wolves near Riske Creek in 1994. *Image courtesy of Wayne McCrory.*

relevant to my final recommendations for the future of Canada's last wild horses.)

Since we had not observed any strong evidence typical of wild-horse overpopulation in the Brittany Triangle, such as habitat damage, the Tŝilhqot'in caretakers of the land and the ecosystem were doing something right to hold a natural balance. Horse numbers in the new wild-horse preserve, while varied, appeared stable except for the mix of domestic horses that free-roamed in the Nemiah Valley. Here the local livestock association periodically does roundups.

Was the apparent natural balance of horse numbers in the remote areas of the wild-horse preserve related to the role of the top predators in population control? Since we still had limited understanding of the complex interrelationships between wild horses and large predators in multi-species predator-prey ecosystems in North America, we

Eagles and other animals are also killed by deadly poison targeting "problem wildlife." It is still not banned in Canada. *Image courtesy of Wayne McCrory.*

decided to look deeper, starting with the wolf. We felt this to be a unique opportunity, since the West Chilcotin and Alberta foothills are the only wild-horse ecosystems left on the continent where the guild of large predators, including the wolf, has not been wiped out by historic predator-eradication programs run by the livestock industry.

The gray wolf was also intriguing to us, since the predator-prey interrelationship between wolves and free-roaming horses is an ancient one dating back to the last Ice Age, in the Pleistocene.[2] For example, 26,000 years ago the gray wolf once thrived with the now-extinct Yukon Horse in the unglaciated savannah steppes of the northern Yukon. It coexisted with such meat-eaters as the scimitar cat and short-faced bear. When gold miners near Dawson City unearthed from permafrost the near-intact remains of a late Pleistocene Yukon Horse, puncture wounds in its neck and leg bones matched wolf-bite marks.[3] The Yukon Horse, the same species as today's horse, went extinct in North America about 5,000 years ago.[4] [5] However, the gray wolf today survives with free-roaming Chilcotin horses just as its long-ago ancestors lived alongside the Yukon Horse.

Some of the local ranchers and others still shoot, trap and poison wolves, often blaming them for killing cattle. In 1994, when I worked on the Chilcotin military block out in the East Chilcotin, there were only a few wolves left. One winter day, I came across the frozen carcass of a cow baited with Compound 1080 for wolves.

Out in the West Chilcotin, I once came across three wolves in the Nemiah Valley that had been shot and left, I was told, by a Xeni Gwet'in. They would have been from a pack with a known den in the area.

A dead wolf shot in the Nemiah Valley, one of three shot and left on the range that apparently had a family den in the area. *Image courtesy of Wayne McCrory.*

I found that the history of the Tŝilhqot'in relationship to wolves is complex; any interpretation, including my own, is subjective. For one thing, the Tŝilhqot'in relationship and coexistence with the wolf, which they call *Nun*, goes back into the deep time of their peoples' ancestors (*ʔEsggidam*). According to Xeni traditional knowledge, animals with *Nun* in their name, such as the wolf, are known to hold a special energy.[6] The grizzly bear, called *Nunistiny*, is also in this category.

Xeni researcher and knowledge keeper Alice William told me that some of the Tŝilhqot'in elders felt control was necessary when there were too many wolves. Others felt the wolves needed to be respected and protected. She said the Xeni believe that if you kill a wolf, you shouldn't touch it right afterward, to avoid transference of negative power from the dead animal. After this energy-transference process, when the blood has cooled down, it is okay for an adult—but not a child—to

Following wolf tracks in winter is often a good way to learn about the hunting strategies of wolves. *Image courtesy of Sharon MacDonnell.*

touch the dead wolf.[7] According to the Smithsonian Institution's *Handbook of North American Indians*, the wolf was a special animal feared by most of the Tŝilhqot'in. If one was accidentally killed, the hunter made an apology.[8]

Many years passed while we searched for a biologist or graduate student to do a wolf study in the wild-horse preserve. While waiting, we continued to track wolf packs in winter and gather anecdotal information.

One winter day, I was able to track a pack of wolves in the Nemiah Valley area of the wild-horse preserve. I was working on a wildlife tourism study for the Xeni Gwet'in. I was staying in a rustic one-room cabin that trapper Lester Pierce rented to me in return for a bottle of Jack Daniel's whiskey. The tiny cabin was secluded, down a bush road from Lester and Rosie's main house. The small woodstove barely took the subzero chill off the air, so I was glad to be able to venture out one day to explore for wolf tracks.

Biologist's Field Journal. March 9, 2009
Tracking Wolves in the Nemiah Valley

A fresh skiff of snow had fallen at Lester's cabin overnight, ideal for wildlife tracking. I drove along the gravel road to the Nemiah Valley with Lucy, ever-loyal bear dog, beside me in the passenger seat scanning for wildlife. The valley has spectacular winter mountain scenery, rivalling Lake Louise. I was delighted to encounter the fresh tracks of six wolves heading down the road not too far from the Xeni office. I surmised that the pack had moved through the area of small ranchsteads at night. I worried that if they were detected by anyone early this morning, they might end up shot on sight. Becoming more nocturnal was probably one of their long-term survival strategies.

I drove off on a side-road and parked; Lucy and I started following the tracks, hoping we might catch the wolves interacting with a band of free-roaming horses. Lucy, excited about following fresh wolf scent, seemed nervous. All was quiet except for a lone dog barking in the distance. After we'd been tracking about an hour, the sun came up, warming the surrounding peaks with its first golden rays. Snow-blown by the latest blizzard, the surrounding mountains seemed higher today; I felt humbled by their beauty.

Hiking across the open prairie, I felt that everything belonged. Far off to the west, across blue Chilko Lake, was the massive Coast Range that marked the boundary between the pocket grasslands of the Tŝilhqot'in wild-horse country and the coastal rainforests.

To the south rose sacred Mount Ts'il?os, where the legendary Man Who Turned to Stone stood as a guardian to protect the Xeni Gwet'in homeland. At the edge of a large prairie, I got out my binoculars to see if the wolf pack had stopped to rest on the other side. No such luck. However, high on a windswept ridge on Mount Nemiah, I was able to glimpse through the binoculars the speck of a California bighorn ram standing against the skyline. Even at that distance, the telltale curl of its horns suggested it was a large, probably old, sheep.

Once in a while, the wolf tracks would traverse the tracks of a small band of free-ranging horses that had criss-crossed the open meadows earlier, but the pack showed no interest in following the horses' trail. Instead, it veered back onto the main valley road, took a ninety-degree turn north across the open grasslands around Bald Mountain, and moved into the willows along Nemiah Creek. The

A lonely grave site in the Nemiah Valley with a storied history. *Image courtesy of Wayne McCrory.*

wolves walked out onto a frozen pond to inspect a beaver lodge, then continued along the frozen creek past a large corral with wing fences made of pine poles. The Nemiah Valley Livestock Association periodically rounds up wild and domesticated (branded) horses here in an effort to control some of the overgrazing. Unlike the Brittany Triangle, where there was little evidence of overgrazing by the wild horses, here both cattle and domestic free-ranging horses had taken their toll on the grassland ecosystem.

Near the corral was an old grave with a collapsing wooden fence. I had been told that the grave's history involved conflicts between ranchers. Throughout the wild-horse preserve lie ancient Xeni Gwet'in burial and cremation sites, including graves where many people were buried after the 1860s smallpox epidemic. It's a cultural/heritage layer over the land that we respect when doing field research with the Xeni knowledge keepers. They are willing to share storylines from their oral history about places and timelines, including the names of their ancestors kept alive in memories and not forgotten in now-unmarked graves.

A set of large tracks from a wolf travelling with a pack in the Nemiah Valley. *Image courtesy of Wayne McCrory.*

Following Nemiah Creek, the pack of wolves had crossed the scattered tracks of a herd of wild Hereford "bush cows" but had not bothered to follow them. These feral cattle had overgrazed the bottomland and streamside that the Xeni hoped to restore, so the sockeye salmon could return to spawn in their ancestral birth-waters. The wolves tracked back to the main road for a kilometre to avoid a small ranch, then lit out across country along a partially dry lakebed and through the large rolling prairie at the bottom end of the Nemiah Valley.

The tracks passed by the remains of four or five cattle, the leftovers from a die-off the previous winter when a strange ailment depleted many people's herds. Ranchers had dumped the carcasses in the meadow next to the dried-up lakebed. I had periodically checked the carcass pile earlier in the season in hopes of photographing a grizzly or wolf. None showed up that I could tell. As the weather got hotter over the summer, the carcasses had become a tangled pile of hide, shrivelled leg bones and skulls.

As I kept following the wolves' tracks across the frozen, rolling grasslands, I began to notice that they had turned over some frozen horse droppings, but for what? Years back, when I visited Yellowstone National Park, I observed sites where coyotes had flipped over dried buffalo droppings to feed on dung beetles. But it was winter here and dung beetles were long gone. One of the wolves left its large imprint in an area where the mud had started to thaw from the morning sun.

Just as I looked up from examining the track, I saw the tip of a black Stetson appear over the top of a nearby knoll. The wearer then showed his handsome tanned face. I felt a wave of delight when I recognized Harry Setah, the Xeni Gwet'in BC Parks wild-horse ranger, who lived nearby. He had a large dog with him. Harry was friendly, a true horse expert, and always shared his wealth of traditional knowledge. Normally most at home on the back of a horse, he was walking this morning.

"That's not my dog with me," Harry said, holding back a large dark dog with a big head. It eyed Lucy in a not-so-friendly manner that made me nervous. The dog had a thick bundle of orange binder twine tied loosely around its neck for a collar. "That's my granddaughter's dog. I'm taking care of it. It wanders too much. Wanders to people's places. Going to get into trouble."

"Maybe this wolf pack will get him sometime," I said, pointing to the tracks. "They've been wandering all over the place. I even collected a dropping for our wolf study."

"There's a pack of real black ones," Harry said. "Likely the ones that came through this morning or last night that you're following. There's also about six grey ones, one nearly white, in the valley, too. I saw them once all together. Fourteen all in one bunch, last year . . . I think that's why those cayuses wintering down towards Chilko Lake were bunched up into thirty. That's what the cayuses do in winter to protect themselves from those wolves, bunch up."

"Hey, Harry," I said, "I noticed the wolves are going around turning over frozen horseshit. What's that about?"

"That's to eat them white worms . . . the horses have these worms." He held out his hands to indicate they were about a foot long. "That's what the wolves are eating. This dog eats them too."

Ugh, I thought to myself.

"Are they round worms or flat?" I asked. Mammals generally get two types of parasitic worms: round worms, otherwise known as nematodes, and flat worms, known as tapeworms or cestodes.

"I think they are those round ones," Harry replied.

"The wolves didn't seem to be interested in eating those dead cows piled over there," I said, pointing across the prairie. "That bunch that died last winter from that weird illness." We could still see in the distance the dead cow remains, frozen legs sticking skyward.

"No," said Harry. "Maybe they knew it was diseased cow meat."

Several years earlier, a wild horse had died on the open range near Harry's ranch. Harry had told me that in the spring a mother grizzly and her young cleaned up the carcass. I wished I had been around to photograph them.

"So, are those your horses?" I asked, pointing to the band of six standing on a far grassy ridge, alertly watching us. The band included a large bay, a black, a brown mustang-looking stallion, a paint mare with a paint two-year old, and another bay.

"Nope. Mine are always at home, where I feed them hay. These are wild cayuses. I don't know why someone branded two of them and then just left them run loose. But they're two domestics now, the rest are wild ones, slicks. They're cayuse slicks."

Harry explained that to his people a slick is any unbranded wild cayuse over two years of age that is considered unowned. As it has no brand, any Xeni has the right to capture it for their own use.

"We are trying to find out who told the newspapers about the horse roundup we did last year in the Nemiah Valley," said Harry. "We sold those six slicks we shot to the Wildlife Branch to use for bait to shoot wolves that are killing mountain caribou. Wolves supposed to be bad for the mountain caribou. Shooting those wild horses . . . has given our people a bad name in the newspapers. Don't know why the shooters didn't see the brand on the one horse . . . that was owned by someone local who got upset."

"Word was bound to get out anyhow," I said. "But clear-cut logging and snowmobiling in the caribou's winter range is really the problem, not the wolves."

"We only shot six horses for wolf bait," said Harry. "No one came to claim them and pay the fee. We caught and moved twenty-six horses out of the valley. Not supposed to be out on the range all winter. People need to keep them at home, like I do, feed them hay. Too much grazing's not good for the range.

"People have always been shooting cayuses, and some still do," Harry continued. "That rancher up the Brittany, he still shoots cayuses there. So do others. Still do. Not just white ranchers shoot them. Our people used to shoot them, too, to get the bounty. Shoot them, cut the ears off, then find out some of the cayuse still alive, trying to get up without the ears, shoot horse again. That's what I heard anyhow. Now we don't shoot wild cayuses for a bounty anymore. There's no more bounty."

The winds had picked up. Our dogs were restless, and we were both chilled, exposed to the cold westerlies now blowing strong off Chilko Lake. Harry and I shook hands. Lucy and I continued our grassland morning meanderings. It became difficult to follow the wolves' tracks in the blowing snow, so we hiked back to my vehicle.

I'd enjoyed meeting Harry, who had taught me so much about the history of cayuses in the area and his people's traditional relationship to the land. I pondered the relationship between wolves and wild horses: maybe the wolves would only eat wild horses when they could, but the horses were also providing a sort of winter snack bar via the white worms. Wolves, moose and other wildlife travel the packed horse trails when the snow gets very deep. When wild horses pawed through deep snow for the grasses and sedges, they opened the meadows to ease wolves' hunting of the mice and voles that overwintered in their subnivean burrows lined with tiny rounded dried-grass nests. During our field studies in spring, we often observed the remains of these burrow networks and nests in various meadows.

I wondered how much wolves actually depend on wild horses as a food source throughout the year, especially in winter, when most of the range cattle have been herded back to the home ranches and most of the mule deer have migrated to easier wintering grounds along the Fraser River. This pack, and other wolves that travelled in the Nemiah Valley, did not even touch the dead cattle left on the range. I knew that wolves sometimes attack cattle, but I wondered how often wolves actually kill and eat ranchers' cattle. I suspected many innocent wolves get scapegoated and shot on sight.

As one of the local Nemiah Valley tourism outfitters had told us when we interviewed him about wolves for the Xeni tourism study: "Well, I've lived here in the Nemiah Valley for thirty-some years and the odd wolf does get shot, but you know there has always been one or two packs running around. The wolves are still here, just as strong as ever." A pack of wolves had attacked his horses in their corral one winter but killed none.[9]

Wildlife survival rates showed the tolerance of most of the Xeni Gwet'in and their willingness to protect the ecosystem under the joint umbrella of their *Aboriginal Wilderness and Wild Horse Preserve Declaration* and Ts'il?os Provincial Park. If the Xeni Gwet'in had not fought hard in the early settler days to keep out most of the large cattle ranchers, they would have been crowded onto the three tiny reserves the government granted them in the early 1900s. Hordes of settlers' beef cattle would have been moved in and overgrazed the native grasslands, as had happened in Tŝilhqot'in–Tl'esqox (Toosey) territory in Becher's Prairie and in the Canadian Forces' military block in the East Chilcotin. The wolves and grizzlies would no longer be here. The wild qiyus would also be gone, the range cleansed for the exclusive domain of cows.

It seemed to me that we could learn about coexisting with an ecosystem from the 250 Xeni Gwet'in residing in the Nemiah Valley on their small ranches and Indian reserves. They had creatively integrated some of western society's modern rancher culture with their ancestral ways of living off the land, showing tolerance for wild horses, wolves, grizzlies and other predators. In comparison, the East Chilcotin settlers' rancher society and government range managers created killing fields where any wolf or grizzly bear that ventured down from the mountains had its lifespan significantly reduced. If the Xeni tourism-lodge project went ahead, they still had an intact ecosystem with spectacular scenery, Ts'il?os Provincial Park and the Eagle Lake Henry ?Elegesi Qiyus (Cayuse) Wild Horse Preserve for their clients to enjoy.

The First People in the Nemiah Valley worked with nature, despite some overgrazing by free-ranging horses and the killing of a few wolves and problem grizzly and black bears. Their waste transfer station was bear-proofed by an electric fence.

"Was there more to learn here about Indigenous coexistence with wildlife and the intact ecosystem?" asked a voice in my head.

"Look and listen more deeply, and learn!" the voice answered back.

My backpack held the smelly fresh wolf droppings I had placed in a plastic bag for a hoped-for wolf-diet study. It sat in my freezer at home for many years until finally biologist Sadie Parr agreed to start a wolf study in the Brittany Triangle and Nemiah Valley.

Two leading Canadian academic carnivore biologists, Dr. Paul Paquet and Dr. Chris Darimont, helped with the design of Sadie's 2013–2017 wolf-diet study. The research would focus on collecting wolf scats in the wild and analyzing them in a lab for food content.

Sadie's research required her to walk hundreds of kilometres of wild-horse trails—whether during early summer clouds of mosquitoes, scorching hot summer sun with threats of wildfires, or −35°C deep-freeze spells and blizzards. Her research area did not just include wild-horse areas but some areas where cattle free-ranged. This was because we needed to get some idea of how much, if any, the wolves were feeding on cattle. Her wildlife cameras and mapping of wolf tracks and sign indicated a low number of wolves in the Brittany Triangle and Nemiah Valley.

Sadie also donned hip-waders and, armed with bear spray, carefully waded creeks where Chinook salmon spawned, looking for evidence of wolves feeding on fish. Although there was some sign of wolves frequenting the salmon spawning areas, there were no tell-tale field signs of wolves capturing salmon and eating them, as was common with coastal wolves.

Biologist Sadie Parr heading off on one of her many field trips for her wolf-diet study in the wild-horse preserve. *Image courtesy of Wayne McCrory.*

Sadie's study concluded that wolves enjoyed a cosmopolitan diet in both the Brittany Triangle and Nemiah Valley study areas; their menu included free-ranging horses, deer, moose, cattle, beaver, small mammals, birds and insects. Wild horses were the most important and regular component in the annual diet of wolves. For the Nemiah Valley study area, where both free-ranging horses and cattle were common, horses topped the list, while cattle were seldom eaten. Considering the large size (biomass) of horses, Sadie concluded that there was a high ecosystem energy transfer from

Winter 2015. Wolf researcher Sadie Parr examining the remains of an adult wild horse that had been shot and left in the Brittany Triangle. Wolves had consumed most of the carcass. Sadie is collecting wolf scat for her study and horsehair for the wild-horse genetics study. This type of open meadow is prime winter habitat for the horses, as evidenced by their numerous tracks and feeding craters. *Image courtesy of Wayne McCrory.*

horses as a prey species to wolves as an arch predator in the wild Chilcotin food chain.[10] She felt that wolves probably played a key role in helping control wild-horse numbers in the Brittany Triangle.[11]

Sadie's discovery that wild horses were an important component of the wolf diet in the wild-horse preserve was not surprising, given the similar results of a 2009 wolf study in wild-horse country in the Alberta foothills. It was the first such study in North America, and the biologists used Global Positioning System (GPS) radio units on collared wolves from eleven packs to locate winter kill sites. Some fifty-three per cent of the wolf kills were deer, twenty-four per cent moose, seventeen per cent elk and seven per cent wild horses. This amounted to twenty-seven horses killed by wolves over three winter periods.[12] When I later did my independent review of the management of Alberta wild horses, I compared the wolf kill rate from the above-mentioned study to the overall wolf and wild horse population and concluded that wolves might be playing a key role in helping to regulate horse numbers.[13]

Xeni Gwet'in traditional knowledge informs us that wild horse herds sometimes have large aggregations as protection from wolves. Here we see, from a 2017 Xeni Gwet'in–FONV winter helicopter survey, an unusual aggregation of fifty-seven wild horses in one meadow in the wild-horse preserve. The survey documented a pack of wolves in another meadow attempting to prey on a foal in a smaller herd. *Image courtesy of Chris Harris.*

Sadie's research was a large step forward in expanding our knowledge about the role of wild horses in the annual diet of wolves and the possible role that the gray wolf may play in helping control wild horse populations. Still, both the Alberta and BC wolf studies have barely scratched the surface of the complex relationship between the gray wolf and wild horse in multiple predator-prey ecosystems.

CHAPTER 12

MOUNTAIN LIONS, BEARS AND WILD HORSES

The Tŝilhqot'in know the large wild lion as *Nundi-chugh*; in English, cougar or mountain lion. It is the largest of the three wild cat species commonly found in Chilcotin wild-horse country, the other two smaller species being the Canada lynx and bobcat. Knowledge keeper Alice William and her siblings recall that when they grew up on the family ranch deep in the heart of the Xeni Gwet'in wilderness, their dad, Jimmy Bulyan, used the paws or the hide of a *Nundi-chugh* to initiate a baby or a youth to the power of the animal.

Adult mountain lions can weigh 40 to 60 kilograms (95 to 135 pounds) and measure up to 2 to 3 metres (6 to 9 feet) long. Their size is enough, under the right conditions, to bring down a full-grown deer, moose or horse. Unlike the gray wolf, which is social and hunts in packs, the cougar is solitary and hunts alone, unless it is a mother accompanied by subadult young. We know from local ranchers and traditional knowledge passed on by the Xeni Gwet'in that cougars do kill and eat wild and domestic horses. But how often?

Pete, a domestic horse in the Nemiah Valley, on the road to recovery after being treated by a vet for a night attack by a cougar in his corral. Cougars most often attack large prey around the head and neck, hoping to get a tenacious chokehold on their wind-pipe. *Image courtesy of George Colgate.*

So secretive is North America's largest cat that we never actually observed one in the Brittany during our several decades of field research. However, our wildlife cameras often revealed their stealthy presence, as did tracks and droppings.

Our only example of a mountain lion–wild horse interaction occurred when, one winter, we were able to follow the tracks of a mountain lion following those of a horse. The lion was able to walk on top of the crusted snow, while the horse sank up to its knees. We

Five years after being attacked as a foal, "Medicine Bow" still bears the scars of a cougar attack. He was one of only four surviving foals from the twenty-eight known to be born in 2004 in the Pryor Mountains Wild Horse Refuge, with the rest believed to have been killed by cougars. *Image courtesy of Nancy Cerroni.*

followed the trail to where the big cat had forced the horse into a series of downed windfalls buried under the snow—treacherous footing for the horse. Then darkness fell, so we never knew the outcome for certain. In short, we learned little from our fieldwork about the interactions between cougars and wild horses in the preserve.

The Xeni Gwet'in say that cougars not only prey on foals but periodically take down healthy adult wild horses, attacking the head and neck area first, savaging the animal's wind-pipe. One such incident involved a winter-night attack in the Nemiah Valley by a large cougar on an adult domestic horse named Pete, owned by George Colgate.

The attack happened in the fenced-in field with knee-high dried grass and six inches of snow. Judging by the injuries, Pete had his head down, George postulated, possibly challenging the cat, and got clawed across the face. The cougar then sank its jaws into Pete's throat and hung on for quite some time. Biting a prey's wind-pipe is apparently a characteristic attack tactic when cougars are unable to bite through the vertebrae on the back of the neck to sever the spine. The tracks in the snow showed that Pete had dragged the cougar, with its jaws clamped on his throat, in circles for 50 or more metres. Finally, Pete shook the cougar off. Tracks showed the cougar had rolled in the snow and left a puddle of blood before leaving the scene. Although Pete's throat wound was evidence of the severity of the cougar's attack, the horse survived.

The cougar's role as a predator of wild horses in North America has been studied more than other large predators. The studies reveal that there is considerable variation from ecosystem to ecosystem in the predator-prey relationship between cougars and wild horses. The spectrum ranges from cougars preying very little on Alberta foothills wild horses[1] [2] to the horse being a primary prey species (with the moose) in the West Chilcotin[3] to mountain lions controlling a free-roaming horse population in the Montgomery Pass Wild Horse Territory along the California–Nevada border. In this area, cougar predation on foals in spring effectively regulated the population size of about 150 wild horses.[4] No roundups have been done for thirty years.

When I visited the Pryor Mountains Wild Horse Refuge on the Montana–Wyoming border in 2012, Matt Dillon of the Pryor Mountain Wild Horse Foundation explained that cougars sometimes killed a lot of foals in the spring. Matt knew every horse by name and its family history going back decades. After the spring of 2004, wild-horse herd monitoring in the Pryors revealed that only four out of twenty-eight foals known to be born that spring survived; most killings were attributed to cougars.[5] In stark contrast, a more intensive cougar study seven or eight years later showed no predation on wild horses.[6]

Occasionally, an adult cougar will focus on the wild horse. According to one of the Alberta researchers, "We had one large cougar, a 180-pound male, that in one year killed seventeen wild horses, five elk, four moose, and only two deer."[7]

Closer to home, the 2022 West Chilcotin study of collared mountain lions west of the wild-horse preserve in the Itcha–Ilgachuz

Grizzly bears are found throughout the wild-horse preserve in low numbers. Although they are known to prey opportunistically on young ungulates, we saw no evidence of grizzlies preying on wild horses. *Image courtesy of Wayne McCrory.*

mountains found that of forty-six mountain-lion kill sites examined from April to December, moose and wild horses were the primary prey. Horses accounted for twenty-four per cent of the kill, with beaver and moose calves (not horse foals) selected in the spring. Only a small percentage of kills involved caribou. In May, a collared lion killed and ate a black bear cub.[8]

Although both grizzly bears and black bears coexist with wild horses in the Eagle Lake Henry ?Elegesi Qiyus (Cayuse) Wild Horse Preserve, we did not find any predaceous interactions between either of these bear species and wild horses; in fact, we sometimes observed

Black bears, such as this one in its brown phase, are common in the wild-horse preserve, but again, we found no evidence of them preying on wild horses. *Image courtesy of Wayne McCrory.*

them grazing in the same meadows. Since both bear species have largely vegetarian diets, unlike the carnivorous diet of the gray wolf and cougar, we suspect bears would only opportunistically prey on wild-horse foals or older horses injured or weakened from winter starvation.

We observed only two separate instances of grizzly bears feeding on the carcass of a wild horse. One was that of a horse that died from an unknown cause; the other was a horse that had been shot and left in a meadow. We confirmed the low incidence of the wild horse in the diet of bears in the wild-horse preserve by studying numerous bear droppings that showed largely plant and berry matter.[9]

We can therefore infer, but not prove, that sometimes cougars and wolves, but not bears, likely help keep the wild horse population in

Serious injuries or diseases, such as this wild mare's laminitis, make wild horses more prone to predation by cougars and other large carnivores. This sad image was captured on a remote camera set up along a horse trail in the Brittany Triangle. *Image courtesy of Wayne McCrory.*

balance in the Eagle Lake Henry ʔElegesi Qiyus (Cayuse) Wild Horse Preserve. We suspect that newborn foals and winter-weakened or injured wild horses would be the most susceptible to attacks by large carnivores. Although in our research we only recorded one incident of wild-horse laminitis, a painful condition that affects the horse's hooves, this condition would also make a horse more susceptible to predation.

CHAPTER 13

WILD HORSES AND STARVATION WINTERS

In addition to larger predators, winter starvation stalks wild horses, bighorn sheep, moose and deer in the Eagle Lake Henry ?Elegesi Qiyus (Cayuse) Wild Horse Preserve. Prolonged harsh winters have the potential to effect enough wildlife and wild horse die-offs to cause periodic population declines.

Wild horses and wildlife are all well adapted to survive the six-month-long Chilcotin winters. However, during more extreme weather, when deep "inhumane" snow and ice cover their forage, some animals die from lack of nutrition. Biologists call these "starvation winters."

The Chilcotin is well known for its record-breaking cold winters, with temperatures as low as −52.8°C (−63°F), particularly when Arctic air masses get trapped for months over the plateau. There is some possibility that the East Russian (Yakut) bloodlines we discovered in the Brittany Triangle wild horses may also carry metabolic anti-freeze compounds that help them survive extreme winter, similar to those discovered in the Yakut horses of Russia north of the Arctic Circle.[1]

Periodic warm Chinook winds that descend from the Coast Mountains can make winter survival challenging for Chilcotin wild horses. These winds cause melting and then freezing, creating deep,

ABOVE AND OPPOSITE: In the Eagle Lake Henry ?Elegesi Qiyus (Cayuse) Wild Horse Preserve horses survive the long Chilcotin winters by cratering through deep snow with their front feet. Their splayed hooves act as small shovels to expose buried dried grasses and sedges. In some winters on the plateau, a combination of deep snow and hard frozen crusts make for challenging survival conditions. The warming Chinook winds alternate with extreme prolonged Arctic cold fronts, creating melting-freezing conditions and making for a bad combination. *Image courtesy of Wayne McCrory.*

hard-packed snow-crusts that cover winter forage. Horses require much more energy to paw ice to find dried grasses and sedges. Horses and wild ungulates that become winter-weakened are susceptible to being easy prey for wolves and mountain lions. After the harsh winter of 2016, I photographed two companion horses, one in an emaciated condition, that appeared to have survived a predator attack. Their survival shows how tough and hardy are these wild qiyus.

Wildfires that burn dried grasses and other wild-horse winter foods in the fall can also cause winter die-offs. As noted in Chapter 10, about the 2003 fires, we found the remains of four horses that had starved to death in the winter following the burn.

Image courtesy of Sadie Parr.

Image courtesy of Duane Starr Photography.

The wild-horse preserve in spring 2016. Although it was not a severe winter, the smaller juvenile horse appears to have a large neck injury, suggesting it may have escaped an attack by a cougar and then could not get enough food. Its healthy companion, which may be its mother, always stayed near; it waited for it to catch up before carrying on. Perhaps with the lush new green spring forage, the juvenile might yet survive—a testament to the hardiness of these wild qiyus. *Image courtesy of Wayne McCrory.*

Otherwise, we did not observe any major winter die-offs of wild horses over two decades, though it has been reported in other areas. During the early to mid-1800s era of the Hudson's Bay Company (HBC) in the Cariboo–Chilcotin, fur brigade horses were left to overwinter in the grasslands surrounding forts such as Fort Alexandria. HBC journals recorded that those horses sometimes starved to death around the trading posts. As noted by one historian: "Fort Alexandria was the northern terminus of the land route yearly followed by the Company's pack-trains . . . the letters of the managers of Alexandria are replete with references to the large number of horses that died on the way or at their winter-quarters."[2]

Although moose often share the same meadow-shrub winter habitats with wild horses, a Chilcotin range study showed very little overlap in their diets, as horses mostly grazed dried grasses and sedges, while moose ate mostly shrubs. During severe winters, horse herds also keep trails open and make habitats more accessible for moose. *Image courtesy of Wayne McCrory.*

In more recent times, large winter die-offs of wild horses have been reported by the Forest Service in both the BC interior and in the Alberta foothills.[3] Researchers in the Pryor Mountains Wild Horse Refuge in Wyoming–Montana reported the severe winter of 1977–78 caused a fifty-one per cent loss of the population. The die-off was attributed to alternating periods of heavy snow accumulations followed by warm temperatures that caused icing. In the winter of 1983–84, thirteen per cent of the population died.[4 5]

A male brown-headed cowbird. Although not proven, the cowbird, best known for its association with the Plains bison, may have arrived in the Chilcotin with the first horses brought in by the Tŝilhqot'in in the early 1600s. The female cowbird parasitizes the nests of songbirds. *Image courtesy of Wayne McCrory.*

CHAPTER 14

THE BUFFALO BIRD THAT HITCHHIKED IN WITH THE HORSE

I first noticed brown-headed cowbirds riding on the backs of wild horses when I started research in the Brittany Triangle. Even though I knew of their association from taking care of my son's Belgian logging horses in the Kootenays, seeing cowbirds so far out in the wilds of the plateau was a surprise: how had they got there?

As an ecologist, I always find the intricate interrelationships between creatures fascinating. Take, for example, the brown-headed cowbird's mutually beneficial relationship with wild horses. The birds hitch rides on the backs of the horses as they forage, acting as a portable pest-removal service by catching ticks and flies that harass horses. In turn, the cowbirds feed on seeds and insects, such as beetles and grasshoppers, stirred up as the horses forage for grasses. This mimics the cowbirds' past interaction with bison.

The cowbirds have evolved an additional "easy ride" to aid their reproduction. The female cowbird does not build a nest of her own; she lays eggs in the nests of many other neotropical bird species,

This bachelor stallion, with hitchhiking cowbirds, was grazing new spring grass in the Brittany Triangle, its ribs reflecting a long, tough Chilcotin winter. The cowbirds would have recently migrated from overwintering in the southern US or Central America. The stallion was covered with a swarm of biting flies. The horses benefit from the cowbirds feeding on the insects harassing them, while the cowbirds benefit from eating insects along with seeds disturbed on the ground as the horse feeds. *Image courtesy of Sadie Parr.*

including the mountain bluebird. Usually, one female cowbird lays one egg in each nest she finds, first removing one of the host's eggs. Other female cowbirds also lay single eggs in the same nests already invaded by another cowbird. The host bird incubates the eggs and raises the cowbird chicks as if they were her own. Because the cowbird's egg usually hatches a day or two before the host bird's eggs, and the cowbird chicks grow faster than the host bird's chicks, the cowbird out-competes the host's chicks for food and space in the nest.

Another advantage the female cowbird has over other birds is her long reproductive period. One female can lay as many as eighty eggs

Female mountain bluebirds such as this one nest in tree cavities. They are one of many neotropical birds with nests that are parasitized by female cowbirds. Each cowbird lays only one egg in a nest, timed so that each neotropical mother bird incubates the cowbird egg along with her own. The cowbird hatches a day or two before the other chicks and thus out-competes them for food. *Image courtesy of Wayne McCrory.*

over a two-month period. Because cowbirds lay many more eggs than other wild birds, they have been called "songbird chickens."

While there is concern that cowbirds may be contributing to population declines of many species of neotropical birds and other species that nest in the Chilcotin, several studies elsewhere have not shown a serious impact on songbird populations by cowbird parasitism.[1] Clear-cut logging and destruction of nesting habitat are likely greater causes for declines of neotropical birds in the Chilcotin and elsewhere.

It's likely that the "easy rider" lifestyle of cowbirds began as an adaptation to survival in the pre-colonial prairie landscapes with their great bison herds. Once horses arrived with the Spanish in the early 1500s, and quickly spread across the interior grasslands of the continent through trade by First Peoples, cowbirds likely adapted to the horses' nomadic feeding and breeding ecology. I wondered if the cowbird had hitchhiked into the region on the backs of the first horses

A wild horse with a companion cowbird atop its back, photographed from a remote camera in the Brittany Triangle just before the 2003 Chilko wildfire arrived on August 21, a month after it started. *Image courtesy of Wayne McCrory.*

From the same remote camera the following spring. This appears to be the same wild horse—and possibly the same companion cowbird—at the same wild horse meadow the spring following the wildfire. Note the charred forest in the background. Both the horse and the cowbird survived the huge wildfire. The cowbird was able to fly away from the fire, but the horse would have had to do some intelligent long-distance travel to move out of the path of the fast-spreading fire and then survive a tough winter to return the following spring. *Image courtesy of Wayne McCrory.*

introduced by the Tŝilhqot'in in the early to mid-1600s.

Cowbirds are also persistent in their association with wild horses. A wildlife camera set up in a meadow in the Brittany Triangle captured images of a wild horse with a cowbird on its back as smoke filled the meadow from the approaching 2003 wildfire. The next spring, after the wildfire, the same hidden camera documented what appears to be the same horse with three cowbirds on its back.

CHAPTER 15

WILD-HORSE COMMUNICATION

I have spent hundreds of hours safely guiding groups to view grizzly bears and white- and black-phased spirit, or Kermode, bears on the BC coast. Consequently, I learned to read the subtle and not-so-subtle visual cues between bears, as well as between bears and humans. For example, if a tolerant bear being comfortably viewed by humans at a safe distance suddenly lowered its ears or suddenly stomped its feet after turning towards the group, it was a sign for the group to leave or at least back further away. Periodically, I was able to pick up on a bear's non-verbal communication when it would change from being tolerant to feeling uncomfortable or annoyed by our presence, even with no overt changes in its body language.

I am sure this level of subtle non-vocal animal-to-human communication (or vice versa) also occurs with people who spend a lot of time with their domestic horses; it probably also occurs from horse to horse. When I was still lacking in my horse sense, a seasoned warden in Jasper National Park told me that horses will know, before you even put your foot in the stirrup, whether you are nervous around them or comfortable with them. If a horse is going to act up, it will most likely be in response to your nervousness and lack of experience. We were leaving on a ten-day back-country trip with a few horses with behavioural issues; I appreciated his counsel to act as if confident.

Large piles of horse dung are scattered along travel trails or at bedding sites throughout West Chilcotin wild-horse country. They are called "stallion piles" and are believed to mark territory with the scent of urine. *Image courtesy of Wayne McCrory.*

In our wild-horse research in the Brittany Triangle, we were fascinated to see that both stallions and grizzly bears created communication centres where they left their scented calling cards as a potential means to mark their territory and communicate their presence. Since both species have much larger noses and olfactory systems than humans, their methods made perfect sense.

Bears rub trees for scent-marking; wild stallions leave large mounds of horse droppings, called stallion piles. We commonly found such large piles of droppings. If they were fresh, they often smelled of horse piss. They were commonly found in association with large bedding areas but were also located randomly in meadows and along forested horse-trail networks. In some forested areas adjacent to large meadow complexes, quite often where horse-trail networks interconnected at a crossroads, stallion piles were so abundant that the areas looked like winter barnyards.

We sometimes observed a stallion standing stretched out over a mound of faeces and urinating on it. We speculated that the stallion piles were communication centres similar to the grizzly bear rub (mark) trees along some of the same horse trails. Bears either rubbed their sides along a tree trunk or stood up on their hind legs and rubbed their backs on the trees. Either method left ample body scent for other bears to detect. My remote cameras at bear-mark trees in several of my BC study areas showed that even young grizzly bears joined parents in this ceremonial tree-rubbing behaviour. We called such bear trees the olfactory "smart phone" centres; we speculated that each bear might be communicating to other bears a variety of information through their scent glands: gender, status of female estrus cycle, and individual bear body scent.

A breeding lesser yellow-legs shorebird uses a pile of droppings for a perch. *Image courtesy of Wayne McCrory.*

Not much research has been done in the wild on the use of stallion piles for scent-marking and communication, but some scientists think the practice is a way for stallions to claim their territory. One study in Poland of four domestic Konik Polski stallions found that they defecated equally on both mare and stallion faeces but urinated exclusively on mares' faeces. The researchers hypothesized that stallions pooped on other stallions' faeces to announce their own presence but peed on mares' faeces to mask females' presence from rival stallions.[1] However, captive domestic horses in Europe might practice different marking behaviour from wild horses in BC.

A number of horse researchers working with domestic horses in captive situations have discovered that the vocal repertoire of horses includes five call types: squeal, nicker, whinny, sigh and roar. The longest and loudest call is the whinny. A whinny is typically composed of three parts: a squeal-like tonal part; a second atonal, more or less rhythmical part presenting long units; and a third soft nicker-like, generally rhythmical part with very short units.[2]

One study in France found that different whinnies can communicate the size, gender and social status of the caller, but not their age. I was not surprised by this subtle vocal communication system: researchers have found that elephants have a sophisticated vocal communication system in the infrasonic range at frequencies well below normal human hearing. Elephants are able to discriminate between familiar and unfamiliar alarm calls from other elephants over very long distances because infrasonic sounds carry much further than the higher frequencies humans are used to.[3]

While we heard some of these wild-horse vocalizations during our field research, we never had time to pay much attention or to try to interpret them. We also never heard a horse roar. One vocalization we did hear frequently that does not appear in the above-mentioned categories is the loud, short blow from a stallion to warn the herd of a threat, such as us showing up out of nowhere. It is likely used by a stallion to warn the herd of an approaching predator; I sometimes heard this stallion alarm-snort noise when accompanied by wolf-like Lucy. The short, sharp blow is similar to the warning vocalization used by white-tailed deer. I became adept at imitating this sound to try to keep wild horses confused enough not to run off, so we could observe, classify and photograph them.

Perhaps domestic horses in the above-mentioned European study never exhibited the stallion blow sound simply because they lived tame lives, unworried about wolves, bears or cougars, unlike horses in the wild that had to develop different vocalizations in response to large predators.

As with grizzly bears, it appeared to us that wild horses have a fairly sophisticated way of using subtle body language as a means of inter-species communication. This would help explain how herd animals such as caribou, elk and wild horses are able to flee in a coordinated manner when confronted by predators.

We noticed that after observing us for a short period, herds of wild horses would then quickly decide to run off. It was always the lead mare that led the herd off into the woods, with the stallion taking up the rear. We wondered how they communicated this process since there were no vocalizations, such as whinnying, between them, other than the stallion's warning snorts.

Research on feral horses has found that herding was exclusive to alpha males, but that any herd member might initiate departure. Higher-ranking herd members were followed more often than subordinates.[4] This would explain the pattern we observed of the head mare always leading the herd to run away from perceived danger, with the stallion following. Obviously, much more research is needed for humans to understand the many fascinating ways that wild horse herds communicate.

A typical West Chilcotin cattle drive, when the herds are turned loose in the spring to free-range for six months on Crown grazing tenures in wild-horse country and then gathered in the fall. *Image courtesy of Wayne McCrory.*

CHAPTER 16

THE CHILCOTIN KILLING FIELDS

1860S–1988

Direct competition with authorized users would occur in specific areas, horses removing available forage over a permittee's spring range prior to authorized turnout, one of the problems is that we have 14,800 cattle and 850 horses under permit and it is difficult to convince someone from the outside that 500 feral horses are a serious threat to forage supply, especially when we have identified a surplus of range in the District.

—**1988 BC Ministry of Forests** Internal Grazing Memo[1]

My intent in this chapter is to focus on an evidence-based review to expose the true history of the century of range wars against the wild horse, mostly in the BC Chilcotin. I have used my own long-term field investigations, historic accounts, BC government documents (including some internal range management memos), interviews with Tŝilhqot'in people, various newspaper and magazine articles, range studies and other sources. For parts of this chapter, I am grateful for Dr. John Thistle's 2009 seminal doctoral thesis *Range Wars*[2] and his subsequent book on the same topic.[3]

A wild-horse mare that escaped a neck snare set up along a trail, though her neck is scarred. Such snares sometimes kill horses and also catch and kill moose, deer and other species. *Image courtesy of Darrell Glover.*

Early in my research on Chilcotin wild horses, I quickly learned that the debate around the Chilcotin horse, grizzly bear and wolf killing fields was, and still is in some quarters, characterized by deep prejudice, if not downright animosity, against these last wild horses and large carnivores. I also found that evidence used to eradicate wild horses and large predators could charitably be called slim, full of misinformation and speculative, unproven claims.

While there were many efforts to address range degradation by cattle during the century-long war against the horse, for a variety of reasons it was always easier to focus on the less powerful and less economically valuable claims on grassland by wild horses and other creatures that settlers considered pests.

Government-sanctioned ranchers' weapons against these so-called pests included bullets, bounties, snares, roundups, poisoned baits laced with strychnine, and leg-hold traps. The choice of method depended on whether "the enemy" was wild horses or large predators.

According to Thistle, "The common connection and the point of killing animal pests, such as grasshoppers, wild horses, coyotes, bears, cougars, and numerous other species, were at least partly to claim territory—in this case land and resources—for the colonial state and for immigrant ranchers and their cattle. As part of the range cleansing, First Nations that had occupied the grasslands for countless centuries were unjustly forced on to small reserves, with no Treaties ever being negotiated."[4]

This settler monopoly of the grasslands still exists today, leaving little or no room for the restoration of Indigenous traditional uses of their original commonage landscape; it prevents careful rewilding and coexistence with wild horses, wolves, grizzly bears and a multitude of at-risk grassland species. An exception occurs in the more remote areas of the West Chilcotin where the Xeni Gwet'in–Tŝilhqot'in First Nations have been able to sustain much of their traditional lifestyle in a still-intact wild-horse ecosystem.

Since first being introduced by the Tŝilhqot'in about four centuries ago, the Chilcotin wild horse has been able to roam free and thrive within a fully functioning predator-prey ecosystem. Horses and other wildlife also benefitted from improved habitat that resulted from the Tŝilhqot'in's carefully controlled burns. To the Tŝilhqot'in, the horse was a special being, *Nen*.

This stasis continued during the early fur-trade era, during the first half of the 1800s, but changed abruptly with the subsequent arrival of thousands of cattle during the Cariboo gold rush of 1858–1860. According to Thistle, cattle ranching arrived "just after Native populations had been decimated by smallpox and at a time when the government of British Columbia offered land for purchase or lease for next to nothing. Ranches and cattle quickly took over the grasslands and cattle competed there with other creatures the ranchers soon considered pests."[5]

Between 1859 and 1868, 21,216 cattle from the US were tallied crossing into the colony at the government's Customs House at Osoyoos.[6] [7] These first bovines were a mix of British shorthorn and Spanish cattle that originally came from Mexico via California.[8]

It was a long journey for the drovers to trail their large herds through the Okanagan grasslands following the well-established Indigenous and Hudson's Bay fur brigade–Okanagan Trail to Fort Kamloops, then on to the Cariboo. After the gold rush waned in 1860, some of the cattlemen stayed and started cattle ranches. The carpets of pristine, knee-deep bunchgrass that cloaked the interior prairies and sagebrush hills were too hard to resist. Many new immigrants followed once the word was out that the colonial government was allowing the cheap pre-emption of the grasslands.

By 1863, the flood of immigrant settlers had rafted across the Fraser River into the remote Chilcotin grasslands. They poured into the Chilcotin from many foreign countries, in a steady trickle or in surges, using horses, wagons and pack horses to transport their families and possessions.

The Tl'esqox (Toosey) Horse Nation in the East Chilcotin were the most vulnerable and thus the first of the six Tŝilhqot'in groups to feel the brunt of the immigrant influx and have their traditional lands pre-empted for cattle ranches. The Tl'esqox (Toosey) were forced onto reserves too small for their herds of wild horses or to support their traditional subsistence lifestyle. Today, they still keep their own special herds of horses for teaching their youth equestrian skills and for cultural revival related to their deeply ingrained relationship to the horse.

Given that the roots of formal regulation related to the use and control of natural resources run deep in European culture,[9] it did not take long for the British colonists to form a legislative assembly and pass laws to establish British sovereignty over the influx of American gold-seekers and other immigrants.[10] Some of these laws facilitated the pre-emption of Indigenous traditional lands and, eventually, allowed the new settler culture to get rid of wild horses. No consideration was given to the sovereign rights of numerous First Nations who had been living on the land with their own horse herds and governance systems.

By 1870, previous colonial government claims were consolidated into the *BC Land Ordinance*, giving more vested powers to the provincial commissioner of Lands and Works. All white men over eighteen and "British Subjects" could continue to pre-empt 320 acres (129 hectares). The 1870 ordinance also allowed large pastoral leases for the established cattle ranchers.[11] The interior Horse Nations, isolated to small reserves, were not allowed to pre-empt land for about eighty years, until 1949.

It was not until 1891 that the colonial government's Department of Agriculture awakened to the problem of cramming First Nations and their horse herds and other livestock onto small reserves. By the early twentieth century, the Anaham Tŝilhqot'in had as many as 350 horses and 120 cattle on their reserve. This was a common ratio for reserves throughout the grasslands.[12]

Despite repeated protestations by the Tŝilhqot'in and other interior First Nations, the reserves were deliberately kept small.[13] As early as 1863, interior ranchers had started scapegoating Indigenous horses to cover up range degradation caused largely by their own cattle. They escalated their calls for the eradication of the wild horse. Grasshopper outbreaks from 1889 to 1891 exacerbated the problem of the depleted East Chilcotin rangelands.[14] In 1896, the colonial government passed the *Act for the Eradication of Wild Horses*. This made it lawful for "any person licensed by the Government to shoot or otherwise destroy any unbranded stallion over the age of twenty months which may be running at large upon the public lands, provided that such person shall theretofore have unsuccessfully used reasonable endeavours to capture such stallion."[15]

Not surprisingly, this early legal killing of unbranded wild stallions did not solve the ranchers' overgrazing problems.[16] During the 1890s, some Chilcotin settlers also started their own community wild-horse roundups as two- and three-day family sporting events.[17] By the turn of the century, Chilcotin wild horses were also being rounded up and sold to Alberta[18] or shipped overseas to the Boer War.[19] Even with these aggressive control measures, in 1908 a government surveyor's report titled "Horse-Raising in the Chilcotin" claimed there were still "large bands of wild horses frequenting the hills and open country on both sides of the Fraser River although they were not as numerous as before . . . since the opening of the North-west, they have greatly increased in value; consequently many of the wild horses have been corralled and sent out of the country." The report also stated that Indian horses, or cayuses, were generally small, rarely over fourteen hands, but "they are, however, stoutly built and tough, making excellent saddle and pack horses."[20]

By 1912, the appalling social injustices of confining the wide-ranging Horse Nations and their livestock to small reserves finally came to a head. The Dominion government initiated a Royal Commission on Indian affairs. Nearly every interior First Nation made a submission requesting an increase in pastureland for their horses and other livestock. However, again, the government took no action. By then, cattle ranchers had done a thorough job of monopolizing the grasslands. By 1915, there were 100 ranches and 30,000 head of cattle in the Cariboo–Chilcotin.[21]

Over most of the interior, ranchers escalated their war on wild horses. According to John Thistle, by 1919 "state enclosure of the open range, ridding the range of wild horses became, for ranchers and provincial range managers alike, a powerful imperative." However, by 1922, BC's first grazing commissioner finally admitted the truth—that a great deal of the destruction of the rangelands was caused by the stockmen. Nonetheless, backtracking on his original claim, in 1925 the same commissioner initiated legislation that allowed for the continued roundup of free-ranging horses on Crown land, while he also turned to the old mantra of blaming First Nations' horses as "responsible for the heavy damage to the range."[22]

According to Norma Bearcroft of the Canadian Wild Horse Society, the BC government inaugurated a wild-horse bounty system in 1924 that remained in effect until 1967. In the early days, the bounty paid $1 for a set of ears, but later paid $5 for a set of ears, and $7.50 for a stallion's ears and testicles, plus horse-hunters' out-of-pocket expenses.[23]

In 1926, anti-wild-horse sentiments were further fuelled in the Canadian psyche by the publication of a feature article, "Hazers of the Cariboo," in *Maclean's* magazine. The article claimed that the 15,000 wild horses scattered across the interior BC grasslands were "too numerous" and had "outstayed their welcome."[24]

According to Bearcroft, between 1924 and 1946, 10,000 wild horses were shot on the spot and "the Chilcotin region is said to contain a valley knee-deep in the carcasses of slain horses."[25] Chilcotin naturalist and renowned author Eric Collier summarized the 1920s "broomtail" eradication program as follows: "Winter of '24–'25 the hunting got underway and continued through the winter of '25–'26. Working as a team on Becher Prairie–Meldrum Creek units was Wes Jasper and Dave Chersney (now gone). Dan Weir, working from the old Slee and Benner ranch fifteen miles east of Becher House, hunted Harper, Beaumont, and Bald Mountain ranges."[26]

Collier reported that the mustangers were paid $60 a month and $1.50 for each wild-horse scalp turned in. Ammunition was free. He claimed that by March 1926 "the grisly business was all pretty well taken care of. The odd band remained, so wild and elusive that it seemed they were able to outpace the track of the bullet itself. But some twelve-hundred-odd head of wild horses that were there two years earlier were now dead."[27]

Unfortunately, the continued killing of wild horses in the Chilcotin did not appear to make much difference to range quality because it did not address the real overgrazing problem—the cow. A 1936 government range study concluded that cattle had reduced the 9,000-hectare Becher Prairie at Riske Creek "to weed stage."[28] Range ecologist Dr. Bert Brink lamented the dismal state of the interior grassland ranges caused by too many cattle: "You can't imagine what some of these ranges were like by the 1920s . . . much dust. Dark, black dust."[29]

As if the 1920s mass slaughtering of wild horses in the East Chilcotin grasslands were not harsh enough, the 1930 Grazing Commission decided that the government should turn its gun-sights westwards and aim them at Tŝilhqot'in wild horses in the wilderness enclaves.[30] Few records, if any, of this westward wild-horse eradication program appear to have been kept by government. One West Chilcotin old-timer recalled that in 1930, two bounty hunters hired by BC Forestry killed over a thousand wild horses. The last big hunt occurred in the winter of 1939 when BC Forestry hired the old-timer and his brother to shoot 400 wild horses. Their killing fields ranged across much of the West Chilcotin and into the Nemiah Valley.[31]

In 1940 a Vancouver *Province* article trumpeted to its readers "War is Declared on Wild Horses of the Cariboo Area," stating, "Once more the fiat has gone forth, 'Kill the wild horse.'" The article claimed that over the past twelve years over 10,000 had been slain, mostly west of the Fraser River (i.e., in the Chilcotin).

A *Victoria Daily Times* article again headlined that war was declared on wild horses, observing that over the past thirty years a type of guerilla warfare had been carried out against BC's wild horses and that they were steadily being reduced. The newspaper fanned the issue by promoting total eradication: "This year they must all go, if possible."[32] In 1965, nearly seventy years after the *Wild Horse Eradication Act*, wild horses, including those from the West Chilcotin, were still being rounded up and marketed for horsemeat.[33]

Records kept by the provincial grazing branch indicate more than 13,000 horses were removed from BC over the three decades between 1924 and 1955.[34] After World War II, warhorses were in demand for human consumption.

Old, weathered wild-horse bones are scattered across Chilcotin wild-horse county. If bones could talk, they would tell the story of horse deaths by natural causes or of death caused by the colonial government's aggressive wild-horse eradication programs. Tŝilhqot'in elder Norman William tells a story of a large area of wild-horse bones in Nabas, where a whole herd of ponies was shot by government-paid bounty hunters in the 1920s. *Image courtesy of Sharon MacDonnell.*

According to a 1965 *BC Outdoors* article, "wild horses were flushed from every part of BC, cornered, and shipped for butchering." British Columbia horses and those from the prairies were still shipped to Alsack in Edmonton, where government inspectors checked the horsemeat. From there, it was shipped to Europe and Japan, and also sold in stores across Canada, two of which were in Vancouver. According to the article, "Mr. Foss Hoy of Cloverdale, who operates one of the few remaining slaughterhouses on the lower mainland, says that up to eight or nine years ago he used to kill about 100 horses a week, but now his horsemeat trade is largely restricted to the pet food market. The last real wild-horse shipment Mr. Hoy received was fifty-four a year ago from Alexis Creek area in the Chilcotin."[35] Whatever the true numbers of wild horses slaughtered during the century-long era of the Chilcotin killing fields, it is obvious that the grasslands had been turned into a wild-horse boneyard.

By the mid-1960s, some Canadians, such as the newly formed Canadian Wild Horse Society, looked askance at the government's wild-horse eradication program. The society published a book in 1966 that documented, for the first time, the appalling history of the bounty hunts. The society recommended that a number of wild-horse reserves be established in BC.[36] It was a wake-up call: if Canadians did not speak up to protect the last wild horses, they would soon all be gone.

BC government range managers responded to the adverse publicity by adopting new strategies and rationales to deal with the "horse preservationists," while admitting in internal documents that their previous semi-official policy from the range management office had been to muffle any publicity about their horse-control program.

In January 28, 1977, an internal memorandum to all range supervisors and agrologists in Cariboo Forest District from Williams Lake District range manager Lyle Resh issued the following public relations instructions: "We do not wish you to over publicize our horse program, but if asked, explain with range management reasons why we do not recognize horses as having a wild status in the ecology of BC."

Reasons cited for the wild-horse control issue included: "Headaches to our administration of Crown ranges were seasonal trampling and grazing, competition with cattle where ranges were fully stocked, competition with wildlife and areas with 'little winter rustling' causing . . . inhuman conditions to the horses during the winter." I could find no evidence that any of these claims had ever been independently verified in the field. It seemed a far-fetched rationale to be saving wild horses from "inhuman conditions . . . during winter"[37] by rounding them up and shipping them off to slaughterhouses.

Media attention to the plight of the last Chilcotin wild horses came and went; it reached a critical head in March 1988, with a major exposé in the *Vancouver Sun* by author Terry Glavin. In "The Killing of the Wild Horses: Problem Worsens in the Chilcotin," Glavin reported at length on the controversial wild-horse cull in the West Chilcotin in winter 1987–1988. A total of twenty-three horses were shot on the range, and another 120 rounded up and shipped to Williams Lake and auctioned off to a slaughterhouse for pet food.

Glavin's article pointed out that only ranchers were allowed to bid on the wild-horse roundup permits, which included a subsidy of $80 per horse, with the permit-holders being allowed to capture as many horses as they saw fit. For wild horses too difficult to round up, there was a bounty of $40 for each scalp taken. According to range officer Steve Demelt of Alexis Creek, a horse scalp was defined as "the piece of skin between the ears and the adjoining tuft of hair."[38] No mention was made in the account as to how many pregnant mares and foals born the previous spring were shot on the range or rounded up and sent to slaughter.

I was shocked to learn from Glavin's article that the roundups were also allowed in the final weeks of winter, when the wild horses were at their weakest and mares were heavy with foal. The *Sun* article described how the wild horses were chased by mounted cowboys through unbroken snow. According to Demelt, "Each animal is usually individually run down to the point where they are exhausted." While Demelt admitted that running down wild horses to exhaustion might be controversial, he justified it as "more humane, in many cases, to round them up for slaughter, rather than leave them to succumb to the elements, which often happens." As with a similar argument used in the past by range managers, it seemed to me a twisted rationale for the government to claim that it was "humane" to run down wild horses in late winter until they were exhausted or simply shot in order to save them from "inhumane" natural conditions in the wilds—when such animals had survived in the Chilcotin wilderness for centuries. As well, the 1988 BC range management's population estimate for the West Chilcotin was about 500 wild horses versus 850 domestic horses and 14,800 cattle.[39] It is hard to imagine how 500 wild horses were the root of the overgrazing problem when for every wild horse on the range there were 30 cows.

In reaction to Glavin's *Vancouver Sun* article, the Integrated Resources Branch of the Ministry of Forests and Lands in Victoria swung into defensive mode. It faxed a "strictly confidential" interim briefing note to Chilcotin range officer Steve Demelt advising his office how to best deal with the adverse publicity. This included citing that "horses can reach population levels that cause deterioration of the Range, pose serious competition for native wildlife, and also compete with domestic livestock."[40]

It was highly misleading for headquarters to omit mention of the only range study ever done in the Chilcotin (in 1984) that attributed most of range damage to cattle, not wild horses.[41] Furthermore, when I examined the Range Management Division's wild-horse aerial counts for West Chilcotin that started in 1989, I did not see any convincing evidence that there was an overpopulation of wild horses.

Public controversy over the 1987–88 Chilcotin wild-horse bounty hunt should have ended the culls, but it did not. The war on wild horses just continued. In 1990, the Vancouver *Province* trumpeted headlines: "War is Declared on Wild Horses of Cariboo Area" and "Once more, the fiat has gone forth 'Kill the wild horse!'" The article claimed that in the last twelve years, over 10,000 of these "wild steeds have been slain throughout the vast ranges of Cariboo and chiefly on land west of the Fraser River." Range manager Lyle Resh was quoted as stating that, although the bounty on wild horses had ended, the ministry in 1990 still contracted out wild-horse roundups for slaughter because they were "still classified as undesirable by the provincial government."

In addition to government-sanctioned wild-horse roundups in modern times, Chilcotin wild-horse control measures also included an unofficial tourism roundup, private snaring, and even a BC government-licensed Chilcotin game outfitter allowing his trophy hunters to shoot a herd of wild horses.

In the fall of 1990, an ad appeared in a local newspaper for a "Once in a Lifetime" opportunity to participate in a wild-horse roundup in the Anahim Lake area of the West Chilcotin for a $500 fee per client. The government's attorney general and range managers said there was nothing they could do to legally stop the tourism roundup since there were no wild-horse protection laws.[42] People were also setting out snares for wild horses in order to catch them and sell them to the slaughterhouse in Williams Lake. Alexis Creek conservation officer Mitch Kendall did not show much concern, claiming the horses were not wildlife and thus not protected under the *Wildlife Act*. He said they were an introduced species and the only thing illegal was setting snare traps.[43] A guide outfitter hunting big game bragged about allowing his trophy hunting clients to surround a herd of wild horses in a box canyon: "We shot them all down, the stallion, every mare, every colt. They were all down dead in the meadow. . . There is nothing wrong with shooting horses. I've shot lots of horses."[44]

And so, on and on, continued the Chilcotin wild-horse war in the modern age, fanned by the media and biased, ill-informed government officials. In April 1995, the *British Columbia Report* published an article titled, "Mange on the Range. The Chilcotin wild horses are judged to be a nuisance." The article quoted Mitch Kendall as saying the horses were mostly strays that the owners had neglected. He claimed, "They just start breeding like feral cats . . . they're undesirable and breeding in the wild, like starlings . . . They're a pain . . . the wild horse [is] just an overbred house cat and they're destroying the species that do belong here."[45]

In 1996, the BC *Livestock Act* was changed to allow the capture of animals at large if they are livestock, including "stallions" over one year old. At last official count, in 1999, thanks to the Tŝilhqot'in some 2,800 wild horses still survived in the West Chilcotin, the remainder of the tens of thousands of the Indian horses that used to inhabit the interior grasslands. The survey also proved that horse numbers had not increased in the previous decade;[46] they were not "breeding like cats."

A wild horse, one of a herd of five—including a pregnant mare—that were all shot and left near the road to the Nemiah Valley. This was a favourite herd for visitors and photographers to view. The RCMP was unable to do anything. *Image courtesy of Wayne McCrory.*

Except for the West Chilcotin, the century-long bounty hunts had finally achieved the government's goal of wild-horse eradication from BC rangelands. There was no longer any need to continue the large bounty hunts. However, because there was no law protecting these last wild horses, some random killings still happened in the West Chilcotin. In spring 2005, five free-roaming horses were found shot on the range near Tatla Lake. This included a mare whose young foal was left to fend for itself. Our researchers also found a few horses shot randomly far out in the Brittany Triangle in the new wild-horse preserve. In December 2016, Yuneŝit'in (Stone) author and knowledge keeper Linda Smith and I investigated the case of five wild horses shot at Chensqwedeten Meadow on the road to Nemiah. This herd was a favourite of Linda's and others for photographing. It was obvious a sharpshooter had killed them from the road. Written complaints by Linda and me to the authorities went nowhere since there were no legal statutes to protect the horses.

A Chilcotin resident who had captured a number of wild horses, taming some and selling the rest for slaughter, summed the situation up quite accurately: "Chasing wild horses in the Chilcotin is a national sport."[47]

In his book *Resettling the Range*, John Thistle claimed there was a much better way to deal with what ranchers perceived as pests, including wild horses: "There was nothing inevitable about the decisions early British Columbians made: They might have restored the range rather than simply put poison in it. They might have reclaimed wild horses rather than simply annihilate them. They might have listened more to what First Nations peoples were saying rather than simply dismiss and blame them for not valuing property or knowing how to use the land properly and they might have looked closer at their own land use practices than simply demonize those of others."[48]

The last 2,800 wild horses still roaming free in the West Chilcotin wilderness and those maintained by First Nations on scattered Indian reserves in BC are cultural reminders of the rich Indigenous equestrian past. They are promises for a better future. The thousands of wild-horse bones scattered across the BC grasslands are reminders of what once was. According to writer Larry McFadden, "They are nearly all gone from BC now, these wild horses of our quiet valleys and hills—the blacks, greys, whites, browns, sorrels, roans, duns, appaloosas, and palominos—once seen in great herds described as 'a sight . . . as beautiful and life-fraught as any the grass ever showed.'"[49]

CHAPTER 17

THE MUSTANGERS

After the publicity in 2002 surrounding the new wild-horse preserve, I accepted a number of public-speaking engagements on our wild-horse research. It was interesting to see a few old cowboys show up, distinguished in the audience by faces weather-worn from riding in the wind; their stained Stetsons concealed their grey hair and balding heads. During the public comments, these old-timers would regale the audience with their colourful memories of their long-ago mustanger years.

Their stories also brought a human dimension to the cruel history of the Canadian wild-horse bounty-hunt era. In telling of these long-ago wild-horse roundups, their voices were tinged with melancholy, seemingly a lament for the last wild horses they helped to eradicate. Their stories also reminded me that we are all living out and creating our own histories as the river of time moves inexorably along.

One old mustanger, Maurice Graydon, from a retirement home in Maple Ridge, BC, gave Friends of Nemaiah Valley a short and barely legible handwritten memoir of his BC interior roundup days in the 1930s–40s: "Some of the cowboys and wild horse trainers and catchers of the greatest wild-horse country in all of Canada, Cliff Tucson, Jack Smith, Harold Turner, Maurice Graydon, Clifford Brucaw, Warren Christians, Natives Able Sam and son George, Hyson Taylor, Jimmie Peters, and 'The Chief' McNab, all of us broke, rode and sold wild horses to the people who were not equipt—& the Secrets of our Wild Horse Roundups, our secret corrals hidden deep in the willow thickets around waterholes; ten feet high and quarter mile long wings. We snowshoed them down & trapped them in the deep snows of winter & caught them in their favourite pastures & on their annual migration trails."

Graydon wrote that he started riding broncs when he was eight years old. Later, as a mustanger, he had favourite saddle horses for roping and leading wild horses and snubbing them to be ridden. He also described his experience of catching and breaking them: "We had our ways of driving them also to plough, seed, hay, etc. Breaking and training wild horses is to catch them on the high ridges windblown and the beautiful alpine meadows of Indian paintbrush, tiger lilies and waist high grasses with lupines, vetches, fireweed, all colours in the beautiful valleys."

He claimed that the Fraser River was the centre of all wild-horse country north of the Thompson River and east and west of the Fraser on the high ridge interior plateau, from the Coast Mountains to the Rockies and foothill country. He wrote that, "Thousands of wild horses roamed over British Columbia. The wild stallions with their manes and tails and fetlocks trailing on the ground; always on the alert & watching over their harem of mares, colts and young stock. Couple of hundred horses in most herds, all colours, clay banks chestnuts, blood bays, pintos, roans, white, grey, black, and buckskin. A sight to behold & a memory of a great time in my childhood. Moose & deer with black & brown bear & cinnamon also roamed in our wild beautiful BC Savona Range, Red Lake Cliffs, Tranquille, Deadman Creek, Hume Lake & Bonaparte Range. Some of our wild horse ranges. 'The kings of their domains in the wild windswept ridges.'"[1] Sadly, thanks to the mustangers' roundups and bounty hunts, the wild horses are now all gone from these very ranges, except apparently for a few stray herds.

In 1927 *Maclean's* magazine featured a roundup of wild horses that lived in the depths of the rugged canyonlands of the Chilcotin River:

"Daybreak was just beginning to send its messengers of light streaking across the hollows of the far hills when the hunt resumed. Down below the trail—three hundred feet down, perhaps—the Chilcotin [River] boomed and thundered as it rushed through the canyon in a white froth, but its surging waters were hidden by the morning mist. We could imagine only the sheerness of the cliffs that sloped down to the mad stream. Wild country, this—the last place on Earth where one would imagine that outlaw horses would find their paradise, yet Long Paul, riding in the lead, threw back over his broad shoulders . . . the assurance that the landscape was no wilder than the horses which it harboured."

This hunt for wild horses was to go on for several days with their guide "Long Paul" and his piebald mare following the wild-horse sign:

". . . Only the night before, just as darkness commenced to settle upon the winding valley, he stopped up suddenly to listen. He told us that he had heard a noise that sounded like the whinnying of a wild stallion, and for fully ten minutes we waited, silent, trying to penetrate with our eyes the gathering dusk . . . But neither Long Paul, with his years of experience in following the wild horse trail, nor Chilcotin Joe was the first to sight the band. That remained for the wise old piebald mare in the lead, whose white ears pricked up suddenly as we reached a curve in the canyon path. The mare stopped dead still, her nostrils distended, breathing in the misty early morning air."

As the mist lifted from the canyon, the horse hunters saw a band of about fifty wild horses of varied sizes and colours gathered at their watering hole. The herd was already aware of the intruders, their leader, a black stallion "with his head arched high, snorting defiance at us" then clambered with the herd up a gravelly cliff. Led by Long

> Paul, the mounted troupe began a casual pursuit of the horse band so as not to alarm them too much. After some distance "the wild horse's tendency to double back on his tracks became apparent. The farther they were driven, the more desperate they seemed to get back to the canyon. A score of times they separated, the black stallion striving in vain to hold his following together." The pursuit did not end until dusk the next day when Long Paul spurred his piebald to a gallop "as though to strike the knockout, final blow at the exhausted, frightened fugitives." Long Paul then cut out, lassoed and hobbled the horses he wanted "and brought them into reluctant submission." This left a dozen sturdy-looking horses still trapped in the natural enclosure. Two of them then got away "dodging like a flash from the sure aim of Long Paul's lariat, and one of them was the proud black stallion whose final snort was one of victory as he thundered away to gather in the remnants of his herd."
>
> The article ended with the following: "In the vast sage-brush and bunchgrass plateau of the central British Columbia district, from the Seven Lakes country and the Thompson River Valley in the south, to Ciena Ciena and the Naimia Valley in the north, the snow-tipped Coast Range in the west and Windy Mountain and the Horsefly River in the east, ten thousand wild horses are roaming today. The area is one of the greatest wild horse ranges on the continent—and that means, in the world."[2]

All I can say about this overblown narrative is that if these areas were the greatest wild-horse ranges on the continent, a century later they are not anymore. The only exception is the West Chilcotin and the wild-horse preserve.

Another interesting mustanger author was R.D. Symons, whose book *Where the Wagon Led* provides a vivid portrayal of wild-horse roundups in the Cypress Hills of Alberta and BC's Peace River Country in the late 1800s and early 1900s. Symons was considered the Canadian equivalent of American artist Charles M. Russell. This is Symons's wild-horse lament:

> "Today, we old men of an almost forgotten life still thrill in thought of those wild rides, when we threw our hearts ahead into the dust of galloping hooves, forcing those wild ones by our will and the strength of our mounts to turn this way or that . . . we rode in a sort of exultation, little heeding the sharp snags, the crumbling banks, the tide of dark water, or the badger holes that pockmarked the ridges . . . our eyes were with our hearts, watching that foxy, long-maned gray or that striped buckskin. . . . The days draw in for us. What matter? We have seen and felt the best the West could offer, and I feel sure that when all things are made new, there will be horses for our delight in New Jerusalem; for is it not written that into the city shall enter no evil thing? And was there ever evil in a horse?"[3]

CHAPTER 18

NO ROOM FOR WILD HORSES

The unceded territory of the six groups of the Tŝilhqot'in Horse Nation is a vast, complex and diversely rich landscape. Avoiding colonialism and the impacts of the immigrant cattle-rancher culture, including bounty hunts of their herds of free-roaming horses, depended largely on their degree of remoteness, thus isolation from mainstream immigrant incursions.

The eastern Chilcotin grassland prairies and wild canyonlands within the traditional territory of the easternmost of the Tŝilhqot'in alliance, the Toosey (Tl'esqox) Band, are some of the most beautiful in Canada. Some areas, however, such as the Fraser–Chilcotin Junction bighorn sheep range and Becher's Prairie, are now severely overgrazed by cattle in some places. The shrill, haunting mating call of long-billed curlews still echoes over the grass-covered bench lands where herds of California bighorn hang out in the rugged cliffs and canyons overlooking the Chilcotin River. Here, each summer and autumn, millions of wild salmon struggle up through the rapids and whirlpools on their ancient journey to their spawning grounds. Native bluebunch wheatgrass and other species that only rarely occur west of the Rocky Mountains still sway in the evening breezes in areas not taken over by needlegrass and other plants, the result of cattle overgrazing.

The ancestral homeland of Tl'esqox (Toosey) Horse Nation looking down on the confluence of the Fraser and Chilcotin rivers. Wild horses, introduced and caretaken by the Tl'esqox, coexisted here for centuries with grassland grizzly bears and wolves but were all extirpated after the cattle industry moved in and pre-empted the best grassland starting in the late 1800s. This range is still recovering from heavy overgrazing by cattle. A significant population of California bighorn survives in these spectacular canyonlands. *Image courtesy of Wayne McCrory.*

These Chilcotin grasslands are distinguished from their interior ecological counterparts to the south in Oregon and Washington by a greater proportion of boreal plant species, making them unique.[1]

Nearly half a century after the government's big 1920s bounty hunts that eradicated most or all of the Tl'esqox Nation's last wild horses in the East Chilcotin grasslands, I learned firsthand in 1994–1995 that, while all of their wild horses were gone except for free-roaming herds they kept on their small reserve, the wild herds still lived on in the Horse Nations' memories and dreams. At the time

I had been commissioned to do an environmental impact study on the Chilcotin Military Block west of the Williams Lake for the Tl'esqox.

Owned by the Federal Department of National Defence (DND), the 41,000-hectare military block was originally part of the Tl'esqox ancestral caretaker area. There, Tl'esqox horses once roamed the rolling prairies dotted with numerous small lakes and aspen parklands. The Tl'esqox Indian reserves are about fifteen per cent of the size of the military block.

My study involved systematically documenting habitat damage caused by military exercises.[2] The Tl'esqox had previously been arrested for blockading the military after troops from a number of countries had conducted their big Nordic Warrior winter exercise that included low-flying jets over their reserve land. The judge in Quesnel said he would not sentence the Tl'esqox if they agreed to do an impact study of military exercises to help prove their case against the military exercises. The DND approved me to do the study on their land, but each time I went there I had to inform them in advance and check in at the guardhouse.

At that time, some 24,000 cattle owned by private cattle ranches enjoyed nearly free grazing on the Crown range in the East Chilcotin from spring until fall. This included a portion of the military block. Cowboy rancher Jack Palmantier, one of the Tl'esqox wildlife researchers working with me, said that he and his wife, Loretta, were refused military permission to rewild some of their horses on the military block grasslands where he grew up; apparently all of the grazing allotments were leased to private ranchers. Jack and Loretta were still hoping to have their horses roam free the way they had in the time of his ancestors. Jack told me that his mother had raised him on the military block. They used to run a winter trapline to survive, travelling from cabin to cabin by horse and wagon, with a milk cow trailing behind.

One day on a field-trip to the military block with Chief Francis Laceese and other leaders, I was shown a field with numerous scattered bones where it was said that early bounty hunters had eradicated some of the Tl'esqox free-ranging horses.

The Toosey were this day inspecting some of the extensive grassland habitat damage caused by the military, which I had been mapping. This included numerous craters and trenches and excessive roads, not to mention small lakes that had been blown up over the winter as part of military "ice demolition" training. Overgrazing by cattle added to the cumulative effects on these rare northern grasslands.

One day Chief Laceese asked me to review the BC government's 1977 Coordinated Resource Plan for the Becher Prairie. I found that the BC Range Management Division did not intend to welcome any First Nations' hopes to rewild their horses on lands outside their reserve. The provincial government's plan had been signed off by area ranchers, the West Fraser logging company, the Canadian military, BC's Fish and Wildlife Branch, Forest Service, Ministry of Agriculture and others. The Toosey were not invited to have input or comment, even though most of them still resided in the plan area, on their small reserves with their horses and cattle. The plan did acknowledge that a small portion, 5,500 acres (2,226 hectares) of the total area of 210,000 acres (84,983 hectares) was "Indian."

Nearly $200,000 of taxpayers' funds were to go towards improving grazing allotments on Crown land that was open range for thousands of cattle. This included grasshopper control with poisons, construction of extensive cattle fences, corrals, cattle water stations and other measures.

One of the final signed-off objectives of the plan was to "prevent the establishment of a wild horse herd because there are no known free-roaming horses on the area or in the vicinity and their presence would be completely incompatible with the objectives of this plan."[3] In other words, the objectives were to continue the cattle monopoly of the Becher Prairie Crown range.

At the time, any attempted recolonizing of the grasslands by wolves and grizzly bears was also considered unwelcome. I was told

A cattle ranch near Riske Creek, south of the military block. *Image courtesy of Wayne McCrory.*

by one old rancher who worked as the band manager for the Toosey (Tl'esqox) that a grizzly that had moved down out of the mountains some years back had been hunted down and shot. "Ha, ha," he said mockingly.

One sub-zero winter day, near the edge of the military block, I found the frozen snow-covered carcass of a dead cow with yellow warning signs on nearby fence posts warning that game officers had laced it with Compound 1080 to poison wolves. Bald eagles, coyotes and other species I had seen in the area would also become innocent victims and suffer terrible deaths.

While working on this book, I phoned Jack Palmantier to see if the Canadian military or the BC government had met his applications to rewild some of his horse stock on the military block. Jack, now seventy-three, told me that he still could not get approval. The night before I phoned him, he told me, he'd had the following dream, which I found a strange coincidence: "I never could have remembered when awake the details that were in my horse dream last night. In my dream, I was able to go back and remember when I was a kid and recall the details of each and every horse that was owned by the people around me . . . I could remember the colour of each horse owned by each person: bays, buckskins, and others, and which were mares and geldings. I could also remember the name of each horse. I remembered my grandmother Lizzie Grandbush's horse. It was a bay gelding named Dixie. I don't know what my dream meant."

I told him that I hoped things would change and that his dream of rewilding some of the qiyus in areas where his people used to follow their old ways would come true. This could happen, since Toosey (Tl'esqox) have been busy mapping and defining key areas of their original pre-colonial caretaker ecosystem in order to apply for Aboriginal Title lands, similar to the large Xeni Gwet'in Title area recognized in the 2014 Canadian Supreme Court landmark ruling.

Horses are a herd animal and form strong social bonds necessary for survival in the wild. *Image courtesy of Duane Starr Photography.*

TOP: Battling it out during the spring mating season, these two stallions are part of about 1,500 "wildies" that survive in the Alberta foothills, where they are still subject to century-long controversial culls. *Image courtesy of Duane Starr Photography.*

Canada has only about 5,000 wild horses left, many unprotected and in need of strong legislative protection. *Image courtesy of Duane Starr Photography.*

OPPOSITE TOP: First introduced to Nova Scotia's remote Sable Island by settlers in the late 1700s, these unique wild horses are today the most protected in Canada, part of Sable Island National Park Reserve. *Image © Patrice Halley for Sable Island.*

OPPOSITE BOTTOM: This stallion ekes out a hard living amidst the Sable Island sand dunes. Surviving huge Atlantic winter storms, Sable horses are a testament to the hardiness and adaptability of *Equus. Image © Patrice Halley for Sable Island.*

Mountain horses enjoy an early spring in the high mountains of the Eagle Lake Henry ?Elegesi Qiyus (Cayuse) Wild Horse Preserve, in British Columbia's West Chilcotin. At 770,000 hectares (1.9 MILLION acres), it is North America's largest wild-horse preserve, thanks to the Xeni Gwet'in Tŝilhqot'in Nation. *Image courtesy of Kelly Wilson.*

OPPOSITE TOP: These combative stallions belong to Canada's largest wild horse population, some 2,800 individuals in the remote Chilcotin. About 600 survive in the wild-horse preserve. The Tŝilhqot'in call the horse "qiyus (cayuse)." *Image courtesy of Kelly Wilson.*

OPPOSITE BOTTOM: This herd of Chilcotin Plateau wild horses enjoys a spring evening in a landscape burnt over by a recent wildfire, which improved their habitats through nutrient recycling. *Image courtesy of Kelly Wilson.*

Only a few days old, this foal starts a new life in the wild-horse preserve. *Image courtesy of Kelly Wilson.*

Genetic studies show two distinct horse populations in the wild-horse preserve. Brittany Triangle horses have Canadian Horse and East Russian (Yakut) ancestry, with some Spanish bloodlines. The rest of the Chilcotin wild horses, including this stallion, are descended from Spanish Iberian horses brought to the Americas in the 1500s by the conquistadores. *Image courtesy of Alice William.*

The Spanish Iberian ancestors of this blue dun stallion were spread across the Americas by Indigenous cultures, arriving in the Chilcotin in the early to mid-1600s, two centuries before the white man. *Image courtesy of Wayne McCrory.*

Genetic studies were not done on these mountain horses in the Nemiah Valley because the Xeni Gwet'in domestic horses mix with them on the open range. *Image courtesy of Wayne McCrory.*

Wild horses run free in the Nemiah Valley. Here, the mix of wild and domestic (branded) horses are periodically rounded up by the Xeni Gwet'in as one of their means of controlling overgrazing by horses and cattle. *Image courtesy of Wayne McCrory.*

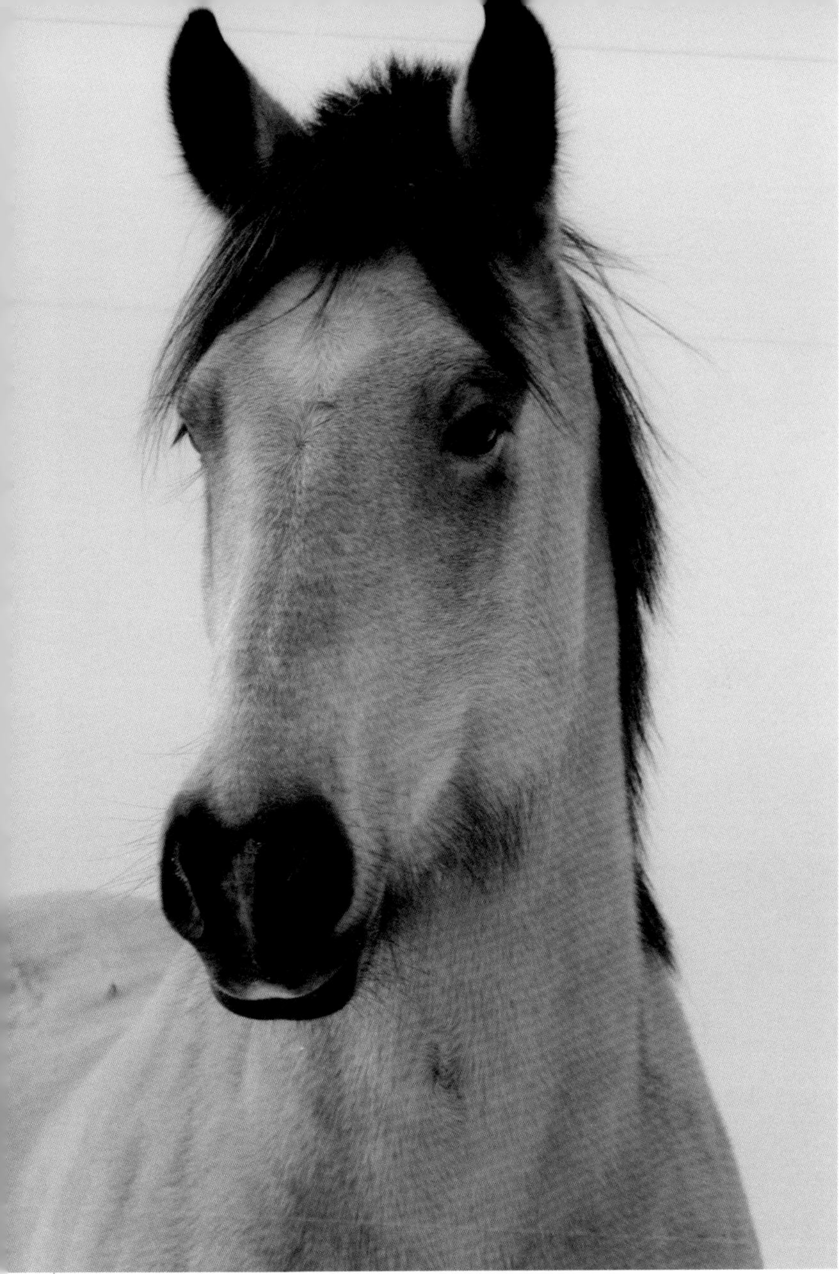

The Tŝilhqot'in First Nation brought horses to the Chilcotin in the early to mid-1600s. While they were wrongly persecuted by settler-cattle ranchers as a "feral" and "alien" species, new evidence strongly supports Canada's wild horses being a native species reintroduced to their evolutionary birthplace. *Image courtesy of Wayne McCrory.*

Yuneŝit'in elder Orry Hance on a horse trip in the wild-horse preserve and the new Indigenous Protected Conservation Area declared by the Yuneŝit'in and Xeni Gwet'in Nations. Both First Nations protected areas helped stop a large open-pit mine and clear-cut logging. *Image courtesy of Jeremy Williams.*

OPPOSITE: Horses and bronzed cowbirds have a symbiotic relationship. Cowbirds get free rides and eat the bugs that harass the horses. They also eat bugs and seeds stirred up as the horses feed. *Image courtesy of Sadie Parr.*

While wildfires can improve habitat for wild horses and wildlife, the growth of new lodgepole pine makes travel a challenge. *Image courtesy of Sadie Parr.*

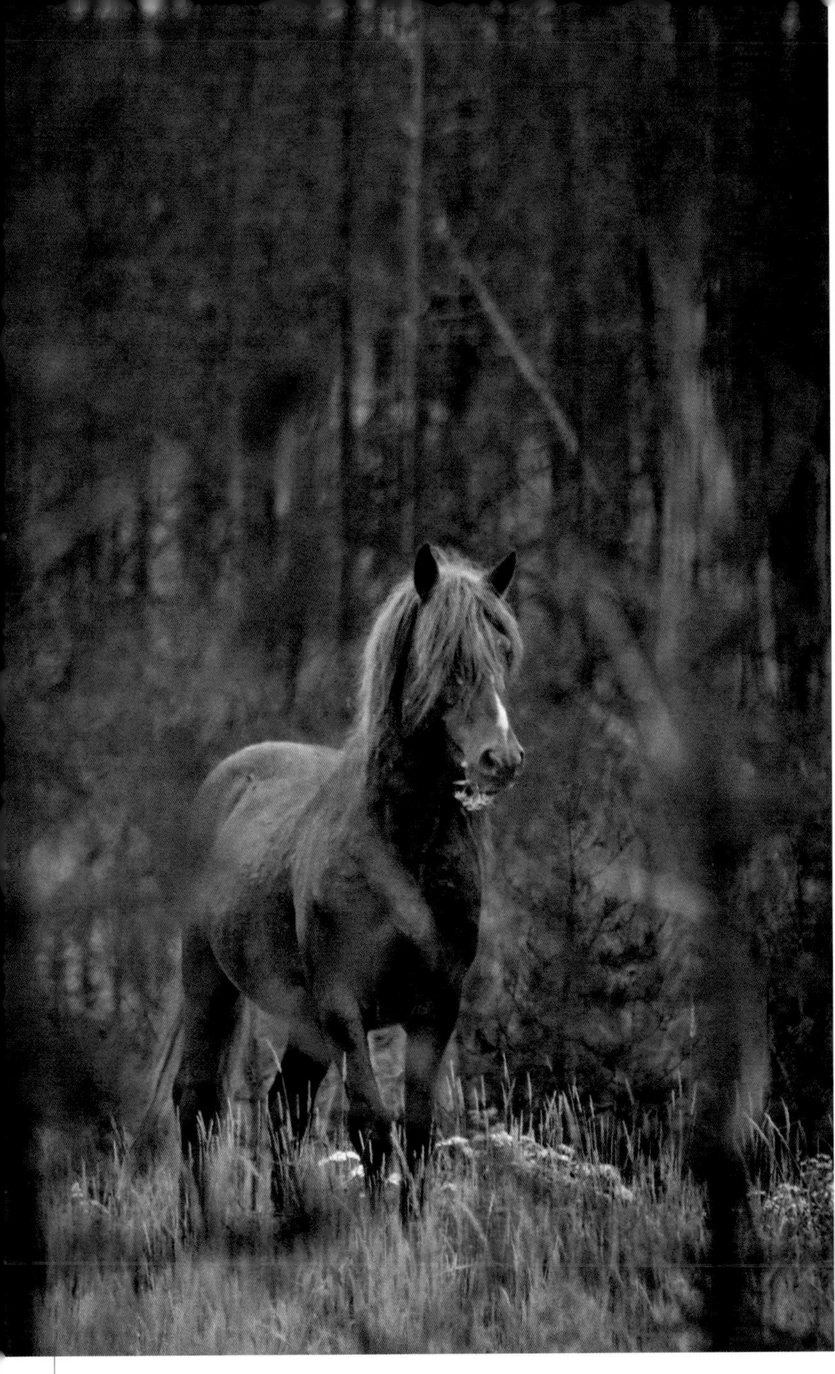

A stallion enjoys a purple aster flower that grew back after a wildfire. The Chilcotin wild horses survive today thanks to the Tŝilhqot'in. *Image courtesy of Sadie Parr.*

The black colour of this stallion, scarred from a serious injury, may reflect its Canadian Horse ancestry. *Image courtesy of Sadie Parr.*

Like these American wild horses, the wild horses of the Alberta foothills and BC Chilcotin survived a century of cruel roundups, bounty hunts and persecution by the cattle industry and government range managers. *Image courtesy of Ann Evans, The Cloud Foundation.*

Xeni Gwet'in Nits'il?in (Chief) Roger William (seen out for a morning ride in the Nemiah Valley) led his people in the protection of their wild-horse preserve and traditional territory. *Image © Patrice Halley, Canadian Geographic.*

TOP: A lone dun stands guard in the wild-horse preserve. The provincial and federal governments still do not recognize such Indigenous protection, so clear-cut logging remains a threat. *Image courtesy of Wayne McCrory.*

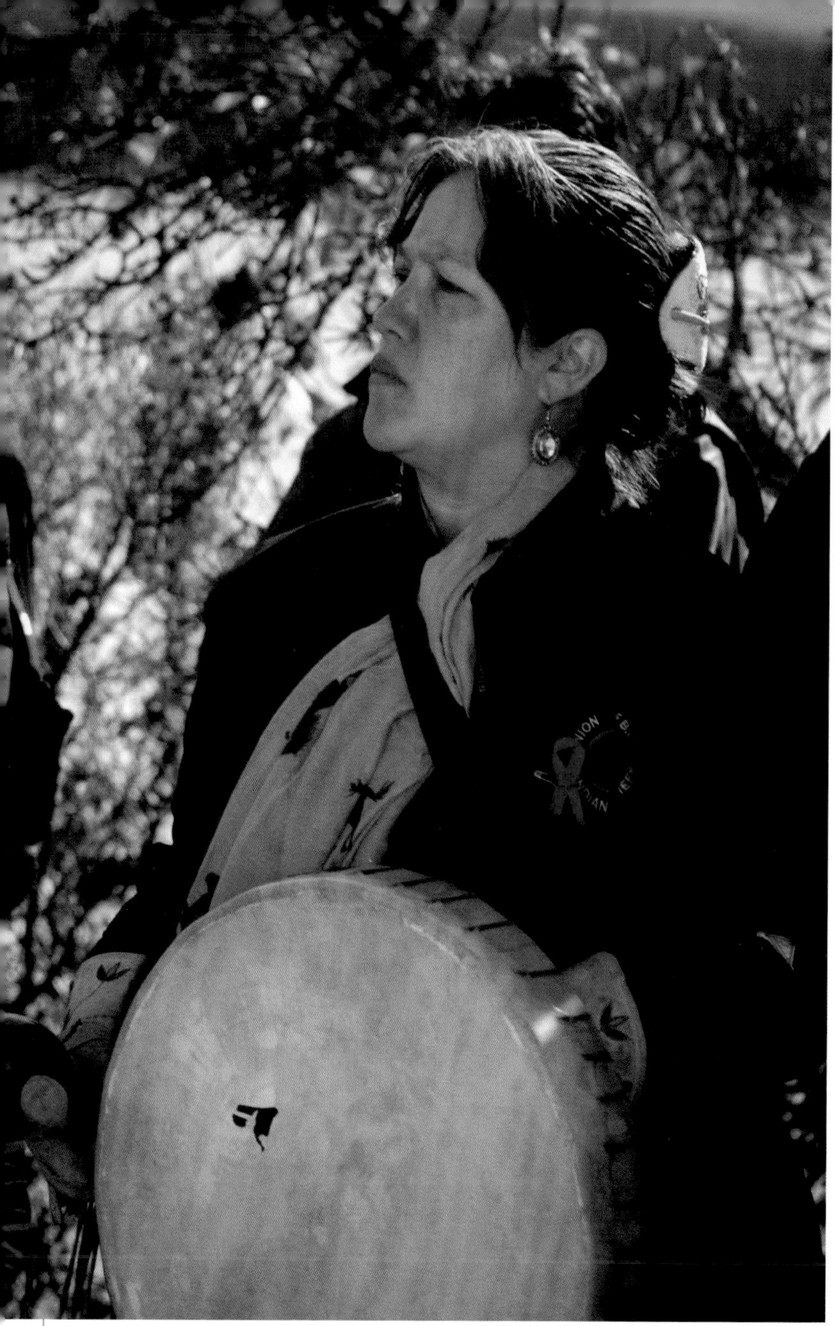

International environmental award-winning former Xeni Gwet'in Nits'il?in (Chief) Marilyn Baptiste helped her people stop Canada's largest open-pit mine and protect the land. *Image courtesy of Wayne McCrory.*

The harsh Chilcotin winters can be a survival challenge for the wild qiyus. *Images courtesy of Sadie Parr.*

During long Chilcotin winters, wild horses have to use their front hooves to crater through deep snow for food.

During winter blizzards, wild horses stay near trees for shelter. *Image courtesy of Wayne McCrory.*

A lone horse grazes on a wetland in the wild-horse preserve on the Chilcotin Plateau. Such wetlands, pocket grasslands and pine forests allow these horses to survive in a vibrant wilderness ecosystem with North America's top predators. *Image courtesy of Sadie Parr.*

Here we see a Yukon Horse, which evolved with many other mammal species, including the gray wolf, in the ice-free northern Yukon during the Pleistocene. *Image courtesy of Julius Csotonyi, © Government of Yukon.*

OPPOSITE: Chilcotin and some other North American wild horse populations are partially controlled by mountain lion predation. *Image © John E. Marriott.*

Research by biologist Sadie Parr found that Chilcotin wild horses were a primary food for wolves and that wolves may help control wild-horse numbers. *Image courtesy of Kelly Wilson.*

TOP: In the Chilcotin and the Alberta foothills, wild horses coexist with North America's top predators, such as the gray wolf. *Image © John E. Marriott.*

Small Nemiah Valley ranches in the wild-horse preserve coexist with grizzlies, wolves and other large wildlife. *Image courtesy of Suzy Chaston.*

TOP: A Chilcotin grizzly bear family marking territory near a salmon river. Wild horses and grizzlies coexist, with very little apparent predation on horses by bears. *Image © John E. Marriott.*

A large herd of Chilcotin wild horses enjoys the lush green forage at a wetland in a burnt landscape on the plateau. *Image courtesy of Wayne McCrory.*

TOP: A pure white stallion in the wild-horse preserve. Such horses are called "ghost horses" since they are so hard to see in the winter. *Image courtesy of Wayne McCrory.*

The annual mountain race has long been a tradition for the Xeni Gwet'in. *Image © Patrice Halley*, Canadian Geographic.

LEFT: The abundant wild Pacific salmon that spawn in the pristine rivers in the wild-horse preserve provide annual sustenance for many First Nations people. *Image courtesy Gary Fiegehen.*

For the Tŝilhqot'in, re-establishing their culture with their youth and maintaining a close relationship with the horse are key parts of preserving the old tradition after two centuries of colonialism. *Image courtesy of Daryl Visscher.*

OPPOSITE TOP: Tŝilhqot'in children learn equestrian skills at an early age, a tradition going back many centuries. *Image courtesy of Gary Fiegehen.*

OPPOSITE BOTTOM: The wild-horse preserve provides Labrador tea and an abundance of traditional medicines and foods for the Xeni Gwet'in. *Image courtesy of Wayne McCrory.*

Canada must protect all wild horses with strong federal and provincial laws that recognize their rich Indigenous cultural relationship to the horse, as well as the horse as an integral part of a healthy and functioning ecosystem. *Image courtesy of Wayne McCrory.*

TOP: A lone horse watches over its homeland in the wild-horse preserve. *Image courtesy of Wayne McCrory.*

CHAPTER 19

BLOODLINES

UNRAVELLING THE ORIGINS OF THE CHILCOTIN WILD HORSE

One very cold winter day knowledge keeper Norman William and I stood silently at the edge of a frozen meadow in the Brittany Triangle, holding steady the gazes of a nearby herd of wild horses. Time hung suspended between us, wind blowing their manes. Lingering questions whispered on the wind: "Where did you horses really come from? How long have you been here? What are your bloodlines?"

Early in our research, my colleagues and I were becoming increasingly annoyed that the healthy and somewhat refined-looking middle-to-large-sized free-ranging wild horses we had observed in the Brittany Triangle and West Chilcotin were still being referred to as "nothing but inbred, stunted, hammerhead cayuses and only worthy of being shipped to slaughter for pet food."[1]

During those first years, we also learned that there was a wide range of "local expert" settler opinions about the origins and bloodlines of the Chilcotin wild horses. Not only were settlers' horse-origin stories often contradictory, they were almost as numerous as the wild horses still left in the Chilcotin. For example, in an article on Chilcotin wild horses in 1946, local historian Louis LeBourdais claimed that wild horses originated more than a century ago from the pack trains of the Hudson's Bay Company (HBC) fur brigades. If he had looked deeper, he would have learned that HBC horses originated from the First Nations' foundation breed; there are no records of the HBC having imported new European and American breeds to their early trading posts in the West, including the Cariboo–Chilcotin.

In 1995, Jodie Kekula, rangeland specialist for the BC Ministry of Forests at Alexis Creek, stated in a Canadian Press article that Chilcotin wild horses might be descendants of workhorses left behind by homesteaders who gave up the land: "You can't compare them to horses of Nevada, where they have a mustang background and date back to the Spanish."[2]

It seemed obvious to me that the rancher and government horse-origin stories were exceedingly self-serving. Such distorted history served to give settlers the "ownership" right to implement the century-long BC bounty hunts and near-eradication of the wild horse.

No one ever bothered to ask the Tŝilhqot'in elders and knowledge keepers about their horse-origin stories and legends, which portray a different, truer history.

Other horse-origin stories being bandied about shone a different light on when First Nations in the interior first had horses. Four years after the Forest Service range manager at Alexis Creek claimed to the national media that the horses likely came from workhorses left by homesteaders, the biologist who produced the 1999 Royal BC Provincial Museum publication on hooved mammals claimed that BC's interior feral horses had early Spanish origins before the white man came: "Some were present in the interior when European explorers first arrived in British Columbia. Presumably, they originated from horses brought to the southwestern United States by the Spanish in the 17th century; later, First Peoples brought these horses northward."[3]

Thoroughbreds were also thrown into the origins debate around Chilcotin campfires. Charlie Stump, an elder with the Tŝilhqot'in National Government, claimed when I interviewed him in 2002 that "some of us believe that the wild horses in the Chilcotin today represent a special breed that we call 'the Chilcotin Horse.' This was the result of the release of a special type of Thoroughbred stallion many decades ago that improved the stock. We want the horses today to be recognized as a special Chilcotin breed and to market them as such."

I also talked to Dan Wilson of the Canadian Horse Society, who claimed Chilcotin horses still had bloodlines of the Canadian Horse introduced by the early French-Canadian fur-traders, who brought the breed to the West from Quebec after they were first imported from France in 1665. (Our later genetics study showed him to be partly right.)

At first, I naively thought it would be a simple matter of having some of the Tŝilhqot'in knowledge keepers and researchers interview the elders about their horse-origin stories and legends, then I would research some of the early fur-trader and explorer accounts, and then follow with a genetic study. In fact, it turned out that these were only some of the pieces of a complex puzzle. In the end, not only did the research involve investigating the above-mentioned facets, it also meant searching the evidence about the evolution of the horse, including the Yukon or Ice Age horse, and exploring studies of horse fossil remains found in this region of British Columbia.

At the end of my initial review, I was left with three different storylines on the possible origins of the Chilcotin wild horse:

- Horses that escaped from various European and American domestic breeds brought in during the 1858 gold rush followed by early white cattle ranchers.
- Escapee horses from the first European horses brought to the Americas by explorers, primarily the Spanish, then spread by Indigenous tribes across the interior of North America.
- Survivors of the late Pleistocene Ice Age horses that may have been domesticated long ago by some Indigenous cultures.

Over time, after hundreds and hundreds of hours of research, with the help of Friends of Nemaiah Valley, Xeni Gwet'in knowledge keepers Alice William, Norman William and other Xeni Gwet'in, as well as leading genetic experts Dr. Gus Cothran and Dr. Ludovic Orlando and many others, I was eventually able to assemble the many disparate pieces of the puzzle into a much deeper, more credible framework that better revealed the origins of the Chilcotin wild qiyus.

Mine was a long, long ride but, discouraged as I was sometimes, I never gave up. Ultimately, I was able to document a deeper understanding about where Chilcotin qiyus came from, their bloodlines, and their rich significance in Tŝilhqot'in Indigenous lifeways. It's a story that's never been told before. In doing so, I have also deconstructed the historic myths, misinformation and strong anti-Indigenous biases by many in the cattle industry and BC government range management division.

The storyline of the genesis of the North American horse begins with Indigenous dreams and prophesies of their coming as sailing caravels with European horses ply westward across the Atlantic towards the continent. It ends with some fascinating and unexpected findings but some still mysterious threads that may have no end.

CHAPTER 20

HORSE DREAMS AND PROPHECIES

February 1519: Ancient Tŝilhqot'in village— Biny Gwechugh (Canoe Crossing)

It is the Tŝilhqot'in month of the short moon and the month when the female bear gives birth to cubs. It had already been a long, severe winter at the ancient Tŝilhqot'in village of Biny Gwechugh, nestled in a grassy meadow alongside the blue ice-choked waters of the Chilko River, a major salmon spawning area in autumn, the lifeblood of the community.[1] [2] [3]

Except for the Tŝilhqot'in dogs[4] snuggled outside in snowbanks, the residents of the ancient village are all asleep in the comfort of their warm underground winter homes spread out across the meadow. The short moon slides slowly up over the distant snow-clad mountains and pushes away the valley darkness around the village, its eerie glow revealing the cluster of large mounds, roofs of the Tŝilhqot'in underground lodges.

Shafts of moonlight illuminate the columns of smoke wafting up from the top-down ladder entrances to the lodges. Whole family clans, up to fifty in a lodge, slumber peacefully on their caribou and elk hide, moss and grass mattresses, wrapped in cloaks of marmot and beaver. Tunnels connect several of the underground lodges, making for easier interactions between different family clans.

The Tŝilhqot'in call February the month of the short moon, the month of bear giving birth to cubs, and other seasonal names relating to the month. *Image © Patrice Halley,* Canadian Geographic.

Chunks of ice floating on the river reflect the moonglow, jostling silently for space in the dark unfrozen centre of the Chilko River as it flows seaward. In the gravel below the surface, thousands of baby salmon in eggs laid last fall are nearly ready to hatch. The dogs lie curled up in different snowbanks next to the lodges, their thick fur covered with night frost. Occasionally, they stir and awaken to break the stillness by barking and howling in agitation at the pack of wolves howling from a nearby hill. The wolves are upwind of the village, hoping to lure one of the male dogs away with the wind-carried scent of the estrus of the alpha female wolf. A great horned owl hoots from its perch on the bare branch of an aspen tree along the river's edge, waiting to swoop down and scoop a fat meadow mouse when it emerges from its subnivean burrow to scuttle across a path in the snow-covered grassy meadow where the women go for water every day.

This village of underground *kekules*, or pithouses, is one of many along the salmon-rich Chilko River. It's a land of plenty in good years,

Hibernating black bear mother and newborn cub in winter den.
Image courtesy of Lynne Rogers.

starvation in poor years when the salmon runs are low and there is stiff competition from *nunistiny*, the grizzly bear.

From the village, trail networks radiate out all over the land, linking village to village, and village to hunting and food-gathering areas.

It had been a poor salmon year. Food supplies were now running low. The split halves of sun-dried and smoked salmon from their poor catch in the fall were nearly depleted, as were the hide bags of dried elk, caribou and mule deer jerky, dried *soopolallie* and other berries, and stored bulbs of root foods. Wild potatoes had been harvested from nature's garden up on Potato Mountain in fall. They had to share these with the *nunistiny*, who use their long claws to dig up the nutritious underground corms.

During this late winter, oolichan oil stored in cedar boxes traded from the coast was also running low. The oil was used for cooking, eating and treatment of many different ailments and injuries, such as stomach problems, wounds and skin conditions. The villagers were already dreaming of the next moon, Moon of the Melting Ice, when they could again load up their pack dogs and hike to the coast to barter with the Nuxalk Nation for a new supply of oolichan oil.

At this time, oolichans, an anadromous smelt-like fish, returned by the millions to spawn in coastal rivers. Oolichan, also called candlefish, is so high in oil that it can be burned. For many First Peoples, oolichan was known as the saviour fish, being the first fresh, rich food of the season. It came in from the ocean in huge abundance near the tail end of long winters. (Oolichan oil was made by allowing the fish to decompose for a week in a hole in the ground, then adding boiling water and skimming off the oil that rose to the surface.)

Dried meat and bear fat were also running low in Biny Gwechugh. While waiting for the Moon of Melting Ice to signal the time of their oolichan journey to the coast, hunters were readying their dogs and spears to hike up the mountain to the grizzly den they had noted in late fall. They had found it when they were hunting bighorn sheep after the onset of the first snows. They had seen a large, fat grizzly bear digging its earthen tunnel into a steep alpine hillside, then bringing in grass and twigs to make its hibernation nest. They would spear the hibernating bear, as it would not yet have used up most of the stored body fat it needed for hibernation. Hunting was the Xeni's way of having a backup food supply for the village during shortages in famine years.

The dogs would be able to sniff out the frosted air hole in the snow that now blanketed the den's entrance. If they heard the crying of new cubs, they would not kill the mother. Along the way, the hunters could snack on the red bearberries on windswept hillsides, which grow sweeter over the winter. In the high-elevation whitebark pine forests, they would also search out squirrel middens under the snow and raid them for the whitebark pinecones that contained nutritious pine nuts. Some of these might be left over from the squirrels and from the grizzlies that also raided the middens in fall.

It had been a long night of drumming, singing and dancing around the campfire in the earthen floor of the central pithouse, with elders sharing in their descriptive ancient tongue their winter dreams, stories and legends. Some men sat in a circle playing *lahal*—a gambling game that uses sticks, beaver teeth and small bones—to the rhythm of the drumming and singing. Sometimes their wives gambled, too.

It had also been a season of mourning, when some elders passed on, some mothers died in childbirth, or children died of strange illnesses the medicine people could not cure despite their access to wild herbs and roots. With the ground frozen, the dead were taken out of the lodges and downriver to a special place where ceremonies were held as the remains were cremated on beds of dried fir, pine logs and branches. Each deceased's ashes were placed in a small painted box set on a pole that had been planted before freeze-up.[5]

Yes, it had been a long winter and now, on this night of the short moon, the tight-knit community slumbered away within the comfort of Mother Earth beside the ice-choked river, just like the bears in their winter dens in the high mountains. Newborn babies whimpered and suckled at their mothers' breasts, men snored, children stirred and talked in their sleep. Some people had long winter dreams of spring and flowers while the temperature dropped so low it was unsafe to go outside. The dogs huddled for added warmth while ignoring the wolves now prowling closer, still trying to lure them away. They were hungry, too.

One wonders if any of the Tŝilhqot'in elders, prophets and medicine people at Biny Gwechugh had dreams or visions that foretold the coming of the horse to their mountain haunts. This strange four-legged animal had one hoof on each foot, unlike the elk that had cloven hooves. Other First People on the continent had such dreams and visions foretelling the coming of the animal that would eventually revolutionize their societies forever. For example, the Thompson (Nlaka'pamux), a tribal culture in the canyons and grasslands to the south and east of the Tŝilhqot'in homeland, have a tale about the creation of the horse when the Earth was young.[6]

During the early 1500s, far down the continent, in the huge stone mountain palace in the ancient city of Tenochtitlán (now within modern Mexico City), the ninth Mexicali (Aztec) emperor, Moctezuma II, dreamt that the fair-haired god *Quetzalcoatl*, who had deserted his people, would return riding a fierce animal breathing fire, and that day would start the beginning of the end.[7] Moctezuma was aware that his ancestors had also prophesied that men with beards would come from the direction of the sunrise and rule over them.[8]

CHAPTER 21

THE FIRST SIXTEEN HORSES OF CONQUEST

The Conquistadores with their high saddles, powerful curb bits, their lances, armour, and their fire-arms, broke upon the New World, horseless since the Tertiary, like creatures of another race . . . Indians took the horse and rider to be one flesh, and thought the gunfire was the bellowing of the monstrous animals.

— **R.B. Cunninghame Graham**, *The Horses of the Conquest*[1]

February 1519

Far, far away from the ancient Tŝilhqot'in village of Biny Gwechugh, in the month of the short moon and the birthing of bear cubs, a small flotilla of Spanish caravels gained wind in their sails and departed Havana harbour. Loaded with sixteen warhorses, the caravels were headed from Cuba to the east coast of Mesoamerica to plunder the wealthy Mexicali (Aztec) empire ruled over by Moctezuma II. The Spaniards would wage one of history's most brutal colonial assaults on a rich Indigenous civilization.

The Spanish method of loading horses onto their caravels using a sling system and a windlass. *Image from 1769 Spanish horsemanship guide titled* Manejo Real, *or* True Handling.[2]

The sixteen Spanish horses, the first of many still to come from Spain, would symbolize the forebears of the Spanish horse that would eventually be dispersed by the First People across the North American interior, the evolutionary birthplace of the horse. Over a century later, the Spanish horse dispersal would be so widespread as to reach the northernmost grasslands of the continent, including the large homeland of the Tŝilhqot'in and one of their ancient villages known as Biny Gwechugh.

The initial sixteen Spanish horses came from breeding farms in Havana. The original foundation horses were brought across the Atlantic as a result of a Royal Decree by King Ferdinand and Queen Isabella of Spain, inspired by Christopher Columbus's first voyage in 1492.

The expedition was headed by Fernando Cortés. Bernal Diaz, one of Cortés's most trusted soldier-captains and a dedicated expedition historian, listed the owner of each horse and gave a description of each horse's main qualities. The thirteen described below give us a hint of the 500-year-old ancestors of today's Spanish Iberian wild horses in the West Chilcotin:

- Captain Cortés: vicious dark chestnut horse which died upon arrival at San Juan de Ulúa.
- Pedro de Alvarado and Hernando López de Avila: very good sorrel mare, good both for sport and as a charger. When the expedition arrived at New Spain, Pedro de Alvarado bought the other half share in the mare or took it by force.
- Alonzo Hernández Puertocarrero: grey mare, very good charger, which Cortés bought for him with his gold buttons.
- Juan Velásquez de Leon: powerful grey mare called "La Rabona," very hardy and a good charger.
- Cristóval de Olid: dark chestnut horse, fairly good.
- Francisco de Morla: dark chestnut horse, very fast and easily handled.
- Juan de Escalante: light chestnut horse with three white stockings, not much good.
- Diego de Ordás: grey mare, barren, tolerably good, but not fast.
- Gonzalo Domínguez: very good dark chestnut horse, a grand galloper.
- Pedro González de Trujillo: good chestnut horse, all chestnut, very good goer.
- Moron: dappled horse with stockings on the forefeet, very handy.
- Baena, a settler at Trinidad: dappled horse, almost black, no good for anything.
- Ortiz, the musician, and Bartolomé Garcia: very good dark horse called "El Arriero;" this was one of the best horses carried in the fleet.

According to Diaz, "at that time horses . . . were worth their weight in gold, and that is the reason why more horses were not taken, for there were none to be bought."[3]

It would take six weeks for the expedition to reach its mainland destination. Lowering their sails, the ships heeled into a safe bay and dropped their anchors next to the jungle shoreline that had been mapped earlier by the Spanish. Cortés, worried that the Indigenous residents on shore were about to attack their ships, ordered the horses "quickly landed" into the shallow sea to swim to shore, the new foal swimming alongside its mother. Here they were guarded for the night.

R.B. Cunninghame Graham, Argentine rancher, horse expert and historian, described what the landing of the horses might have been like: "Once landed, the horses were so stiff that they could hardly move. A curious sight, this first landing of horses on the mainland of the New World, must have presented. In some cove where there were grass and water handy, the ships rode at anchor . . . The horses grazing, hobbled or sidelined, for it would have been madness to let them entirely loose, must have made a strange and unfamiliar note of colour as they grazed for the first time in the New World, where they were destined to multiply in countless numbers at no distant date." And multiply they did, forever changing the way of life for Indigenous peoples across the continent, including the Tŝilhqot'in.[4]

CHAPTER 22

SHARED TŜILHQOT'IN ORAL HISTORY ON ACQUISITION OF THE HORSE

With the planetary context of equids in mind, in 2003 Friends of Nemaiah Valley and I, in cooperation with the Xeni Gwet'in, decided to commission an independent genetic study of the wild qiyus, starting with the Brittany Triangle area of the wild-horse preserve.

One of the positive aspects of the project was that the population of 150 to 200 horses in the Triangle appeared to have been isolated from the West Chilcotin wild horse population outside of the Brittany, including mixed breeds of free-roaming domestic and unowned horses in the Nemiah Valley. Mountain ranges and deep valleys with large fast-flowing rivers appeared to have acted as barriers to gene flow between these different areas. A genetic study would help test this hypothesis. It was to be the first such study of the ancestry of Canada's last wild horses.

Depending on what bloodlines we found in the Brittany Triangle, we planned to expand the study to the wild horse population to the east and north of the Brittany. Because the Nemiah Valley had such a mix of free-roaming breeds, we decided not to include it.

As we would be plowing new ground, I reached out to Dr. E. Gus Cothran at the College of Veterinary Medicine, University of Kentucky (later at Texas A&M College of Veterinary Medicine and Biomedical Sciences). One of the world's foremost equine genetic experts, he agreed to guide our research and his lab would genotype our samples.

He cautioned us that the ancestry of the contemporary wild horse population would likely have changed greatly from the first horses introduced. The mechanisms for changes in bloodlines are many, he said, such as crossbreeding and dilution from the introduction of new breeds, genetic drift and natural selection due to different or changing environmental conditions. He also warned that we should not get our hopes up about discovering unique ancestry, such as the Spanish horse. His genetic research of numerous US wild horse populations found that the majority were a "melting pot" of domestic European and new North American breeds. One exception was the Spanish ancestry in the Pryor Mountains Wild Horse Range that straddles the Montana–Wyoming border. Dr. Cothran also recommended we start by ascertaining the approximate time period when the first horses were introduced to the Chilcotin. Genotyping of horses does not establish timelines for different breed introductions of foundation ancestry.

Our next step was to obtain permission from Chief Roger William to interview Tŝilhqot'in elders for their oral knowledge of the origins of their horses. Indigenous people never kept written records. They passed on their history and knowledge in the vernacular, often bound by ancient laws that governed sharing, a tradition that continues today. This ancient, sophisticated method of retaining and passing on history, stories, legends, myths, family lineages and traditional ecological knowledge has evolved over thousands of years. Xeni Gwet'in schoolteacher Jessica Setah-Alphonse (the late wild-horse ranger Harry Setah's daughter) referred to Tŝilhqot'in knowledge keepers as "walking PhDs."[1]

I was also told that much of Xeni Gwet'in history had been lost after smallpox and other epidemics (introduced by the white man in the 1800s) wiped out entire villages—often over half of the population. Ancestral knowledge has been further undermined by persecution and cultural suppression effected when white society forced Indigenous children into government-mandated, church-run residential and day schools. In such institutions, Christian priests, nuns and teachers forbade children to speak their native language, practice their dances and songs, or learn their own cultural history. Such transgressions are now being exposed as part of Canada's shameful racist past.

I was amazed how Indigenous oral legends spiral into deep time. For example, while doing caribou surveys years ago in the northern Yukon, Vuntut Gwitchin knowledge keeper Charlie Peter Charlie told me their legend about a giant four-legged monster that burst out of the Old Crow flats. Later, when one of the Vuntut Gwitchin elders guided a palaeontologist to the site, they found the bones of a female woolly mammoth that had died 30,000 years ago.

When I helped on the research, conservation and eventual protection of a large area on the BC central coast for the Kermode bear (also known as the spirit bear), I discovered the Tsimshian "Legend of the White Bear" in a book called *Somewhere Between*. The legend was about Raven the Creator going about Princess Royal Island and making every tenth black bear white—as a reminder of the last Ice Age.[2] I found incredible such time depth of 10,000 years. The book was written by a non-Indigenous fisherman, but many years later Kitasoo/Xai'xais Chief Douglas Neasloss verified the legend through an elder just before she died: her gift to help protect large areas of habitat for the spirit bear so revered by her people.

One complexity arose in trying to determine when the Tŝilhqot'in first obtained the horse: their history is not based on Gregorian

This is Xeni Gwet'in elder Francis Setah, one of the many elders who provided oral testimony on the horse and other historical aspects for the Tŝilhqot'in 2007 BC Supreme Court Rights and Title case. *Image courtesy of Wayne McCrory.*

calendar years. Traditionally, the Tŝilhqot'in used a lunar calendar, combining the phase of the moon with seasonal activities or significant changes occurring in nature, such as bear cubs being born in their winter dens or villagers first moving into their underground lodges.[3] For longer time periods, going back in deep time, the Tŝilhqot'in use three oral time periods, which have now been correlated to Gregorian years: *ʔUnidanx* (recent), *Yedanx* (the long-ago period prior to the mid- to late 1700s up to first contact with the white man) and *Sadanx* (very long ago, when legends began and when the ancestors, land and animals were transforming according to supernatural forces).[4]

Our final but incomplete research in collaboration with Xeni Gwet'in knowledge keeper Alice William produced mixed views as to when the Tŝilhqot'in first brought in the horse. These ranged from "time immemorial" to the Chilcotin War of 1864. Some of the written accounts by local historians and cowboys were similar, likely because

Orry Hance, Yuneŝit'in (Stone) knowledge keeper, provided key information on the Tŝilhqot'in origin of the horse in an interview with Alice William. *Image courtesy of Jeremy Williams.*

much of the oral Tŝilhqot'in history on the horse was lost during the epidemics.

When I interviewed former Chief Marvin Baptiste, he insisted the Xeni did not get horses until 1864. Francis Setah, a Xeni elder, testified in an interview for the 2007 BC Supreme Court that the ancestors never had horses until recently: "Our ancestors never did have horses. It's just a little while ago the horses came." Before horses, he said, his ancestors would pack their belongings into tightly rolled hide bundles, which they secured to their backs with straps called *nets'eghish*, and walked to their next destination.[5]

The recent Tŝilhqot'in acquisition of the horse was also echoed by anthropologist James Teit: "Horses were introduced at a much later date than amongst the Shuswap, and probably not before 1870 had they become common."[6] Others felt the Tŝilhqot'in acquired the horse before the coming of the white man. Both former Chief Benny William and Chief Roger William relayed to me in 2002 that the Tŝilhqot'in

Wild-horse ranger Harry Setah provided the longest time frame as to when the Tŝilhqot'in acquired the horse as "time immemorial." *Image courtesy of Wayne McCrory.*

had horses before the white man. Roger William said, "Horses have always been part of the Xeni Gwet'in people. Our forefathers used and trained these wild horses. These wild horses, being part of us, are something we don't want to lose."

According to Orry Hance, a Tŝilhqot'in Yuneŝit'in (Stone) knowledge keeper known for his expertise on the horse, the Tŝilhqot'in first got horses before the 1700s.[7]

Tŝilhqot'in ranger Harry Setah insisted in an interview with me that his people had horses since "time immemorial." Both Hance's and Setah's oral memories would have placed the Tŝilhqot'in having horses in the deep time of *Sadanx*.

To further confuse matters, BC Supreme Court Justice David Vickers, after reviewing oral testimonies about the horse, agreed that the Tŝilhqot'in had horses before the white man but not since time immemorial. However, to be fair, the oral testimonies were not focused on when the Tŝilhqot'in first got horses and also did not include the oral evidence on the acquisition of the horse from Hance and Setah. Justice Vickers stated, "I find that horses arrived in this area at a time that preceded the arrival of the first Europeans. Their use and enjoyment by Tŝilhqot'in people was well established at the time of first contact and that Tŝilhqot'in witnesses acknowledge their ancestors did not enjoy the use of horses from time immemorial. They understand that horses are European in their origin."[8]

As our research on the origins of the Chilcotin wild horse deepened, we found clues in every story shared, document found, chance encounter, and fossils uncovered and carbon-dated. Just when we thought the contradicting data had sorted itself out and we had a grip on all the facts, a voice from the past invited us back into brackish waters.

CHAPTER 23

EXPLORERS RECORD INDIGENOUS SPREAD OF THE HORSE

Just as Mexicali (Aztec) emperor Moctezuma and other First Nations leaders dreamed about the coming of the horse, so did the Nlaka'pamux First Nations and other Fraser Canyon cultures have foreknowledge about the first Europeans' arrival. Travellers' and prophets' tales preceded Simon Fraser's birch-bark canoe brigade into the canyon of the river now named for him. Canyon cultures' stories about their encounter in 1808 with Fraser and his North West Company (NWC) traders add a much-needed balance to the explorer's written accounts.[1 2]

Simon Fraser was the second of the NWC fur-trade explorers to venture west of the Rocky Mountains. Alexander Mackenzie was the first, in 1793, led by a First Nations guide following time-worn Indigenous pathways into what is now the Cariboo–Chilcotin. Both explorers' journals demonstrate the northern spread of the horse and how the horse was already deeply imbedded in Indigenous cultures.

I imagine that both Mackenzie and Fraser penned their journals by candlelight as they rested in their tents or around campfires after dangerous days in their canoes or on the trail. They put their journals in semi-waterproof packets sealed with wax so that they might survive the long fur-brigade canoe trips back across the continent to NWC headquarters in Montreal. From Montreal, the records went by sailing ships to Britain. It's a miracle the journals survived at all.

These two NWC Scottish explorers were the vanguards seeking to expand the lucrative fur trade west of the Rocky Mountains and find a shorter trade route to the Pacific Ocean and thence to England. The further west the NWC went in search of valuable beaver pelts, the greater the distance and expense to send their furs by canoe across the continent to Montreal each spring.

The fur trade in Canada started in 1670 with a Royal Charter by Charles II, King of England, Scotland, Ireland and France. The charter granted the HBC exclusive fur trade for all of the Hudson Bay watershed in what are now Canada's prairies, boreal and Arctic regions—a vast region fully occupied for thousands of years by numerous Indigenous cultures never once consulted by king or company.

By the time of the 1670 HBC charter, the first Spanish horses brought to the Americas had already been dispersed by Indigenous cultures across the continent, including the Chilcotin. A 1493 Royal Decree by Spain's King Ferdinand II sent the first horses to the Americas. His decree stated that all Spanish sailing vessels had to carry a number of horses to the "new" land.

The North West Company was established in 1779 by newly arrived Scottish Highlanders. The company earned high profits because it paid so little to Indigenous people for furs. The NWC usually "paid" for furs with metal axes, steel leghold traps, muskets, woven cloth, beads, wool blankets and other goods brought by sailing ships from England. Unfortunately, rum and whiskey (often watered down) were also traded.

When Alexander Mackenzie ventured across the Rockies in 1793, he canoed only part of the way down the same great river that Simon Fraser had travelled fifteen years later. The Tŝilhqot'in call this river *ʔElhdaqox*, or Sturgeon River. Interestingly, Mackenzie reported no horses west of the Rockies.

When Mackenzie arrived at a tributary called the West Road River (Blackwater River, about 40 kilometres west and north of present-day Quesnel), he decided to stash his canoes and hike to the Pacific Ocean on the Nuxalk–Carrier "Grease" Trail to Bella Coola.

If the Carrier (Dakelh) First Nation people along the grease trail had horses at the time, Mackenzie's expedition (including his dog) definitely would not have trekked for a week with heavy packs, slogging through mosquito-ridden bogs on the Chilcotin plateau before descending a precipitous mountain trail to coastal Nuxalk villages.

Once with the Nuxalk, Mackenzie learned that Captain Vancouver had recently sailed out of Bella Coola; Mackenzie hired a canoe to try to catch up but was turned back by hostile coastal people. As he recorded in his journal: "I now mixed up some vermilion in melted grease, and inscribed, in large characters, on the South-East face of the rock on which we had slept last night, this brief memorial 'Alexander Mackenzie, from Canada, by land, the twenty-second of July, one thousand seven hundred and ninety-three.'"[3]

Fraser's canoe brigade crossed the Rockies in the spring of 1806. He called the region "New Caledonia," in memory of inspiring stories his Scottish mother had told him about his Highland home.[4] He never bothered to consider Indigenous names for the region.

Fraser spent several years building and operating two fur-trading posts he called Fort McLeod and Fort St. James. He also prepared for his 1808 expedition to the Pacific Ocean down the great river.[5] Although Fraser found no horses around his northern trading posts, in a February 1807 letter he penned the first written record of First

Located in the Dean Channel and known today as "Mackenzie's Rock," this is the westernmost point that North West Company explorer Alexander Mackenzie reached during his exploration to the Pacific in 1793. He was aided and guided by Indigenous people at all steps. *Image courtesy of Wayne McCrory.*

Nations having horses further south: "I am Positively informed that the Nascudenees have horses that they get from the east." This appears to refer to a Northern Shuswap (Secwēpemc) village that, at the time, existed somewhere near or south of present-day Quesnel. (I have used today's place names and converted some of Fraser's confusing journal names for the various Indigenous tribes.)

In May 1808, Simon Fraser's expedition pushed four canoes into the river at Fort Fraser and began its perilous 800-kilometre voyage to the Pacific Ocean through one of the most treacherous canyons in the world. The expedition consisted of three white fur traders, nineteen voyageurs and two Indigenous guides. As we will see from Fraser's journal entries, canyon First Nations and their horses would turn out to play an important role in helping Fraser's expedition by portaging some of their baggage around dangerous rapids. Without the help of the First People, their guides and linguistic interpreters (the canyon cultures had different languages between them, including different words for horse), the Fraser expeditioners would most likely have perished.

On May 30, when the canoe brigade stopped at a large Native house at what is probably present-day Macalister, Simon Fraser recorded seeing the first tribes with "some vestiges of horse and in the afternoon some Toohowtins (Tautens) and Atnaughs (Atnahs) arrived on horseback . . . These Indians had heard of fire-arms but had never seen any."

A few miles upstream of present-day Soda Creek, Fraser noted more horse-mounted First Nations: "Those who came to see us from below were on horseback . . . tho' animals are plenty and the country in many places clear of wood, they do not use them to hunt, but use them to carry themselves and baggage, which is the chief cause of their not going much in Canoes."

On May 31, Fraser's crew arrived at the treacherous upper Soda Creek canyon and the start of serious troubles. Here his expedition was forced to make a difficult choice: continue by canoe or travel overland. Fraser and his crew must have felt sheer terror when they heard the thunderous downstream roar of Soda Creek Canyon. They pulled for shore before being swept into the whitewater rapids.

I experienced extreme fear at Soda Creek rapids in the 1970s when I and another biologist were doing wildlife surveys by freighter canoe for the proposed Moran Dam. After managing to reach shore, we crab-crawled along the cliff wall to look at the raging river below, realizing that it most likely would have dragged us into the seething maelstrom. We ended our surveys and made our way back up the river.

It was not surprising to me that, here, a group of Atnahs (Northern Shuswap or Secwēpemc) came to Fraser's camp, warning the crew to stay off the river and travel around the worst part of the canyon by horseback: "Numbers of Natives came to see us in [the] course of the day and remained. They all assured us that navigation for a certain distance below was impossible [impracticable] and advised us to leave our canoes in their charge and proceed on our journey by land to a great river [the Thompson] that flows from the left into this communication. The country they said consisted of plains, and the journey could be performed with horses in four or five days."

On June 2, while waiting for horses, Fraser noted that the river had risen eight feet and that "Mr. Stuart and some of the men agreed to go by land. But on application to the Indians for the horses they had promised, we received evasive answers, and we passed the rest of the day in anxious suspense."

On June 3, Fraser penned more disappointing news: "We only could procure four horses; these were of service in the carrying place, where the road is excessively bad, being up and down hill, and sometimes along the edge of dangerous declivities, over which a horse, with Mr. Stuart's desk [and] our medicine chest, tumbled and [some papers and medicine] were lost."

On June 4 Fraser added: "One of the Indians brought us a Pistol, which Mr. Quesnel lost yesterday when he was on horseback."

Once back on the river on June 5 at Iron Rapids, between present-day Riske Creek and the mouth of the Chilcotin River, First Nation horses were again loaned to Fraser's group for a long portage: "The men took five horses to transport the baggage across, yet were much harassed with fatigue."

We also learn from Fraser's June 5 entry that the Tŝilhqot'in (referred to by him as Chilkhotins) also had horses:

> The natives make use of horses. Near [the] end of [this] course is a considerable river Waccans [the Chilcotin River] on [the] right, with an Island at its mouth, and I suppose to see the River. It is likewise the residence of the Chilkhotins [Chilcotins], a tribe of the Carriers, and by all accounts is very rapidous and full of Chutts [chutes; i.e., waterfalls], Mossu [Moose?], Red Deer, and Cheverau [chevreau], and Beaver are likewise said to be numerous in that quarter, and the natives have horses.

An example of one of the Canyon Horse Nations that Simon Fraser encountered on his canoe and portage expedition in 1808 to the Pacific Ocean. This photo was taken of the St'át'imc (Lillooet) Nation in 1865 at present-day Lillooet in the Fraser Canyon. Some of the mounted St'át'imc photographed in 1865 may have been alive or had relatives who had assisted Fraser when his expedition passed through their traditional territory in 1808. *Image courtesy of Charles Gentile, Library and Archives Canada.*

By June 12, 1808, Fraser's expedition had reached the ancient village of Lillooet and made contact with the First Nations people of the same name. The next day he wrote: "We set out at 5, accompanied by all the Indians and two Horses. Soon after three more horsemen joined our party. I asked [for] one of the horses in order to carry part of our baggage. This the owners declined and left us."

Meanwhile, Stuart continued down the river with the rest of the crew in their two remaining canoes. On June 16, at another dangerous portage, Fraser's expedition was again assisted by First Nations horses. On June 19, 1808, the expedition canoes beached at the Nlaka'pamux village of Camchin (Kumsheen) at the confluence of the Fraser and Thompson rivers (Lytton). Here, 1,200 Nlaka'pamux gathered on the beach to greet Fraser and shake his hand.[6]

As recorded by ethnographers James Teit and Wendy Wickwire, Nlaka'pamux oral history passed down through many generations provides much more detail of fur trader–Nlaka'pamux first encounters than Fraser recorded. Nlaka'pamux elder Annie York recalled that her grandparents had told her that the wife of the old chief sh-PEENT-lum had predicted the arrival of the whites prior to their arrival: "The Lytton Indians seen man coming down in the canoe with his party and Chief sh-PEENT-lum soon spot it and he says, 'That's what my wife foretold. That man is coming to this area. You must never hurt him. See that white, what he got on his head?' He had a white handkerchief that ties around as a band. And he's the head man in the canoe."

Annie also told the story, passed on by her grandmother, that a special woman sang as the Fraser expedition paddled away from the village and that Fraser had tears in his eyes. Another elder told a story about how Fraser had fondled a woman at the mouth of the Stein River. Elder oral history also told of their own use of horses at that time.

Annie York also relayed her grandparents' story that Fraser's captain told the people not to touch them. "If you do it, you're going to get some kind of disease, and it's going to clean you out."[7] As Fraser continued down the canyon, his June 24 journal revealed that smallpox was already present amongst the Nlaka'pamux in the lower canyon. Fraser recorded that there were "upwards of five hundred souls . . . smallpox was in the camp and several of the Natives were marked with it."

I am guessing that the Nlaka'pamux were infected after trading earlier at a fort on the coast or via horseback journeys east of the Rocky Mountains. Smallpox first reached the Pacific Northwest with fur-trading vessels after 1744, killing large numbers of coastal First Nations. Nlaka'pamux oral history confirms long-distance travel to distant lands.[8]

While travelling through the rest of the canyon and out to the coast, Fraser does not mention horses. And we know rainforest coastal areas were unsuitable to horses. However, on his return trip, on July 14, after barely surviving reaching the Pacific, his motley contingent arrived back at the Nlaka'pamux village (Lytton). Here, horses again enter his journal. He includes reports that starving Canyon First Nations ate horses for survival. On July 19 he wrote, "The Chief of the [Thompson Indians] . . . were now starving. They now and then

The Chief's grave near Lytton, 1867–1868, about sixty years after Simon Fraser encountered an encampment of Thompson (Nlaka'pamux) people here, including what has been interpreted from his journal as visiting Shoshone from far away. This Chief's horses were killed when he died, then skinned and hung over his grave for "eternal life." We have no idea if this Nlaka'pamux Chief died of the smallpox epidemic that started in about 1860 and wiped out an estimated 50–75 per cent of the interior Indigenous population. According to one authority (Teit) the Upper Nlaka'pamux were skilled horse people in the late eighteenth century. *Image courtesy of the Royal BC Museum, Image C-09264.*

killed a horse. We saw the one quite fresh hanging from a tree, and this famine, perhaps, caused the disagreeable gloom."

These written records by Simon Fraser are invaluable: they delineate the northern and western limits of the spread of the horse in North America; they also prove that the horse was already well established amongst inland Indigenous cultures by 1808, including the Tŝilhqot'in. They show that the horses *came from the east* and that the interior grassland Horse Nations were "great travellers." Some had been east of the Rocky Mountains for a war where they had also hunted the bison.[9] Also, the Nlaka'pamux (Thompson) First Nation even had several visiting horse-mounted Shoshones, whose territory at the time included what today is the Snake River Plains in southern Idaho.[10] If Simon Fraser's journal has accurately named them, the visiting Shoshones would have ridden a thousand kilometres through the territories of many distinct tribes.

Although both Mackenzie and Fraser reached the Pacific Ocean by different routes, neither would have been successful without the generous sharing of ancient travel routes and guiding by many Indigenous people. The Fraser and Mackenzie journals, along with the Indigenous oral history at the time, are indeed gifts to help us more accurately understand the northernmost spread of the horse in the Cariboo–Chilcotin and the role of the horse in Indigenous cultures at the early onset of colonization.

CHAPTER 24

ANCIENT BREEDS FORM CHILCOTIN WILD HORSE POPULATION

Throughout the ages men have held a special place in their dreams for "the perfect horse." Every generation of man has valiantly tried to improve every generation of the horse, with an effort to come a little closer to the ideal. Had the horsemen of the past been blessed with the voluminous amount of knowledge it is our good fortune to inherit, we all would today be riding horses more nearly approaching "perfection" . . . The earliest record we have of horse breeding was found a number of years ago in the highlands of southwestern Persia. An engraved stone was found among other material dated about 3000 BC . . . There are many more horses in the world of mixed blood than purebred, however, it must be remembered that "purebred" is a relative term. This means that while most horses are of one type or another, there is no such thing as an absolute purebred.

— **William E. Jones and Ralph Bogart**, *Genetics of the Horse*[1]

One of my final background tasks for our genetic study was to assess the introduction of new European and American breeds into the Chilcotin wild horse population since colonial times with regard to possible influences on their ancestral foundation lineage. This was prompted by Dr. Cothran's findings that most US wild horse populations today were mixed breeds. Such changes to foundation populations over time were the result of escaped domestic breeds and deliberate attempts to up-breed wild herds by the introduction of new breeds.

One fascinating early example of up-breeding of wild stock in Canada occurred in 1831 when the Hudson's Bay Company at Fort Gary launched a controlled up-breeding program for the buffalo-running prairie horses they had acquired from First Nations and Métis. This involved the complicated importation from England of a Norfolk Trotter stallion named Fireaway, a red roan. At the time, the HBC was dependent on horse-mounted hunters for bison meat. The delivery of Fireaway involved an ocean-going sailing ship followed by a long canoe journey, incredible as this sounds.

The Fireaway project is a famous story[2] worth repeating as an example of the lengths to which equestrian societies will go to try achieve a superior horse breed—the perfect horse. It's also relevant since I found out that in the Chilcotin there had been over a century of similar up-breeding attempts by settlers and the Tŝilhqot'in through the deliberate release of Thoroughbred stallions and other breeds into the wild-horse population.

Fireaway's move from genteel England to the frontier life as a breeding stud in the Red River colony came about partly due to snobbery. Fort Garry HBC traders felt that the plains cayuses, obtained for a blanket each, were inferior to European breeds. However, anecdotal evidence from that era suggests that the ancestors of the Plains Indian horses were actually the Spanish horse. They are some of the hardiest horses on Earth. Because of their arid origins in Spain as war horses, they made perfect buffalo chasers.

In 1831, the HBC in England arranged to load Fireaway onto an HBC sailing ship. Fireaway then spent two months crossing the Atlantic before being unloaded at the remote subarctic post of Fort York, near Hudson Bay. The horse was then loaded onto a wooden HBC York boat with enough hay to survive the thousand-kilometre boat journey to the Red River hinterland via a complex network of treacherous interconnected rivers, lakes and difficult portages. The trip was replete with the hordes of biting flies and mosquitoes that so typify the boggy northern taiga.

The open boat was propelled by a crew of Orkney oarsmen, with Fireaway having to be unloaded at each campsite and portage, then reloaded. On one occasion, Fireaway fell overboard and swam to shore. One can easily appreciate that the poor horse by this time had developed a strong desire to be free, on dry land, but alas the long-suffering equine was captured and loaded back into the York boat.

Safely at Fort Garry after his long ordeal, Fireaway's just reward was waiting. Fifty prairie mares had been selected for a controlled breeding program. Subsequently, the HBC claimed that the new Fireaway prairie cayuse crossbreeds were the best buffalo runners in the country.[3] This claim was made despite the fact that the First Nations' cayuses across the prairies were renowned for their speed and skills as buffalo runners and warhorses, as well as for their incredible ability to endure long-distance travel.

When I researched the western HBC era at Fort Alexandria covering the first half of the 1800s, I found no written records that the HBC had brought in European breeds to up-breed the fur brigade horses they had obtained from First Nations. The existence of the two centuries-long Cariboo–Chilcotin Indigenous domestic and wild horse populations did not appear to fall under any new breed influences until the 1858–1860 Cariboo gold rush and the subsequent immigrant wave of settler-ranchers. During and after the gold rush, hundreds of horses were simply abandoned or escaped to the wilds. Many released in winter died of starvation, littering Cariboo gold trail and placer mine sites with their carcasses.

It is unlikely that many surviving gold-rush horses made their way across the Fraser River into the Chilcotin. However, the large influx of settlers that moved into the Chilcotin after the gold rush brought in many new horse breeds, some of which escaped to mix with the original Indigenous free-roaming horses. There followed sporadic and isolated attempts by both First Nations and cattle ranchers to up-breed the wild herds by turning loose different breed stallions, such as Thoroughbreds, a practice that continues to recent times. However, I question whether a domestic stallion could successfully compete with battle-scarred wild stallions for herd acquisition and dominance to breed, or survive the harsh Chilcotin winters. Following are examples of more recent attempts to up-breed Chilcotin wild horses with European purebred stallions, either in captive situations or in the wild.

Xeni Gwet'in wildlife researcher and knowledge keeper Alice William (a major advisor to this book) recounts the following history of her Tŝilhqot'in family and their horses when she was raised on their ranch in the remote hinterland of the Dasiqox-Taseko River in the 1950s:

> Tsilhqot'in men and women used horses as far as I can remember; most of the people in our family handled horses from a young age and were in constant contact with horses and their care, it was a necessity for survival and travel. The Tŝilhqot'in cherished their horses and adorned them in fancy halters, bridles, and some groomed their horses in the early mornings, like my dad Jimmy Bulyan did as a ritual that showed his connection with the horse spirit. This connection is lost to some of the younger generation.
>
> From our mom Amelia's story, I calculated around the 1930s Nenqayni (Tŝilhqot'in) from Xeni community had

The Tŝilhqot'in integrated some western cowboy ways into their traditional lifestyle. Here are three Tŝilhqot'in horsemen in the 1950s, from left to right, John Baptiste Labusten, Samuel Bulyan and Jimmy Bulyan. They had their own braided rawhide lariats and went on long rides to trade and acquire horses or to capture wild ones. Jimmy Bulyan had a ranch in what is now the new Dasiqox-Taseko tribal protected area and groomed his horses every morning to connect to the horse spirit. He also attempted up-breeding with a Thoroughbred stallion. *Image courtesy of Alice William.*

bought a Thoroughbred stud horse back when dad was a young man.

Our dad Jimmy had bred his favourite mare to the Thoroughbred stud and out of this came a valued colt called Diamond. This selective breeding of a Thoroughbred and mustang produced a herd of 70 horses and all different colours down from the roan genetics. When Jimmy went back into the mountains to Nabist to chase horses, he chased the horses down to the meadows, and the stud Diamond would help round them into the corral. Our mom Amelia recounted this story in wonderment of Dad's and Diamond's days together as precious memories when she told stories to us.

Graduate student Catherine Card recorded other examples of attempts to up-breed the Chilcotin wild qiyus. The following comes from a non-Indigenous rancher:

> We're out there and oftentimes, if a nice stallion was obtained, they would be released into the wild to introduce that blood into our horse herd. Mind you, we up-bred them a little (the free-roaming horses) because we used to turn Thoroughbred studs loose. It's actually a cheap way of obtaining horses. You turn a good stud loose and three or four years later you go and get the colts. You don't have to raise them, you don't have to keep the studs, and you don't have to feed the mares. You're always getting the strong ones. The strong ones survive and that's what you get. Sounds to me like a good situation.

A Tŝilhqot'in commented specifically on introducing European breeds, including the larger draft workhorses, to up-breed free-roaming horse herds: "I think our membership like the idea that maybe in years gone by Thoroughbred horses were purchased and released. I believe lately more often our membership . . . bring in heavy horses, Percherons, Clydesdales, whatever, throw them into the herd . . . if you're raising part-team horse, part-mustang horse, they're a little easier to round up than part-mustang, part-Thoroughbred horse."[4]

During our genetic research in the Brittany Triangle, a number of well-meaning horse people approached us with a sincere interest in up-breeding the wild horses in the Triangle. Although we felt strongly that the population should not be messed with until we completed our genetic research, any decision was left up to the Xeni Gwet'in.

For example, one local wanted to turn loose an Icelandic stud in the Brittany Triangle and then promote and market an all-new breed of Icelandic-mustang stock; this did not happen. An acquaintance contacted me about releasing her aging "curly mustang" into the Brittany to improve the herds, rather than put her pet down. She could no longer afford its feed.

We now needed to complete our genetic study to assist us in interpreting what the influence might have been on the original foundation wild horse population from these deliberate up-breeding attempts. In the end, this turned out be full of surprises.

CHAPTER 25

CHILCOTIN HORSES' UNIQUE ANCESTRY

Our genetic research program spanned a decade, much longer than anticipated, and involved two different labs. Dr. Gus Cothran, at Texas A&M University, did the primary testing of blood and hair samples for genetic uniqueness based on equine microsatellite loci and mitochondrial DNA sequence variation, and comparison with sixty-nine different domestic horse breeds from around the world. Genome sequencing of a small number of hair samples was conducted by Dr. Ludovic Orlando at the Centre for Anthropobiology and Genomics of Toulouse, France. Genome sequencing is difficult to explain in lay terms but involves in-depth analysis of the DNA of each horse.[1]

First off, we had to determine the approximate distribution of wild horses in the vast West Chilcotin to design our sample areas. A map was prepared using winter aerial counts of wild horses done by the Ministry of Forests and the Xeni Gwet'in–Friends of Nemaiah Valley. Obtaining blood samples from wild horses early in the study proved a challenge, as did collecting wild-horse hair later, after it was found hair basal cells could be genotyped. We first chose the Brittany Triangle since we hypothesized this wild horse population might be

Xeni Gwet'in horse-trainer Terry Lulua lassoing a wild horse he previously captured from the Brittany Triangle. *Image courtesy of Wayne McCrory.*

isolated from the larger population in the West Chilcotin by two river valleys. Genetics would give us an answer.

For blood samples from the Brittany Triangle, we decided not to round up wild horses. Instead, David Williams and retired veterinarian Dr. Corrine Long obtained blood samples from eight domestic horses that had been previously captured wild in the Brittany Triangle.

Collecting hair samples from the Brittany Triangle and the vast Chilcotin wild-horse country took many years; it involved hiking hundreds of kilometres of horse trails and collecting hair snagged on tree limbs along the trails or at bedding sites under trees. Xeni Gwet'in knowledge keeper Norman William and I tried collecting hair during a winter deep-freeze, when it was −35°C, plus the wind-chill. We finally gave up for safety reasons: our fingers risked freezing while we pried wild-horse hair off branches. Extreme Chilcotin winters were not the only danger. Our study team constantly had to be on the alert to avoid grizzly bears feeding on wild-horse or wildlife carcasses.

Veterinarian Dr. Corrine Long preparing to take a blood sample, assisted by trapper Ian Bridges. *Image courtesy of Wayne McCrory.*

Dr. Cothran's first results from the blood samples from the Brittany Triangle horses were surprisingly revealing: "Some probability of Iberian influence and possibly old Spanish ancestry, but inconclusive due to the small sample size."[2]

So far, so good. These exciting but uncertain results, along with news that DNA could be extracted from the basal cells of horsehair, provided the opportunity to expand the sample size in the Brittany Triangle, then expand to the larger West Chilcotin without taking blood samples from horses.

Over the coming years, while we collected our hair samples, a genetics study of Sable Island horses off the coast of Nova Scotia found evidence of light draft and multipurpose breeds commonly found in eastern Canada. This disproved the popular belief that these horses originated from shipwrecks carrying Spanish horses.[3]

When I finally mailed a batch of hard-earned hair samples from eighty-three horses in the Brittany Triangle to Dr. Cothran's lab, and a smaller batch to Dr. Orlando's lab, I wondered if our results would

International equine genetics expert Dr. Gus Cothran (right) and biologist Wayne McCrory (left) explained to an Alberta Wild Horse Symposium group how collecting wild-horse hair left on this pine tree can be used to determine the breed of the horse. The horse's DNA can be extracted from the basal cells of its hair. Here, horsehair clusters had been snagged on the rough bark of the tree when the horses sheltered or when they rubbed against it. *Image courtesy of Dr. Christina Barron-Ortiz.*

be similar to those from Sable Island. We estimated that the hair samples represented about one-third of the Brittany Triangle's free-living horses; in scientific terms a good sample size.

Our final 2014 results proved interesting. Dr. Orlando's genetic sequencing of four hair samples from the Brittany Triangle found results similar to Dr. Cothran's earlier genotyping from blood samples: Spanish-Iberian horse ancestry but with a strong Barb component. A Barb is a blend of horses from the Iberian Peninsula (Spain and Portugal) and the Barbary horse from North Africa.[4] [5] Somewhat different and more conclusive results emerged from Dr. Cothran's laboratory. The difference is most likely related to a much larger sample size than Dr. Orlando's.

Lorna Visser examining a tree with both grizzly bear and wild-horse hair. It was sometimes difficult to tell grizzly bear guard hair from the hair of a wild horse or domestic cow. *Image courtesy of Wayne McCrory.*

While there was some suggestion of Spanish ancestry, the Canadian Horse (our national horse) appeared to be the main ancestor of Brittany Triangle horses. There was also evidence of East Russian (Yakut) ancestry. The genetics also indicated the Brittany horses had been isolated for some time. There was no evidence that pre-Columbian (i.e., Ice Age) horses were involved in their ancestry.[6]

We were excited but wondered if the results would be different outside of the Brittany Triangle. We moved on to collect wild-horse hair samples from the vast West Chilcotin Plateau. Dr. Cothran found all fifty-seven samples had Spanish Iberian ancestry.[7] [8] Dr. Orlando's lab obtained similar results from genome sequencing of a small number of hair samples, finding Iberian horses with a strong Barb component. Again, there was no evidence of the pre-Columbian (Ice Age) horse.

Thus, although the much larger wild horse population outside of the Brittany Triangle had a common Spanish-founder ancestry with Brittany horses, their gene pool proved distinct, as they have no Canadian Horse or East Russian (Yakut) bloodlines.

Wild-horse hair found snagged on trees along their trails and bedding areas were the main source of the hair samples collected. Most samples were sent to Dr. Cothran at Texas A&M University for genotyping, with a small number sent to Dr. Ludovic Orlando at the Centre for Anthropobiology and Genomics of Toulouse for genome sequencing. *Image courtesy of Jonaki Bhattacharyya.*

These results confirm that the West Chilcotin horses both outside and inside the Brittany Triangle have some similarities in terms of a common lineage. At some point, centuries ago, a Spanish breed of horse first introduced by the Tŝilhqot'in most likely formed the founding population. The early dispersal of the Spanish horse across the Americas four centuries ago by Indigenous cultures has been well documented.

The Canadian Horse and East Russia (Yakut) bloodlines in the Brittany Triangle wild horse population suggest multiple introductions at different times. We had no way of determining if these breeds had been brought in later by the Tŝilhqot'in or settler-ranchers and had escaped to the wilds or were deliberately released to up-breed the founding population. However, we found no evidence of Thoroughbred influence from up-breeding attempts by the Tŝilhqot'in and others.

In some ways, our genetic study generated more questions than it answered, particularly the mystery as to how and when East Russian (Yakut) and Canadian Horse types were imported into the region. It

The fast-flowing Dasiqox-Taseko River, with its rugged valley walls and canyons, appears to act as a physical and/or psychological barrier to gene flow between the genetically distinct Brittany Triangle and West Chilcotin wild horse populations, though they have a common Spanish Iberian ancestry. *Image courtesy of Wayne McCrory.*

is very clear, however, that the West Chilcotin today has two somewhat similar but genetically distinct wild horse populations, isolated from each other by fast-flowing wild rivers. This is unique for North America and globally significant. Our genetic findings also suggest that constant high levels of culling or eradication of Chilcotin wild horses could be altering or destroying ancient horse lineages with distinct gene pools that can't be replicated or replaced.

CHAPTER 26

THE EAST RUSSIAN (YAKUT) HORSE CONNECTION

Modern Yakut horses are a small, hardy breed that live in northeast Siberia, above the Arctic Circle, some 3,000 kilometres from the Brittany Triangle. Since our discovery of evidence of possible Yakut bloodlines in this population in 2018, a genetic link to the Yakut horse was also discovered in free-roaming horses far from the Chilcotin, in Theodore Roosevelt National Park, in North Dakota. The researchers, like us, felt that more study was needed of the East Russian (Yakut) DNA, but raised the possibility of the historical transportation of horses from Siberia and East Asia to North America.[1]

For the Brittany Triangle, the most likely pathway by which the Tŝilhqot'in acquired this horse breed would have been with trade on the Pacific Coast between 1799 and 1867, when the Russian-American Company operated a large fur trade. The Tŝilhqot'in regularly traded with First Nations on the Pacific Coast. However, I found no evidence to support the Coastal acquisition of East Russian (Yakut) horses. For one thing, the company established trading posts only in Alaska and San Francisco, not on the BC coast. Secondly, research of logs of Russian fur-trade ships in North America found no mention of the transport of horses from Russia to the west coast of North America. This research was done to see if Russia was the origin of the "curly horse" (a type of mustang with distinctive curled hair).[2] However, other research found that some Yakut horses did reach the western shores of the continent and were used at Russian settlements in Alaska during the late 1700s and early 1800s. In 1817, there were sixteen horses in Russian America, more than likely "the hardy Yakut."[3] (Mixed-breed cattle on Chirikof Island still carry the genes of Yakut cattle brought over during the Russian fur trade.[4]) East Russian (Yakut)–type horses were most likely brought into the Brittany Triangle from the southeast, but their origin storylines will likely remain lost in the past.

Equally intriguing speculation on my part: the possibility that the wild horse population in the Brittany Triangle may have inherited Arctic survival features recently discovered in the modern Yakut horse. This could explain the remarkable adaptation of Chilcotin wild horses to harsh winters.

Recent genome research of the Yakut horse found that, many centuries ago, when Indigenous people migrated north into Siberia with their horses, the horse made physical and physiological adaptations to the extreme Arctic winter conditions over many generations. The rapidity of these high-speed genetic mutations surprised evolutionary biologists. The massive reprogramming of gene expression included an increase in body size from the original founder group of Yakut horses and the possible development of a thicker, hairier winter coat. Other changes involved hormonal responses to thermogenetic requirements and the production of metabolic anti-freezing compounds.[5]

This should not surprise us, since the Yakut horse appears to be the only breed in the world adapted to living outside year-round north of the Arctic Circle, where winter temperatures can average −50°C in January, some of the lowest recorded outside Antarctica. The coldest

Have these hardy wild qiyus in the Brittany Triangle inherited some of the same rapidly adapting Arctic winter-survival genes, such as metabolic antifreeze, from their East Russian (Yakut) ancestors? *Image courtesy of Wayne McCrory.*

temperature recorded in Siberia was −64.4°C (−83.9°F).[6] By comparison, winter conditions for the Chilcotin horse are not as severe; the weather station at Puntzi (in the Chilcotin) recorded a phenomenal low of −52.8°C (−63°F) on December 29, 1968.[7] This is not counting the windchill. The Chilcotin winters are famous for their stalled Arctic fronts and periodic warming Chinook winds. Given such extremes, it's no wonder that the ancestors of the Tŝilhqot'in people adapted by making comfortable winter lodges underground instead of above.

The Chilcotin winters are, in fact, so notorious that they have been integrated into First Nations' oral accounts and cowboy stories depicting cattle freezing standing up. I first learned this from Jack Palmantier, a Tŝilhqot'in cowboy-rancher, when I camped out one −35°C winter in the early 1980s while doing moose surveys on the Chilcotin military block. Jack, one of the Toosey (Tl'esqox) First Nations researchers working on the project, told me I was a crazy white man for working when it was so cold. He informed me conditions were similar to a previous bad winter when some of his cows froze standing up in their corral one night.[8]

Cowboys in a blizzard. *Image courtesy of Duane Starr Photography.*

One of the more famous Chilcotin seasons recorded was the 1939–40 "winter of the blue snow," colourfully described by cowboy author Richmond Hobson in his book *Nothing Too Good for a Cowboy*: "Cows bawled and coughed in the dark and the intense cold. The close-knotted silhouette of their dark bodies sprawled out in bold relief against the vast white world around them. The air rattled and crackled, as the cattle called their cold anguish into the dawn of the forty-below zero day of December 20, 1939 . . . For four months of the year, I don't think there is a colder, more winter-chilled creature on Earth than the inadequately clothed, frostbitten cowhand of the

A Chilcotin wild horse herd with frosted backs in –35°C winter weather. *Image courtesy of Wayne McCrory.*

Cariboo and Chilcotin countries in the interior of British Columbia . . . temperatures also drop to seventy below, and, at a few isolated spots like Redstone in the heart of the cattle country in the Chilcotin, government thermometers have registered even colder."[9]

Unlike Hobson's freezing cowhands, adaptation to fierce Arctic conditions is the hallmark of the Chilcotin wild horse. Perhaps that's because those in the Brittany Triangle with East Russian (Yakut) genes have their own metabolic antifreeze. Only more research will help determine this possibility.

CHAPTER 27

THE CANADIAN HORSE

(*LE CHEVAL CANADIEN*)

We were surprised to discover that the Canadian Horse was the primary ancestor of the wild horses in the Brittany Triangle. Even though we occasionally saw a small number of heavy-set black horses that closely resembled images of the Canadian Horse from Quebec, we had no idea of the close ancestry. The breed was first introduced from France in 1665 aboard King Louis XIV's ships. A century later, the Canadian Horse was probably introduced by French colonists to New Orleans and regions of France's large Louisiana Purchase, which extended as far north as Montana. In recognition of its heritage values to Quebec, in 2002 the Canadian government made it the National Horse. The breed is also now listed as "at risk" by Heritage Livestock Canada.

How did the foundation genes of our National Horse come to form the dominant bloodlines of the wild horse population in the Brittany Triangle and not in the rest of the West Chilcotin?

Dan Wilson of the Canadian Horse Society offered one explanation when he phoned me after he saw a newspaper article on our wild-horse research with a photo of our favourite black stallion. "I studied the pictures and the Brittany–Chilcotin horses are without question the 'Canadian Horse,'" he said. "I know my stock . . . and I have helped them be recognized as the heritage horse of Canada.

This large black stallion in the Brittany Triangle shows some of its Canadian Horse ancestry. *Image courtesy of Sadie Parr.*

Those horses are not from the Spanish mustangs." He said that French-Canadian fur-traders brought the Canadian Horse across the prairies; that is how the Canadian Horse came west.

Although the evidence of the spread of the Canadian Horse across the prairies and the western mountains during the fur-trade era is scant, Wilson's explanation seems to me most credible. However, given that Canadian Horses were first introduced to the Americas 150 years later than the conquistadores' horses, they would have been introduced to the Brittany Triangle much later still.

In his 1952 book on mustangs, J. Frank Dobie noted the occurrence of the Canadian Horse on the prairies during the days of the fur trade:

> As the 19th century advanced, the horses of the Plains Indians ceased to be straight-out Spanish in blood, as did also many bands of wild horses . . . Coming west by south from Canada, were other modifiers. Louis XIV had begun sending mares and stallions to New France in 1665, and this stock had crossed with Spanish stock brought northward by Indians.[1]

Another source confirmed Dobie's conclusion:

> Animals identified as "Canadian," "French," or "Norman" were located in the Great Lakes region, with a 1782 census at Fort Detroit listing over 1,000 animals. By 1770, Spanish horses were found in that area, and there was a clear zone from Ontario and Saskatchewan to St. Louis [Missouri], where Canadian-type horses, particularly the smaller varieties, crossbred with mustangs of Spanish ancestry. French-Canadian horses were also allowed to roam freely, and moved west, particularly influencing horse herds in the northern plains and inland northwest.[2]

It is very likely that the Tŝilhqot'in or settler-ranchers or both first introduced Canadian Horses or Canadian-Spanish crossbreeds to the Brittany Triangle. Again, like the bloodlines of East Russian (Yakut) horses, the history and origins of the Canadian Horse in the wilds of the Chilcotin will likely remain lost in time.

Typical large "Chilcotin wild horses," or qiyus, that inhabit the West Chilcotin, outside of the Brittany Triangle. Although all of the hair samples we collected along horse trails showed Spanish Iberian ancestry, these horses had undergone many genetic changes since the Spanish horses were brought to the Americas five centuries ago and likely bear little resemblance to the original Spanish horses of the conquest. *Image courtesy of Wayne McCrory.*

CHAPTER 28

THE SPREAD OF THE SPANISH HORSE ACROSS AMERICA

Although the Spaniards are commonly credited with introducing the first horses to the Americas, there is evidence that the Vikings might have brought them earlier. Viking colonizers transported horses to Greenland starting in the eleventh century and settled areas along the coast of Newfoundland. However, there is little evidence that Viking horses reached mainland settlements. The "Early Dispersal" study rejected the contribution of any Viking horses to the earliest western Indigenous horses. The study found bloodlines from almost exclusively European origins, with strong genetic affinities to three ancient domestic horses from Spain, France and Iran, and with no evidence of a link to the late Pleistocene horse.[1] Our genetic results for the Chilcotin wild horse were similar, though we found no Iranian horse ancestry.

With few exceptions, the Spanish horse was the most common breed of Indigenous-owned horses recorded by early European explorers and fur-traders on the prairies and Great Plains in the late 1700s and 1800s. This included some horses with Mexican brands. For example, in travels across what is now central Canada in the late 1780s and early 1790s, Alexander Mackenzie wrote that the Plains First Nations had great numbers of horses "which are brought, from the Spanish settlements in Mexico: and many of them have been seen in the back parts of the country, branded with the initials of their original owners' names . . . they are turned out loose winter and summer to provide for themselves."[2] In the same region, Hudson's Bay Company fur-traders had also observed Cree-Assiniboine riders with horses sporting Spanish brands as early as 1750.[3]

Further west, when explorer David Thompson overwintered in 1787–88 with the Piegan First Nations just east of present-day Calgary, he recorded a young Piegan, "Kootanae Appee," coming back from a raiding party to the south with a string of "Spanish mules."[4]

In his book on mustangs, J. Frank Dobie summarized well this early Spanish horse history on the prairies: "Towards the middle of the 18th century, two hundred years after Coronado's expedition, horses were appearing in the Saskatchewan country of Canada, and they were Spanish horses. About the same time, east and west of the Canadian plains, that remarkable aggregation of untribed Indians and half-breed Frenchmen called Bois Brules, or Burnt Woods, became suppliers of Spanish horses and pemmican to the trapper-traders on Hudson's Bay [*sic*] and along the Red River of the North."[5]

Perhaps the first written account of the Spanish horse west of the Rocky Mountains came

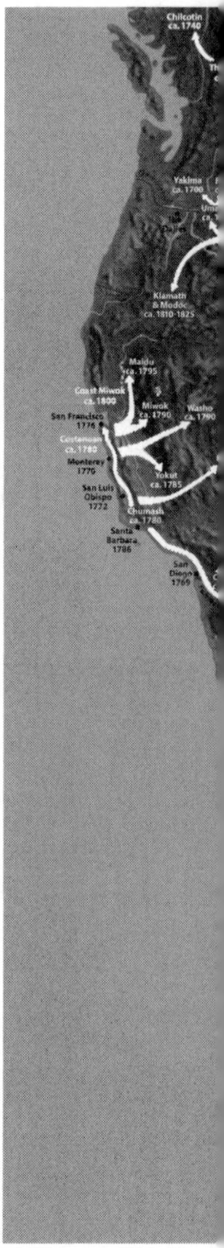

The Spread of the Spanish Horse Across America

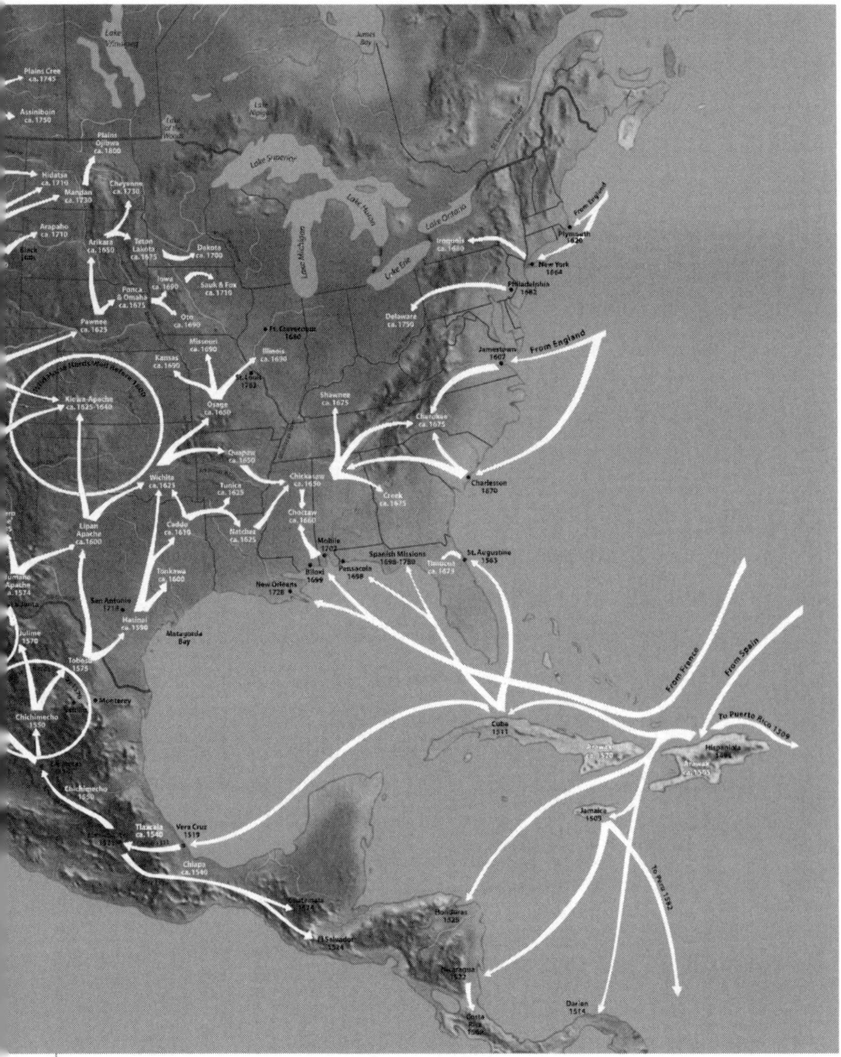

This detail from the map *The Spread of the Horse Across the Americas: 1519–1750* shows the horse reaching the Chilcotin in 1740, but a more thorough study by western scientists and Indigenous knowledge keepers suggests the spread to the Chilcotin was at least a century earlier—in the early to mid-1600s. *Image modified from* The Spread of the Horse Across the Americas: 1519–1750, *courtesy of Mike Cowdrey, Jody Martin and Ned Martin.*

from David Thompson in 1807. He reported large numbers of Spanish horses in the grassland valleys of the Kootenay (Ktunaxa) First Peoples in today's BC east Kootenays. Thompson hunted wild horses for riding and for food and even ate meat from the carcass of one he disputed over with a coyote.[6] Another historian attributed the Kootenay (Ktunaxa) as having introduced the first Spanish horses.[7]

The early ownership of Spanish-type horses by the southern Columbia Plateau cultures, including the Nez Cayuse, Nez Percé and Flatheads in today's Washington, Idaho and Montana, has also been well documented, including the 1805 Lewis and Clark expedition.[8 9]

Closer to the Chilcotin, although the chronology of early Indigenous horse acquisition has been documented by some for First Nations in the interior of BC, I found no reference to the Spanish horse.[10]

Over time, a number of historians have perused early written accounts, primarily of the Spanish horse, to piece together and map the chronology of the dispersal of the horse across North America by Indigenous people. However, very few bothered asking First Nations about their oral knowledge of when they first acquired horses.

Using mostly written accounts, Mike Cowdrey and Ned and Jody Martin, in their book *Horses and Bridles of the American Indians*, provide one of the more well-researched narratives and maps of the spread of the horse across North America between 1494 and 1800.[11]

Prior to publication of their 2012 edition, the three authors contacted me for an estimate of the approximate year of arrival of the horse in the Chilcotin so they could add it to their map. Having interviewed a handful of Tŝilhqot'in knowledge keepers, I guessed it might be about 1740.

While the horse dispersal pathways on their maps are fascinating and informative, in actual fact the recent ground-breaking "Early Dispersal" study proved categorically that the integration of primarily the Spanish horse into Indigenous lifeways occurred at least a century earlier. Domestic horses, spread by First Nations from Spanish settlements in the American southwest, arrived in the northern Rockies and central Great Plains by the first half of the 1600s—at the latest.

This study included an assemblage of historic archaeological horse remains integrated with genomic, isotopic, radiocarbon dating, and paleopathological evidence. Indigenous context included the Lakota First Nations' deep cultural relationship to the horse dating back to the late Pleistocene. Numerous North American Indigenous scholars and knowledge keepers were co-authors, including knowledge keeper Alice William, the Tŝilhqot'in researcher for this book.

The traditional Tŝilhqot'in daredevil mountain race has been around for centuries. *Image courtesy of Wayne McCrory.*

It is thus no accident that Dr. Cothran's previous genetic study of the wild horses in the Sundre equine zone of Alberta's Rocky Mountain foothills revealed there was clearly detectable Spanish ancestry in their mixed origins and that their likely origin was from Prairie First Nations to the south.[12]

Although the study on the early dispersal of the horse did not include a review of evidence west of the Rocky Mountains, I have assumed from the Spanish ancestry of the Chilcotin wild horse from our genetic study, as well as from some of the Tŝilhqot'in oral history and early fur-trader and explorer accounts, that the integration of the Spanish horse into the Tŝilhqot'in lifeway occurred around the same time period as in the northern Rockies, in the early to mid-1600s. This would

A Tŝilhqot'in spruce-root basket. Horse images incorporated into Tŝilhqot'in art and culture, such as in this basket, also reflect the antiquity of the horse in their society. According to Xeni Gwet'in knowledge keeper Alice William, she and her family used smaller versions of this basket with lids that were watertight for berry-picking. They used nice braided rawhide to attach the baskets to their saddle horse when they went on horseback to fill their baskets with soapberries. *Image courtesy of Jessica Bushey, the UBC Museum of Anthropology.*

have been during the Tŝilhqot'in deep time of *Sadanx*—the time of ancestors, legends and creation.

The most likely source of the foundational Spanish-type horses for the BC interior grassland First Nations would have been from trade with the horse-breeding Indigenous horse cultures on the Columbia Plateau to the south, including the Cayuse, Nez Percé, Flatheads and others, though some evidence suggests they may have also acquired horses from the east.

Other evidence of the early Tŝilhqot'in acquisition is how deeply imbedded the horse is in their lifestyle, culture, history, myths and legends. The considerable antiquity of the Tŝilhqot'in horse is also evident in the extensive horse vocabulary, documented from elders in 2011 by Yuneŝit'in researcher Linda Smith. For example, besides the modern-day use of qiyus, their other words for horse are *naŝlhiny* or *nazlhis*; elders also identified an ancient term, *nizex-lhin*. There are at least seventeen original words for the different body parts and other words for the gender, age and type of horse. As well, a whole host of unique sentences and phrases refer to horses.[13] It is worthwhile to compare this rich vocabulary surrounding the horse with the very recent and phonetically simple adoption of *mus* by the Tŝilhqot'in to represent the English word *moose*, a species that did not arrive in the ecosystem until the 1920s, three centuries after the horse.

Many generations passed as domesticated Spanish horses became firmly embedded in the Tŝilhqot'in lifeway, while those that escaped to the wilds would have undergone a long transition to adapt to an ecosystem with large predators and harsh winters. Perhaps such a 400-year-long passage in the Chilcotin enabled the original Spanish horses to evolve to become what some Tŝilhqot'in today consider the perfect mountain horse, the qiyus.

CHAPTER 29

LOST SPANISH CONQUISTADOR EXPEDITIONS TO THE BC INTERIOR AND CHILCOTIN

Indigenous evidence of one or more early Spanish expeditions to the region, including the Chilcotin, suggests intriguing proof of the antiquity of the Spanish horse in BC.

Tŝilhqot'in elder Norman Setah relayed to his son that the Tŝilhqot'in had massacred a group of Spanish conquistadores at Big Creek and that their "metal" had been buried with them.[1] Big Creek is a large tributary of the Chilko River south of Hanceville. Although the Spaniards would have come on their warhorses, there is no mention of their fate. Norman Setah was one of the key elders who provided testimony on his people's history for the Xeni Gwet'in Rights and Title case before the BC Supreme Court. His oral history, including descriptions of many wars, was considered by the court not to have been influenced by books and included lengthy testimony about the Tŝilhqot'in protecting their lands from intruders.

Some corroborating evidence supports Tŝilhqot'in elder Setah's oral account of a Spanish expedition to the Chilcotin. This comes from the story of a so-called "lost Spanish expedition" in BC's south Okanagan, which would have also been the logical pathway for a possible Spanish expedition to reach the Chilcotin on horseback.[2] According to a 1978 book by historian N. L. Barlee, a heavily armed Spanish expedition came to the Similkameen Valley in southern British Columbia around the mid-1700s. Apparently, there was an altercation between a First Nations man and a Spanish soldier that resulted in a battle. The Spanish took several prisoners and then travelled up the east side of Okanagan Lake, following an ancient trail, where they set up a camp and overwintered. In the spring, after some losses, the expedition started south and was massacred by First Nations in the Similkameen Valley. They were then buried with their weapons and armour.[3] The legend has never been fully corroborated.

A panel of pictographs located in a dry sagebrush canyon of the Similkameen Valley is believed by some to represent further evidence of this lost Spanish column. However, this interpretation is disputed by some First Nations. Local legends maintain that both conquistador groups were wiped out by the Indigenous people, so that the Spaniards never lived to tell their story.

CHAPTER 30

INDIGENOUS RELATIONSHIPS TO THE LATE PLEISTOCENE HORSE

The spread of domestic horses and their integration into Indigenous societies contributed to profound social and ecological transformations across western North America. However, the mechanisms and timing of this transition are poorly understood. Horses and other members of the genus Equus find their origins in North America. They sometimes formed an important component of human lifeways across the continent during the final Pleistocene, which is still encoded in some Indigenous oral traditions, including those of the Lakota.

— **W.P. Taylor et al.**, "Early Dispersal of Domestic Horses into the Great Plains and Northern Rockies"[1]

When I asked Dr. Gus Cothran whether there was any indication of Ice Age horses in our Chilcotin genetic study, he said there were no horse variants that could be attributed to pre-Columbian horses, the same as with more than 200 feral populations tested in the US.[2]

The absence of late Pleistocene ancestry in the Chilcotin wild horse was later corroborated by the aforementioned "Early Dispersal" study. Using genetic modelling of thirty-seven different horse populations, including the remains of late Pleistocene North American horses, as well as a representative panel of both modern and ancient domestic horses from around the globe, the study rejected Late Pleistocene North American horses as a possible source for both historic and modern North American horses. However, researchers pointed out that some First Nations, such as the Lakota, have relationships to the horse extending back in deep time beyond the acquisition of European domestic breeds:

> "One possible implication of this finding is that relationships of the kind developed by Lakota peoples could have already been in place by the Late Pleistocene. Such life management practices may even have extended to other members of the horse family at that time, possibly including *Equus lambei* and *Harringtonhippus*. Testing these implications requires further paleontological, archaeological, genetic, and ethnographic research."[3]

The Yukon Horse (*Equus lambei*) and the New World stilt-legged horse (*Harringtonhippus francisci*) were middle-to-late-Pleistocene horses that evolved in North America. While both species lived side by side, they did not interbreed. The stilt-legged horse went extinct about 17,000 years ago, while the Yukon Horse lived much longer, going extinct about 5,000 years ago. But *Equus* evolved in North America and crossed the Beringian land bridge into Eurasia to give rise to all of the members of the horse family today.[4] [5]

Recent research of the birthplace of the Yukon Horse within the traditional territory of the Vuntut Gwitchin First Nations in the northern Yukon suggests, as with the Lakota First Nation, that the Indigenous relationship to the Yukon Horse may go back a very long time. Recently, the 19.65-thousand-year-old jawbone of a Yukon Horse showed evidence of human-made cuts. The bone, from the Bluefish Caves, suggests a hunter-prey relationship between humans and the horse. This is one of the oldest known signs of human occupation in North America.[6] [7]

Regarding the Tŝilhqot'in and other interior First Nations, we won't really know if their relationship to the horse dates back to the late Pleistocene until much more research is done. There are some signs of this possibility. Tŝilhqot'in ranger Harry Setah claimed his people had horses since "time immemorial." Evidence of human occupation in Tŝilhqot'in territory dates back 5,500 years.[8] The Thompson (Nlaka'pamux) First Nation in the Fraser Canyon have a legend about the creation of the horse when the Earth was very young.[9] Fossil evidence shows that prehistoric horses lived in the interior during the last interglacial period.[10] Also, several Tŝilhqot'in knowledge keepers have found what they believe to be horse hoof-prints preserved in stone.[11]

Much remains still to be discovered. Much may also have to be left to mystery in the legendary time of *Sadanx*, the long-ago time of the *ʔesggidams*, or ancestors, when the land, animals and people were transforming pursuant to supernatural powers—the Tŝilhqot'in time of creation.[12]

CHAPTER 31

HORSE EVOLUTION

IN SEARCH OF OLD BONES

Henry Fairfield Osborn, a mammalian paleontologist at the American Museum of Natural History, called horses ". . . one of the gifts of America to the world." He was giving an address titled "Origin and History of the Horse" before the New York Farmers at the Metropolitan Club in New York City on December 19, 1905. His paleontological explorations during the late 1800s had yielded a surprising discovery . . . that horses evolved in North America.

Since Osborn's early finds, fossil remains of the horse, representing every phase of evolutionary modification over 57 million years, have been found on this continent. In fact, horse evolution is cited as a classic example of the evolutionary process where natural selection molds characteristics, both biological and behavioral, that promote survival.

— ***Unbroken Spirit**: The Wild Horse in the American Landscape*[1]

As we proceeded with our wild-horse genetic study, I decided to further explore the evolution of the horse and better understand why

Palaeontologist Aisling Farrell holds a mummified frozen horse limb recovered from a gold mine in the Klondike goldfields, in the Yukon. Ancient DNA recovered from horse fossils and frozen remains has made it possible for scientists to piece together the evolution of the horse. *Image courtesy of the Yukon government.*

some scientists claim that the North American horse is a returned native species.[2] [3] [4]

Fortunately, North America has been blessed with an array of fossilized horse-bone deposits, as well as ancient horse remains preserved in permafrost in gravel deposits in the Yukon and Alaska. The remains of frozen horses recovered with gold nuggets have become another type of "gold" to help palaeontologists piece together the amazing storyline of the evolution of the horse. This work has been significantly aided by recent radiocarbon dating, combined with new genetics tools that allow researchers to study ancient DNA preserved in old horse bones, frozen horse body parts preserved by permafrost, and plant macrofossils preserved in frozen sediments.

The evolution of the horse is actually one of the best documented of North American mammals. While mountains rose out of the Earth's crust and eroded again, the earth ruptured, spewing red-hot lava from deep in its bowels. Lava flowed over vast areas, reshaping the landscape. Glacial ages came and went. There were enough uninterrupted ice-free geological periods over vast regions of the continent, with periodic vegetated ecosystems, to allow for many ancient horse lineages to evolve over 55–57 million years.

The end result is the horse of today: one of the most beautiful and fleet-footed mammals ever created.

Being a boots-on-the-ground biologist, I wished to see in real life, not just in pictures or published palaeontological studies, some of the preserved ancient fossilized horse bones and sites where their bones were found.

My curiosity was also a natural outgrowth of having viewed in our fieldwork many old horse bones of the wild qiyus. Such bones, if they could talk, would tell a story of the life of the horse that they once supported: perhaps the bones of an old horse that died during a starvation winter in a meadow; or the bones of a horse taken down by a cougar, wolf or grizzly bear; the bones of a horse that broke its leg and was then killed by a predator; the crumbling burned bones that turned to dust in one's fingers because the horse could not outrun a raging wildfire.

In the spring of 2015, my wife, Lorna Visser, and I set off on a motor trip to southern Idaho and Oregon in search of fossil horse bones preserved in US government interpretive centres or other sites. We called it our Old Horse Bones Tour.

We first visited the Hagerman Fossil Beds National Monument Visitors Center and fossil excavation site in Hagerman, Idaho. Then we went to the Wilson Butte Cave, on the Snake River Plains near Jerome, Idaho. Finally, we visited the Thomas Condon Paleontological Center in John Day, Oregon. It was truly a fascinating journey into deep time on the history of old horse bones and evolution.

Hagerman is a quaint farm town just off US Highway 30 on the arid Snake River Plains in southern Idaho. It was named after Stanley Hagerman, who helped establish the first post office. As we drove down the main street looking for the visitor centre that featured the Hagerman Horse, we passed old and new farm pickup trucks parked at a café, where farmers were gathered for morning coffee, most likely discussing the latest market values of cattle and grain, the economic

The Hagerman Horse lived on the Snake River Plains some 3.2 million years ago and is the earliest species of *Equus* that the modern horse is related to. *Image courtesy of Lorna Visser.*

mainstay of the vast industrial-agricultural development of the Snake River Plains. When I went into a liquor store to buy a bottle of wine, I was asked for my identification, even though I was over seventy. I told the clerk I was old enough to be her grandfather.

We found the friendly visitor centre in a small historic house on Main Street. We were fascinated by the complete life-sized artificial skeleton of the Hagerman Horse, modelled from fossilized bones. I was surprised to see how much smaller it was than today's average horse.

The zebra-like Hagerman Horse was around much earlier in the planet's history than more recent species such as the Yukon Horse, living in the Pliocene about 3.2 million years ago. It is considered the earliest species of the *Equus* genus that today includes all modern horses, zebras and donkeys. It went extinct about two million years ago, at the start of the Pleistocene glacial period, one stage in the continuing evolution of the horse in North America.

Palaeontologists first excavated five nearly complete horse skeletons at the fossil site on the banks of the Snake River. The horses were believed to have drowned while trying to cross a swollen river, their bodies swept away, then lodged in a river bend and later buried by sediment. Ash from subsequent volcanic eruptions layered over the sediments, eventually forming into rock and preserving these bones.[5]

We continued our explorations of old horse bones by driving east to Jerome and Wilson Butte Cave, a lava dome far out in sagebrush country on the Snake River Plains. We wanted to see for ourselves the cave where archaeologists had discovered early human remains along with bones of an extinct horse and a camel species.

The size of a small house, the dome had been formed during a volcanic eruption some two to three million years ago, when a gas bubble swelled up from hot lava as it cooled. Before being displaced by white settlers, the Snake River plains had been the homeland of the Shoshone-Bannocks and Shoshone-Paiutes and their domestic and wild horses. Now it was all cows. As we drove on the dirt road from Jerome, we passed the remains of a WW II Japanese internment camp. The occasional cow grazed far off in the sagebrush.

Thinking we might be lost, we flagged down a rancher in a large black Ford F-350 truck. Seeing our low-to-the-ground hybrid vehicle bearing foreign licence plates, he asked where we were from. When we told him British Columbia, he said he had recently sold his large dairy farm on the coast of Washington and had moved here to start a much larger operation: a large ranch and cattle feedlot with 4,500 cows.

Thanks to his directions, we eventually spotted the black lava dome far out in the middle of the flatlands. We parked and hiked along a rustic trail, watching carefully for early-emerging rattlers. It was fascinating to enter the cool and dank-smelling world of the large cave, shaped somewhat like an amphitheatre. We saw several small digs in the dirt floor where archaeologists had found artefacts such as tools from humans who may have lived on the plains 10,000 years ago, as well as bones from a late Pleistocene horse and camel that dated back 15,000 years. As we explored the inside of the cave, it was eerie to think that we were in the home of an ancient people who may have dined on horses and camels.[6 7]

Outside again in the hot sun, we paused to gaze over the plains' sagebrush community that had been around for 10,000 years; this landscape had once supported a variety of Ice Age mammals whose remains were found in the cave. I imagined the ages of the different horse species that ranged across these plains. Over three million years ago, the Hagerman Horse galloped free, followed by yet a different Ice Age horse species that disappeared 7,000 to 8,000 years ago and whose remains had been deposited in the lava cave. Kelly Murphey, a friendly local anthropologist, told us that Spanish horses brought in by the Southern Shoshone around 1680 had once flourished on the plains before white settlement and agriculture completely took over.[8]

Here, standing in a 10,000-year-old sagebrush ecosystem near Wilson Butte Cave, I could make sense of the theory that the wild horse of today is a native species returned to its evolutionary birthplace.

Next on the list of our Old Horse Bones Tour was a visit to the Thomas Condon Paleontological Center in John Day, Oregon. Here we spent half a day absorbing the different ages and species of the evolutionary tree of the horse displayed on a wall-sized panel. There were some blind alleys for unique horse species that went extinct. The panel showed how the horse evolved from the Dawn Horse, a dog-sized three-toed (front) and four-toed (hind) browser, to the larger one-toed grazers that led to all living members of today's horse family, *Equus*. Numerous remains of the diminutive 55-million-year-old Dawn Horse have been found in Utah and Wyoming, as well as in Europe, but so far none in Canada.

It was all too complex to retain and digest in one day. We were impressed by the dedication of the palaeontologists who had studied and collated the different evolutionary horse pathways.

After we returned home, I wondered if any fossil horse bones had been discovered in the BC grasslands in our own backyard, including the Chilcotin. Much to my surprise, I found that small Ice Age horses once roamed the BC interior, along with bear-sized ground sloths. Two sites with prehistoric fossilized horse bones had been discovered not too distant from the Eagle Lake Henry ?Elegesi Qiyus (Cayuse) Wild Horse Preserve.

One site is only 350 kilometres southeast of the preserve, as the crow flies, at Westwold, a small, picturesque farming community nestled among low mountains between Kamloops and Vernon. From about 1811 to 1847, the area was used as a camping and grazing area for the 200 packhorses of the Hudson's Bay Company fur brigades. The HBC called the stopover camp near Westwold "Grand Prairie." It was here that the remnants of a small now-extinct prehistoric horse (*Equus cf. E. conversidens*), called the Mexican Horse, along with fossils of bison and other animals, were excavated from a layer of glacial silt and sand. These ancient wild horses lived in the ecosystem during what was known as the last interglacial period, or Sangamonian, which reached its maximum warmth some 130,000 years ago.[9]

Another 120 kilometres southeast of Westwold, near Lumby, BC, fossil bones revealed the existence of a more recent type of small horse. The bones were found with other now-extinct mammal species that appeared to be from 19,000 to 43,800 years ago.[10] [11]

This fascinating evidence of fossil horse bones in the BC interior, combined with our old bone tour in Idaho and Oregon, convinced me, a somewhat sceptical scientist, that the Chilcotin wild horse of today is truly an *Equus* species that was returned to its evolutionary birthplace. According to Dr. Ross MacPhee of the American Museum of Natural History: "Although mammoths are gone forever, horses are not. The horse that lived in the Yukon 5,000 years ago is directly related to the horse species we have today, *Equus caballus*. Biologically, this makes the horse a native North American mammal, and it should be treated as such."[12]

The return of the horse to its evolutionary birthplace in North America is a reminder that despite an apparent intergenerational gap of roughly 5,000 years of the horse in North America after their Ice

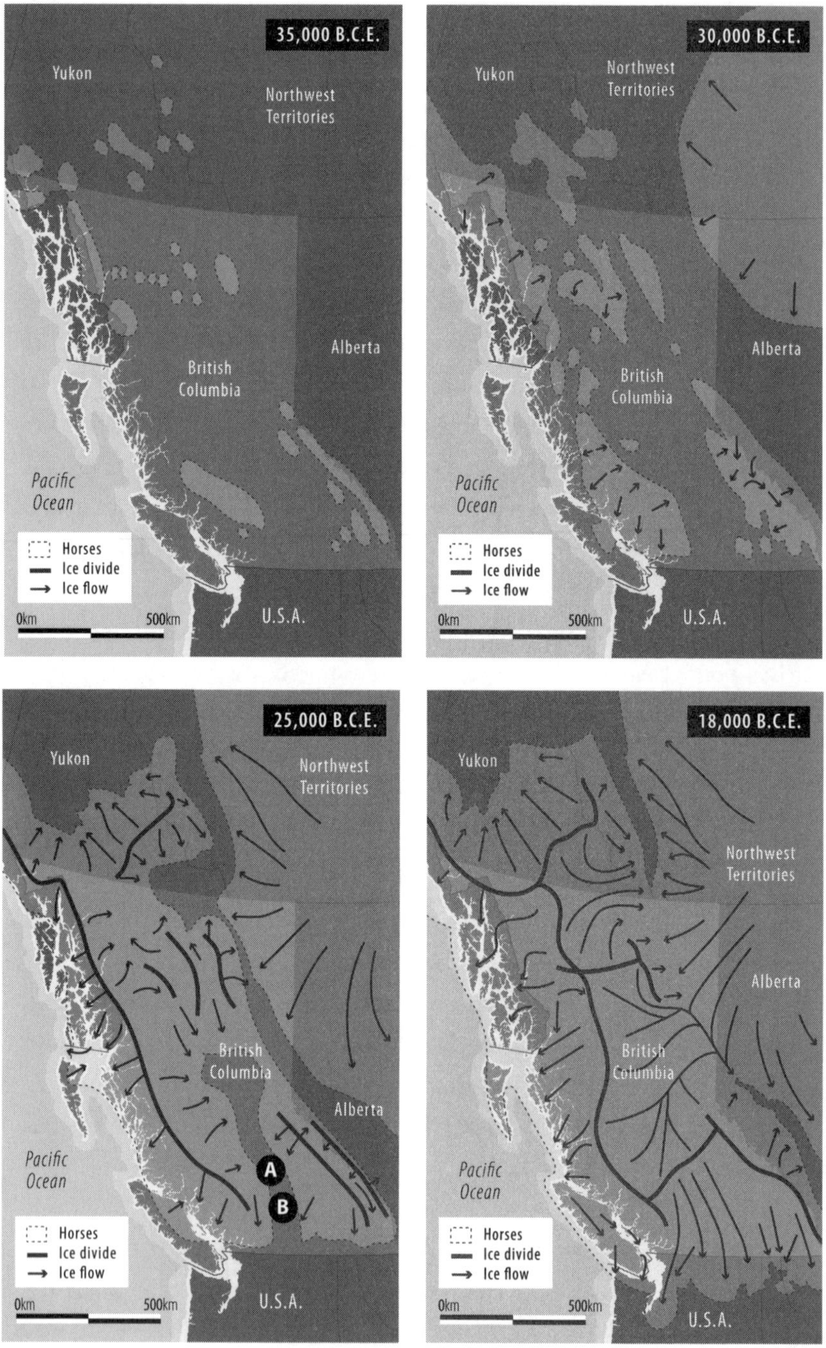
35,000 B.C.E.
Yukon
Northwest Territories
British Columbia
Alberta
Pacific Ocean
U.S.A.
Horses
Ice divide
Ice flow
0km
500km
30,000 B.C.E.
Yukon
Northwest Territories
British Columbia
Alberta
Pacific Ocean
U.S.A.
Horses
Ice divide
Ice flow
0km
500km
25,000 B.C.E.
Yukon
Northwest Territories
British Columbia
Alberta
Pacific Ocean
U.S.A.
A
B
Horses
Ice divide
Ice flow
0km
500km
18,000 B.C.E.
Yukon
Northwest Territories
British Columbia
Alberta
Pacific Ocean
U.S.A.
Horses
Ice divide
Ice flow
0km
500km

OPPOSITE: These are schematic maps of ice cover in British Columbia during the growth phase of the last (Cordilleran) glaciation. The map shows locations "A" and "B" of fossil bone remains from two different Ice Age horses that lived in the interior of BC during the last interglacial period (Sangamonian), which lasted until the advance of the Cordilleran Ice Sheet about 35,000 years ago. "A" shows the location at Westwold, BC, where the fossil bone of a small, now extinct Ice Age horse (*Equus conversidens*), along with the remains of bison and other animals, were uncovered from under a layer of glacial silt and sand. "B" is the location of a fossil bone from a smaller horse type recovered from gravel near Lumby, BC, that appeared between 43,800 to 19,000 years ago. *Map adapted from Clague and Ward, 2011, Fig. 44.4.*[13]

Age extinction, returning the species to their ancestral landscapes and ecological roles was made possible by the introduction of the Spanish horse and other early horse breeds, such as the Canadian Horse. It is nice to think, thanks partly to the Xeni Gwet'in creating a large wild-horse preserve, that the Chilcotin wild horses can still run free with the ghosts of their extinct Ice Age ancestors.

CHAPTER 32

BERINGIA

EXPERIENCING THE BIRTHPLACE OF THE YUKON HORSE

Early in my career as a wildlife biologist, I had no idea that we still had wild horses left in Canada or that the northern Yukon was one of the ancestral birthplaces of the evolution of the modern horse species. I found out differently in 1972 when I went to work in the northern Yukon with a team of biologists and First Nations on a barren-ground caribou study.

Our base was the tiny Vuntut Gwitchin outpost of Old Crow, north of the Arctic Circle. Our assignment was to document the migration patterns of the 200,000-strong Porcupine barren-ground caribou herd. It is one of the largest migratory caribou herds in North America and central to the Vuntut Gwitchin lifeway. The research was needed to determine the potential impacts on caribou of the proposed Arctic gas pipeline planned across the pristine north slopes of the Yukon. The pipeline was intended to convey natural gas from Alaska through Canada to US markets.

It turned out that two of the biologists on our study team had previously studied wild horses and knew about the Pleistocene horses that formerly roamed the northern Yukon during the last Ice Age. I learned that the Old Crow Flats and other areas of northern Yukon, Alaska and Siberia were once part of a vast and ancient Pleistocene landscape called Beringia. During the last Ice Age, when glaciers covered much of the northern half of North America, Beringia was ice-free. The region

It is hard to imagine that this pristine northern Yukon landscape, now protected as the Vuntut National Park, was ice-free during the last Ice Age and hosted a rich Pleistocene ecosystem. This land was the birthplace of the Yukon Horse, a direct ancestor of today's modern horse. *Image courtesy of Wayne McCrory.*

had a climate too dry and devoid of the atmospheric moisture needed to form ice sheets.

Instead, the landscape was an arid steppe grassland and a refugium for many Ice Age species that formed a vibrant predator-prey ecosystem. Besides several species of horse, there were woolly mammoths, caribou, steppe bison, giant short-faced bears, wolves and others. Many of these went extinct at the end of the last Ice Age. As noted previously, the Yukon Horse lived until about 5,000 years ago. Some wildlife species, such as the barren-ground caribou, musk ox and gray wolf, somehow survived the Pleistocene extinctions.

The hamlet of Old Crow, on the banks of the Porcupine River, was an assemblage of small log cabins, including a store and school connected by dirt roads. Our survey crew lived in an old Anglican church called "The Palace." In the evenings, we would sometimes gather to socialize in a tepee belonging to James Dean Feist and his wife, Carol, a talented cellist. Feist had a master's degree on the behaviour of wild horses in the Pryor Mountains Wild Horse Refuge in Montana–Wyoming. Another biologist, part-Mohawk Robert Ruttan, a close friend and mentor of mine, had served as a tail-gunner in a Lancaster bomber in WWII; Robert did wildlife surveys in Saskatchewan in a small Gypsy Tiger Moth. He had also studied wild horses and was involved at the time in trying to help an old Alberta mustanger, Slim Davis, save the Alberta foothills' last wild horses from being rounded up for slaughter. He and Dean were working with Old Slim on a film script to try to help protect Alberta's wild horses.

To add to my new knowledge about the Ice Age, Charlie Peter Charlie, the Vuntut Gwitchin guide and caribou spotter, would often point out to me the eroding sedimentary cliffs along the Porcupine River, which were exposing numerous old bones of extinct Ice Age mammals. He had helped palaeontologists collect some. Thawing and erosion of the permafrost were constantly exposing the ancient bones.

Biologist's Journal. September 12, 1972
Old Crow Flats, Northern Yukon

From the window of our droning Cessna 185 floatplane, I saw the vastness of the Old Crow Flats, sprawling hundreds of kilometres in every direction to merge seamlessly with the surrounding rolling tundra hills and mountain ranges. Willows and other plants that carpeted the flats and hillsides showed various shades of rose and gold. The mountaintops were dusted with the first snow, a reminder that using the floatplane for surveys would soon end, as the lakes and rivers would be icing over.

As I gazed over the vast subarctic landscape—so beautiful that it felt almost surreal at times—I imagined herds of now-extinct ancient horses coexisting alongside the ancestors of the caribou. It was hard to imagine why the well-adapted horses and many other Ice Age mammals, like the Scimitar cat and cave bear, had gone extinct but the caribou, musk ox and gray wolf still lived on here.

We had been monitoring and mapping the fall migration of small herds of barren-ground caribou across the Old Crow Flats. The herds were making their way along ancient migration trails deeply rutted into the muskeg and tundra, trails they had followed for thousands of years to their wintering grounds in the taiga forests to the south. Their quick pace across the flats was a reminder of their urgent need to get to their wintering grounds before freeze-up. The bulls' manes were now white; they were more majestic than their tattered appearance in the spring after their antlers had dropped.

"Flats" does not do justice to this huge 6,000-square-kilometre northern Yukon wetland basin complex, with its 2,000 small lakes, ponds, and marshes, formerly part of Beringia. The flats are so vast and boggy that the caribou we were tracking often took more than a week or two of steady plodding to migrate from one side to the other before swimming the Porcupine or Yukon rivers on their way south.

Charlie Peter Charlie mentioned that in about a week his people would start taking their fall quota of winter meat when the herds swam the Porcupine River near Old Crow. The small herd we had been following ducked into a thicket of dense willows at the low-level approach sound of our plane, as we attempted to get close enough to count the number of cows, bulls and calves.

As Charlie had spotted another small caribou herd, I dropped my musings about the evolution of northern Yukon's Ice Age horses. The plane motor had started to sputter, miss, stall, then start again. Hans Lammers, one of the most competent young pilots in the Yukon, started to lift the plane from our low pass over the caribou herd. He announced in a calm voice that we should try to head for Old Crow while there was still enough daylight. The motor had never acted up before. As we climbed to gain enough altitude to be able to glide safely to one of the lakes if the motor conked out altogether, the knot in my stomach tightened.

"I dunno," said Hans, "it's not sounding so good . . . I really don't think we should leave the flats and try to make it back to Old Crow . . . Charlie, where is that rat research camp of Ruttan's?"

"Rat" was the local term for muskrat, a small aquatic member of the weasel family, its soft, thick fur an important source of trapping income for the Vuntut Gwitchin. Robert Ruttan and the Vuntut Gwitchin were running the muskrat research camp on the flats as part of the pipeline study.

While Charlie studied the landscape he knew intimately, I shuffled through the maps I kept on my lap to mark our daily caribou migration data, then turned around to consult. After he pondered a while, he pointed to one of hundreds of lakes and said we should go in a southerly direction. Soon, with relief, we spotted a number of small white specks at the edge of a lake: the wall tents at Ruttan's camp.

After we landed safely and sputtered to shore, we were greeted with friendly but quizzical looks from Robert Ruttan, James Dean Feist and Mary Kassie, the cook. When we explained our situation, they said they could give us some extra sleeping bags with caribou hides for mattresses, and we could sleep in the spare tent. By the time we set up our beds, Hans had fixed the partially plugged fuel filter. However, it was now too near dark to fly to Old Crow. Supper at rat camp was not "muskrat stew," as Robert Ruttan had threatened, but a delicious moose stew with bannock.

Darkness comes early in September in the land north of the Arctic Circle. Soon everyone had settled into one of the tents for a pleasant evening of socializing, getting caught up on our research projects and the inevitable storytelling. We sat in a circle on dried caribou hides, warmed by the wood stove, drinking Mary's Labrador tea sweetened with white sugar. The hissing Coleman lantern cast a soft glow over everyone's faces. Both Charlie and Mary brought up their concerns about how the giant Arctic gas pipeline might affect their community and all of the wildlife they depended on for survival. They felt the whole northern Yukon should be protected, not developed.

Eventually, the conversation drifted to the ancient Ice Age history of the landscape, including woolly mammoths and ancient horse species. Ruttan and Feist compared notes about one of their favourite conversation pieces: wild horses. Feist maintained that the wild horse, as we know it today in the United States and Canada, evolved in North America in places like the northern Yukon and should be protected.

Charlie then mesmerized us with one of his favourite legends. He delved into the Vuntut Gwitchin oral library about the legend of the Whitestone mammoth. A long time ago, a monster broke out of a lakebed on the Old Crow Flats, trudged up the Porcupine River and died. "Its bones are still there scattered all around on the riverbank," he said. "It was one of those ancient mammoths that used to live here that the palaeontologists who come here told us about. You can also see their tusks melting out of the riverbanks when it thaws in the summer."

In 1967, Gwitchin resident Joe Kaye told the mammoth story to federal government palaeontologist Richard Harington of the Canadian Nature Museum. Harington and

Vuntut Gwitchin elder and knowledge keeper Charlie Peter Charlie told our research group the legend of the Whitestone mammoth. A federal government palaeontologist was later guided to the area and found the partial remains of a woolly mammoth that died about 30,000 years ago. *Image courtesy of Wayne McCrory.*

Peter Lord then boated up the Porcupine River and found the partial remains of an adult female woolly mammoth along the riverbanks near Whitestone Village. A radiocarbon date indicated that the mammoth died about 30,000 years ago. It was the most complete mammoth fossil skeleton ever found near Old Crow.[1] [2]

Over 20,000 fossils and mummified bodies of Ice Age mammals have been collected from the Old Crow area, representing over sixty mammal species. Horse fossils represent the most bones found. Due to environmental, First Nations and other concerns, no pipeline was ever built. Some of the former birthplace of the Yukon Horse is now protected by large Vuntut National Park.

After I left, James Dean Feist was killed in a plane crash in the mountains north of Old Crow, taking all of his wild-horse expertise with him. After my Yukon experience, I carried the memories of his passionate stories of Wyoming's wild horses and Ice Age horses with me for a long time.

CHAPTER 33

CANADA'S LAST WILD HORSES

Neither paleontology nor molecular genetics lends any support whatsoever to the idea that horses evolved into their modern form anywhere but in North America. Nonetheless, most state and federal land agencies continue to insist that horses, with 50 million years of evolutionary history here, are still "non-native."

— **Dan Flores**, *American Serengeti* [1]

When I first started studying wild horses, I often wondered how many were still left in Canada. I discovered that most were gone, and they were so undervalued that the Canadian government had never even bothered to count those still left on public lands, unlike the US. My own rough estimate is about 5,000. That's not very many, considering the tens of thousands that used to run wild in our vast, once pristine grassland ecosystems. In 2022, the US Bureau of Land Management had over 64,000 feral horses in their herd management areas in four western states.

My estimate for Canada includes 2,800 horses in BC's West Chilcotin, 250 in BC's Highland Valley, 1,400 in the Alberta foothills, 35 in Saskatchewan's Bronson Forest, and 500 on Sable Island off Nova Scotia's shore. This estimate does not include small pockets of

Wild horses are a celebration of evolution and the spirit in all living things. They are the embodiment of that wild spirit we can discover within ourselves, that which loves wide, open spaces where we can wander with no bounds and race free as the wind towards an unknown destination. *Image courtesy of Duane Starr Photography.*

free-roaming horses still hiding out in BC sagebrush hills and various herds kept by First Nations on reserves. Also, this is by no means a complete inventory, as there appear to be small numbers of free-roaming horses in Manitoba and Ontario. In the Yukon, about a hundred free-roaming horses of unknown origin frequent the Alaska Highway.

Not many of the wild horses on public lands in Canada today are protected. By my estimate, 600 West Chilcotin horses are protected by Indigenous governance in the Eagle Lake Henry ?Elegesi Qiyus (Cayuse) Wild Horse Preserve (including a portion on Aboriginal Title lands), 35 in the Saskatchewan Bronson Forest under provincial law, and about 500 in the Sable Island National Park Reserve.

The following is a horse-protection inventory.

This Chilcotin wild horse foal is part of western Canada's largest remaining wild horse population. It starts a new life in a vast wilderness wild horse stronghold partly protected as a wild-horse preserve declared by the Tŝilhqot'in Horse Nation. *Image courtesy of Wayne McCrory.*

British Columbia

West Chilcotin
Partly protected

Detailed information about the West Chilcotin wild horses is found throughout this book. Of the 2,800, an estimated 2,200 survive outside the Eagle Lake Henry ?Elegesi Qiyus (Cayuse) Wild Horse Preserve in a heavily logged and fragmented landscape. Although negotiations between the Tŝilhqot'in and the province on governance and land-use practices are ongoing, the horses on public lands outside of the preserve are still mainly subject to outdated provincial laws and thus have an uncertain future. The province also has yet to recognize the wild-horse preserve created by the Xeni Gwet'in.

Highland Valley
Not protected

About 250 animals roam the grassy reclaimed areas of the Highland Valley open-pit copper mine and surrounding area in southern BC. Since 2014, Teck Resources (the mining company) has been working on a feral horse-management plan with a steering committee made up of the six groups of the Nlaka'pamux First Nation, the government range manager, grazing licence holders and the BC SPCA. Annual counts have been done and a genetic study may occur.[2] Some residents are calling for provincial protection of the horses.

Saskatchewan

Bronson Forest
Protected under provincial law, law not enforced

This small population of free-roaming horses is the only one in Canada protected by provincial legislation. Located in the Bronson Forest in west-central Saskatchewan, numbers have dropped from 125 to 35, apparently due to random killings and other causes because the protection law is simply not enforced.

The law was passed in 2009 due to public pressure. The *Act to Protect the Wild Ponies of the Bronson Forest* designated the ponies as a heritage breed and made it illegal to molest, interfere with, hurt, capture or kill them. Violation meant a fine of up to $1,000 and/or up to two months in prison. The act does not protect habitat.

Alberta

Rocky Mountain Foothills
Not protected

The Rocky Mountain foothills in Alberta is an ecosystem I know well, having worked there on wildlife studies for several government agencies. In 2015, my consulting firm was hired by Zoocheck Canada to do an independent assessment of the historic and current management of the foothills wild horse population.[3]

Up until 1994, Alberta had two large wild horse populations: about 1,500 in the Rocky Mountain foothills and about 1,200 on the Canadian Forces Base Suffield, in southern Alberta. The Alberta population was cut by nearly one-half in 1994 when the Canadian military ordered the removal of all of the Suffield horses.

The Alberta foothills wild-horse ecosystem is a fescue-grassland complex, a remnant of a fifty-million-year-old ecosystem on the prairies. Long ago, it was traditional habitat for grazing herds of wild ungulates, including bison, horses and wild camels.[4] Horses evolved here through the ages.

Although ranchers and government range managers have long claimed the foothills horse originated from domestic escapees brought in by settlers, as I have already noted, Spanish horses were brought in by Plains Horse Nations in the early 1600s. This was confirmed by Dr. Gus Cothran in a 2021 genetic study of the Sundre Equine Zone. He found that the Alberta horses show mixed origins, with a clear association with Spanish-type horses.[5] The population is also part of a complex predator-prey ecosystem with all top carnivores, as in the West Chilcotin.

In the early colonial days, most of the grass in the foothills fescue ecosystem was allocated to private range tenures for seasonal cattle-grazing by the settler-ranchers. No allocations were ever made for the wild horses. As with the West Chilcotin, the Alberta foothills

Alberta's last free-roaming horse population has been squeezed into the foothills between the high, snow-capped Rocky Mountains in the west and a barrier of thousands of kilometres of barbed-wire fences on private agricultural land in the foothills, prairies and parklands to the east. Research has shown that cougars, wolves and severe starvation winters play a role in wild-horse mortality levels and likely help control the population. Foothill grizzly bears and black bears also share the range. Although some 33,000 cattle free-range in the foothills, the estimated 1,500 wild horses are most often blamed for range damage, without sufficient evidence. Government culls remain mired in controversy and questionable justification. *Image courtesy of Claudia Notzke.*

horses are survivors of a century-long range war involving bounty hunts, roundups (including use of aircraft) and eradication programs that continue today.

Since the Sundre Equine Zone has the highest number of wild horses, it is here that the beef industry and others have focused their claims of wild-horse overpopulation and overgrazing. In 2013, over

Alberta foothills wildies nurse their foals. *Image courtesy of Wayne McCrory.*

200 wild horses were removed. It is likely that many of the horses went to slaughter. The culls were sanctioned by the government-appointed Feral Horse Advisory Committee, which, to their credit, did strive to put some horses up for adoption.[6]

Many opposed the culls, and some protesters were arrested. Since then, there have been no further removals. Many now want the Foothills Horse recognized as a distinct breed and protected by legislation similar to Saskatchewan's 2009 *Bronson Forest Act*.

In many ways, the Sundre Equine Zone has become the focus of a polarized battleground and test case for protection, pitting, on the one side, those who want the wild horses protected, including a united group of scientists, horse-lovers, photographers, Zoocheck Canada and "Save the Horse" groups such as HAWS (Help Alberta Wildies Society), against the entrenched cartel of the influential livestock industry and the Alberta government's range-management division.

When I began my independent study of foothills feral horse management in 2015, I was half expecting to find significant evidence of too many horses and overgrazing in the Sundre Equine Zone. I started by making numerous requests to a senior government range official to provide me with the locations of sites where their range-condition surveys showed damage by horses so I could go look myself. Eventually, the official admitted in writing that she had no evidence of range degradation. I admired her honesty.

I then made numerous written requests to the Rocky Mountain Forest Grazers Association for their 2015 Rangeland Health Reports. Their claims of feral-horse damage apparently contributed to the 2013–2014 government culls. My requests went unanswered. The range-health surveys are done by the Grazers Association, not at arm's length by the Alberta government. I finally phoned the Grazers Association office and made a verbal request. There was about a one-minute-long response of heavy breathing and then the phone went click.

I then decided to go out and look at the range myself, expecting to find the damage that was being claimed. After covering many kilometres of wild-horse country, mostly in the Sundre Equine Zone, I found limited evidence of damage that could be attributed directly to horses, though some damage likely exists in riparian zones. For example, range studies in Idaho and Nevada show that feral horses were causing some damage to stream-bank and riparian areas.[7] [8] In 1980, a range study done in the Sundre Equine Zone showed that combined grazing by free-roaming horses and cattle caused localized damage along stream courses and around both natural and artificial salt-licks.[9]

After my 2015 study, it would take another seven years for my client to finally obtain the 2015 Rangeland Health Reports for the three equine zones, including Sundre. An independent review by agrologist Brian de Kock helped us understand why the range health reports were withheld from scrutiny for so long. There was only scant evidence of horse damage. Out of 485 sites surveyed, only 17 had evidence of damage that could be exclusively attributed to horses. Four times as many sites were damaged by cattle. Brian de Kock concluded: "Wild horses are not the cause of the vast majority of the problems; they have simply adapted to the changes in the landscape being driven by recreation and industrial activities on the Eastern Slopes. A continued

While some of the Alberta foothills' wild-horse country has some protection, most of it is highly developed, with extensive road networks related to clear-cut logging, oil and gas development, cattle-grazing, outdoor recreation and off-road vehicle access. *Image courtesy of Duane Starr Photography.*

reduction in wild horse numbers will do little if anything to reverse these changes."[10]

My final report concluded that many of the government's claims against the wild horses were not supported by much evidence and were sometimes contradicted by mainstream scholastic and academic studies published in peer-reviewed scientific journals.[11]

Overall, when you have an estimated 1,314 foothills wild horses (2021 surveys)[12] and some 250,000 cattle (2015) on seasonal foothills grazing allotments,[13] it is hard to imagine that the wild horses are causing significant enough damage to warrant culls.

Equally disturbing to me is that the Indigenous Horse Nations in Alberta have been marginalized from management of the Foothills Horse despite their deep wealth of oral knowledge related to horse history and husbandry. After all, the new evidence shows it was they who first introduced the horse to the region.[14]

This photo is called "Three Chiefs" and it is from the Piegan Blackfeet, a prairie grassland Horse Nation from Montana and Alberta. The Plains Horse Nations were responsible for the spread of European horses to the northern Rockies and prairies in the early 1600s, including the foothills where Alberta's last wild horses still survive today. In 1994, the last 1,200 prairie horses on public lands in Canada were ordered to be removed by the military from Canadian Forces Base Suffield, in Alberta, under questionable circumstances. *Image courtesy of Wikipedia Commons.*

Alberta is far behind most other regions in North America in recognizing the value of protecting their last wild horse population, though some politicians, old cowboys, scientists [15] [16], authors, famous Alberta musicians and wild-horse groups are making valiant attempts. Maureen Enns's recent book *Wild Horses, Wild Wolves* builds a strong case for protection of a wild-horse conservation area in part of Alberta's Ghost River region.[17] In reality, all of the foothills horses should be protected.

The Lost Suffield Horses
"Caught in the spin." Gone.

The Canadian Forces Base (CFB) Suffield, in southern Alberta, is the largest expanse of undeveloped mixed-grass prairie left in Canada.

For decades, CFB Suffield grasslands had been the home to up to 1,200 free-roaming horses. Although it was always assumed that the horses originated from local ranches, it was never determined if their history goes back to Niitsítapi (Blackfoot) historic occupation of the area; Blackfoot had horses by the early to mid-1600s.

On January 15, 1994, Major Dan Davies made the executive order that all remaining 1,160 horses had to go, instead of a previously planned partial removal. He tried to blame animal-rights groups for his decision, though citizens' groups and scientists had already agreed to some reduction of horse numbers.[18] In 1993, a range study had shown that excessive horse use had caused considerable damage to some of the grasslands, riparian areas and waterholes. However, the majority of the range, the study said, was still in healthy condition.[19]

Some Suffield horses went for adoption, while some apparently went to the slaughterhouse. Their permanent removal represents about twenty per cent of the total number of wild horses remaining in Canada. As a result, there are no wild horses left on Canada's mixed-grass prairies, where historically there were tens of thousands.

Before she died of cancer, zoologist Dawn Dickinson, an authority on prairie grasslands who had participated on one of the Suffield horse-management committees, wrote a book exposing all of the back-room politics that led up to Major Davies's decision. The horses were "caught in the spin," she claimed.[20]

Ironically, after all the horses were gone, in 1997 and 1998 the military allowed the transplant of 200 elk onto Suffield to replace the role that horse-grazing had played in reducing the threat of prairie wildfires. With no native predators, such as the long-gone mountain lion and prairie wolf, to help keep them under control, by 2014 the elk multiplied to an estimated 8,000 animals—far greater numbers than the horses. This created new overgrazing issues and problems with adjacent ranchers.[21]

As to the fate of the Suffield horses, not all of them disappeared. The Suffield Mustang Association was formed by a number of citizens who had adopted some of the culled horses. They are promoting the Suffield Horse as a new domestic horse breed.

The story of the Suffield horse is a sad chapter in Canadian wild horse history that never should have happened. It serves as a wake-up call for Canadians who care about protecting our last wild horses in BC and Alberta. According to Dawn Dickinson: "No one in the Canadian prairies will have the opportunity of ever again seeing wild horses coming through the sage to drink at the river with a Cree name, or of watching a wild band racing across the sunlit grasslands, their manes and tails streaming in the wind of their passage. That opportunity was extinguished by National Defence. A quality of wildness in these grasslands has been lost, and with what dishonesty, and for what small purpose?"[22]

Sable Island, Nova Scotia

Protected

Tiny Sable Island rises unexpectedly out of the Atlantic Ocean some 160 kilometres off the east coast of Nova Scotia. The island is a narrow, crescent-shaped sandbar 42 kilometres long. The Sable Island horse originated mainly from horses confiscated from French settlers in Nova Scotia in the late 1700s and some put out on the island. Genetic research has shown they are light draft and multipurpose breeds commonly found in eastern Canada. Due to their long isolation, for many centuries, they are now considered unique. However, they have also been shown to be more inbred than their domestic counterparts.

Sable Island is not where you might expect to find 500 free-roaming horses, let alone ones that have survived for centuries. There are no trees; in winter, the horses have to survive the battering of Atlantic storms, with winds so powerful they move sand dunes and bury the coarse beach grass the horses depend on. Lacking predators, starvation in severe winters is a frequent cause of death.

A sand-dune island in the Atlantic, far off the coast of Nova Scotia, is an unusual habitat for Canada's most protected wild horses. Today, they are the most studied horses in Canada and are recognized by Parks Canada as "naturalized wildlife" in Sable Island National Park Reserve. *Image © Patrice Halley,* Canadian Geographic.

The behaviour, ecology, population dynamics, genetics, origin and other Sable Island horse life history variables have been researched *more* than any other free-roaming horse population in North America. Since 2007 they have been intensively studied and monitored by Dr. Phil McLoughlin, his students and colleagues. Over twelve years, they have been able to keep track of the life histories and movements of about 900 horses.[23]

The horses were first protected in 1961 under the *Canada Shipping Act* as a result of a public campaign to save them from the threat of roundups and removals. Further federal protection came in 2013, when Sable Island was officially designated a National Park Reserve.[24] The horses are recognized by Parks Canada as naturalized

Image © Patrice Halley, Canadian Geographic.

wildlife to be managed as equal to other species living on the island and not as an invasive or second-class species.[25] [26] As well, the population is considered a breed of significant conservation interest due to its distinct genetic heritage.[27] [28]

There is, however, still some debate among ecologists as to the negative and positive impacts of the Sable Island equids on the island biota and whether they should continue to be protected or removed. Nonetheless, federal government protection of the Sable horses as wildlife—in a region where no wild horses previously existed—sets a precedent for appropriate federal and provincial legislation to protect Canada's other last wild horses. It's long overdue.

Artist, author and educator Chelsea Robinson writes, "I see Canada's last wild horses as gatekeepers to this kinship with the wild things many of us crave—a reminder that we all belong to nature, an ancient legacy deeply embedded in all Indigenous horse cultures. We think it is the 'human' who tamed the horse, but perhaps it is the untamed spirit of the wild horse which is our greatest teacher and window on how to re-wild our own true spirit."

CHAPTER 34

RECALIBRATING CANADA'S LAST WILD HORSES

The non-native, feral, and exotic designations given by agencies are not merely reflections of their failure to understand modern science, but also a reflection of their desire to preserve old ways of thinking to keep alive the conflict between a species (wild horses) with no economic value anymore (by law) and the economic value of commercial livestock. Native status for wild horses would place these animals, under law, within a new category for management considerations. As a form of wildlife, embedded with wildness, ancient behavioral patterns, and the morphology and biology of a sensitive prey species, they may finally be released from the "livestock-gone-loose" appellation.

— **Kirkpatrick and Fazio**, "Wild Horses as Native North American Wildlife"[1]

As I have documented, some positive things have already happened recently to protect wild horses in Canada. Sable Island horses are federally protected, Saskatchewan's Bronson horses are partially protected by a provincial law, and the Tŝilhqot'ins' wild-horse preserve offers significant First Nations protection for a portion of the West Chilcotin wild horse population. These are very important Canadian milestones for a species that was once considered a pest on the grasslands. May more good things happen to protect all wild horses left in Canada; if we destroy the remainder, our society will lose something of the wild spirit that exists in all of us.

Today the situation in Canada offers much stronger and more compelling science-based and First Nations cultural/heritage arguments than in the past to protect the wild horses in the Alberta foothills and British Columbia's West Chilcotin, outside of the wild-horse preserve. In addition, the genetic uniqueness of wild horses in both regions falls under the 1992 International Union of the Conservation of Nature (IUCN) Action Plan for Wild Equids, intended to conserve feral equids as part of the planet's biodiversity.[2] Canada is a signatory of the IUCN mandate.

To ensure that Canadians can enjoy a much-improved holistic relationship with their last wild horses in the West, not only is strong federal and provincial legislation needed, but the laws must be enforced. The laws also need to embrace First Nations governance, traditional knowledge and cultural/heritage values that are crucial to collaborative protection. As part of this necessary protective legislation, outdated and archaic provincial grazing and livestock laws related to the free-roaming horse need to be taken off the books. Horse-protection legislation must also be strong enough to avoid default compromises that commonly undermine well-intentioned laws, such as the US *Wild Horse and Burro Protection Act* that today sees over 50,000 once "protected" wild horses living an uncertain future crowded in Bureau of Land Management holding pens.[3] [4] [5]

As I end my long ride through the intricate and wonderful world of the wild horse, I have to remind myself that it all began with my strange dream about a magical stone horse twenty years ago. There was no conclusion to the dream, and I still cannot visualize one. On dark winter nights in lonely Chilcotin cabins, when awakened by wolves howling from across a frozen lake, I have reached out to that dream for inspiration and guidance.

Some of this inspiration was needed as our research group struggled with the many complexities of the genetic study which, along with Tŝilhqot'in oral knowledge, led to the unlocking of the fascinating history of the Chilcotin wild horse across deep time and space. They are unique, with a wild spirit that belongs only to them, as untamed as the wind.

Calling themselves the "three musketeers," the Chilcotin wild-horse research "bush" team spent many dedicated years as the backbone of the Chilcotin wild-horse project. Left to right: biologist Wayne McCrory, Friends of Nemaiah Valley president David Williams, and tree planter and volunteer John Huizinga. *Image courtesy of Jonaki Bhattacharyya.*

It is my hope that my book will stimulate many, many Canadians to speak up to ensure adequate protection of the last two large wild horse populations remaining in western Canada; we must save them for the enjoyment and benefit of all present and future generations. The Tŝilhqot'in have shown us the way.

We are the Horse People. The world is watching.

— **Alice William**, Xeni Gwet'in elder and knowledge keeper.

ACKNOWLEDGEMENTS

Lorna Visser and Lucy the Bear Dog. *Image courtesy of Wayne McCrory.*

David Williams. *Image courtesy of Wayne McCrory.*

The creation of this book project came out of my own personal inspiration. I funded, out of my own pocket, all of the background research, writing and early edits. But the book could not have happened without many, many angels along the way.

A substantial number of key people helped to make this book possible. Above all, I have deep gratitude to my loving wife, Lorna Visser, for her enduring patience, advice and support throughout this two-decades-long project, including our hiking many wild-horse trails, exploring archeological sites in the US, and other wild-horse adventures. Thank you, Lorna!

The wild-horse field research that ended up being used in the book would have never happened without David Williams, Pat Swift and other board members of Friends of Nemaiah Valley (FONV). They provided dedicated help, research funding and assistance. Special thanks to FONV director David Williams for all his field assistance, knowledge, guidance and dedication, and for the use of the

Far Meadow cabin as a base for the wild-horse research. FONV director Pat Swift was supportive in so many ways, including providing background material and photographs.

Pat Swift. *Image courtesy of David Williams.*

My longtime good friend and biologist colleague Maggie Paquet was key in critiquing and editing many of the early drafts. As a book designer and publisher, she provided excellent guidance and technical expertise over the duration of the project. Without Maggie's encouragement and strong belief in the importance of saving our last wild horses, it's likely this book wouldn't have happened.

Maggie Paquet. *Image courtesy of Maggie Paquet.*

Particular thanks go to the many Xeni Gwet'in people of the Tŝilhqot'in Nation for showing me the way and for all of their efforts to save their land and their qiyus/wild horses. Xeni Gwet'in knowledge keeper and researcher Alice William deserves special recognition for all of her background research, guidance, patience, and kind assistance as a Tŝilhqot'in consultant, editor and contributor throughout. I also thank her brother, knowledge keeper Norman William, for his field assistance and for sharing, around many campfires on the long trail, so much of the local history and storylines of his people from his encyclopedic

Alice William. *Image courtesy of Lindsay Burrows.*

Norman William. *Image courtesy of Alice William.*

Marilyn Baptiste. *Image courtesy of Goldman Environmental Prize.*

memory. He brought landscapes alive with Tŝilhqot'in place names, events and stories.

Without the positive support and guidance of Xeni Gwet'in Chiefs Marilyn Baptiste and Roger William, none of the wild-horse research that was the foundation of the book would have happened. I thank both for their shared vision to protect qiyus, including the Xeni Gwet'in 2002 declaration of the Eagle Lake Henry ?Elegesi Qiyus (Cayuse) Wild Horse Preserve. Both Marilyn and Roger also assisted with questions related to Tŝilhqot'in traditional oral knowledge and interpretation used in this book. Marilyn also kindly provided the foreword.

Special mention also goes to the late Xeni Gwet'in wild-horse ranger Harry Setah for so willingly sharing his personal stories and

Roger William. *Image courtesy of Wayne McCrory.*

Harry Setah. *Image courtesy of Wayne McCrory.*

intimate knowledge of the wild qiyus. I am grateful, as well, to the many other Xeni Gwet'in who generously shared their knowledge and stories.

John Huzinga. *Image © Patrice Halley, Canadian Geographic.*

My wild-horse sidekick John Huizinga donated hundreds of hours of volunteer work and advice, always willing to bring out his toolbox to fix vehicle breakdowns in the wilds, put out peat fires, collect wild-horse hair and share many a campfire story.

Wolf biologist and conservationist Sadie Parr spent many years researching the diet of wolves in the

Sadie Parr. *Image courtesy of Wayne McCrory.*

Range ecology surveys in the Brittany Triangle. Left to right: Wesley Alphonse, Jessica Setah and Jonaki Bhattacharyya. *Image courtesy of Jonaki Bhattacharyya.*

Getting ready to take blood samples from captive wild horses. Left to right: veterinarian Dr. Corrine Long, Lester Pierce, Ian Bridge and David Williams. *Image courtesy of Wayne McCrory.*

Brittany Triangle and Nemiah Valley and provided meaningful advice and photographs for the book. Sadie's shared wolf study results and sheer passion for wolves was the foundation for the wolf chapter in my book.

I thank Dr. Jonaki Bhattacharyya for her years of research on range ecology in the Brittany Triangle and the Tŝilhqot'in cultural relationship to their horse. She helped with early book edits that encouraged much more Tŝilhqot'in content and storylines.

Many thanks to Lester Pierce and Ian Bridge for their many stories, local knowledge and logistical support when our wild-horse research team was out in the field: to Lester for sharing his wild-horse bounty hunt experience and to Ian (and Terry Lulua) for helping with obtaining blood samples from their captive wild horse herd for our first genetic analysis.

Many thanks also to Zoocheck Canada, especially Julie Woodyer for her knowledge and background on the Alberta wild horses used in the book. Zoocheck's sharing of legal expertise and advice on the future of Canada's last wild horses was invaluable.

I thank artist and educator Chelsea Robinson for her constructive book editing and for teaching me about chapter transitions and context.

I want to pay special tribute to the two wild-horse biologists whose pathways I crossed during my earlier years of ignorance and learning. They were important teachers on my wild-horse journey, and both have now passed on to the next campfire up ahead. The late biologist Robert A. Ruttan was my wonderful elder

Julie Woodyer. *Image courtesy of Wayne McCrory.*

Chelsea Robinson. *Image courtesy of Wayne McCrory.*

Robert Ruttan. *Image courtesy of Wayne McCrory.*

and mentor and researched the history of Alberta's wild horses used in my book.

I thank the late biologist Dean Feist, my first teacher of wild horses, for his patience with my early and ignorant anti-feral horse arguments and for his passionate dedication in helping Wild Horse Annie and others get the US law passed that protected wild horses and burros.

I will forever be grateful to Harbour Publishing/Douglas & McIntyre for their enthusiastic review of the raw manuscript and for keeping their promise to make the book "better than I ever imagined." University of Victoria professor emerita Lynne Van Luven deserves very heartfelt thanks for her patient guidance in working with me on the big edits and refinement of the raw manuscript for Harbour Publishing; Also, thanks to copy-editor Noel Hudson and project manager Zoë Mackenzie.

I deeply appreciate Dr. Claudia Notzke, professor emerita, Aboriginal and International Management Programs, University of Lethbridge, Alberta, for her sage advice and critical chapter reviews. I thank Alberta agrologist Brian de Kock for providing range information on the Alberta wild horses, and Darrell Glover of the Help Alberta Wild Horses Society (HAWS) for guiding field surveys and for providing insights into the government's mismanagement of Alberta wild horses. I thank the Valhalla Wilderness Society for allowing me to fundraise for the genetics research now used in the book and for their general support of the wild-horse project. The Valhalla Foundation for Ecology very kindly let me use their research cabin at the Jas–Chinook Nature Preserve in order to have quiet, creative times to work on the book project.

I am grateful to Lush Cosmetics and the Fitzhenry Family Foundation for funding much of the genetics research that ended up being used in my book.

Many volunteers also contributed to the wild-horse project, including bear biologist Marty Williams, my nephew Shea Pownall, and others.

Special thanks to lawyer Jack Woodward, who cajoled me to "stop and listen to the elders," for his law firm's provision of in-depth qiyus historic and cultural research used in the Xeni Gwet'in Rights and Title cases against the BC and Canadian governments. Nancy Opperman, project coordinator for the Xeni Gwet'in, helped make invaluable background research possible.

I thank international genetic scientists Dr. Gus Cothran, Texas A&M University, and Dr. Ludovic, Orlando of the Centre for Anthropobiology & Genomics in Toulouse, France, for their expert analyses in the Chilcotin wild-horse genetics and genome research used in the book. Dr. Cothran graciously reviewed and critiqued genetic sections of the manuscript. Dr. William Taylor, associate professor and curator of Archeology at the University of Colorado Museum of Natural History, also kindly reviewed several critical sections of my book. The Vuntut Gwitchin Heritage Committee reviewed and approved the use of the legend of the Whitestone mammoth. I thank Erica Mallam for her excellent proofreading of an earlier draft. Husband-and-wife team Gail and Stephen Mitchell, both biologists and longtime university teachers, were "critical readers," providing useful comments on all of my early chapters. Rayola Creative Graphic Design did the initial experimental book mock-up and thus helped build the vision for the end product.

Special thanks to the host of photographers and others who generously let me use the photographs and graphics that make the book so special: Patrice Halley Photography/Canadian Geographic; Duane Starr Photography; Chris Harris; Zoe Lucas; Gary Fiegehen; Ginger Kathrens; Friends of Nemaiah Valley; Sadie Parr; Dr. Jonaki Bhattacharyya; Jeremy Williams; John E. Marriott; artist Julius Csotonyi/Yukon Government; Alice William; Family Estate of Jimmy Bulyan; June Draney; Sage Birchwater; Prescott Patterson; Goldman Environmental Prize; Sharon MacDonnell; Ana Evans; Susy Chaston; George Colgate; Museum of Anthropology at the University of British Columbia; Royal British Columbia Museum; Charles Gentile, Library and Archives Canada; Lorna Visser; Dr. Claudia Notzke; Dr. Christina Barron-Ortiz; Mike Cowdrey, Jody and Ned Martin (Hawk Hill Press); Darrell Glover; Bonnie Myers; Nancy Cerroni; Daryl Visscher; Maggie Paquet; Lindsay Borrows; Lynne Rogers; Tŝilhqot'in National Government (TNG); and Wikipedia Commons.

Blessings to my sister Maureen Tickner and her late husband, Jerry, for welcoming the wild-horse team to Williams Lake with countless meals, spare bedrooms and warm hospitality.

Last but not least, "Lucy the Bear Dog," now passed on to the next trail up ahead, deserves special mention for keeping me safe in bear country, being my companion on many lonely research trips, and for putting up with me during our joint wolf-howl experiments, during which I tried to lure in curious wild horses while wearing a hat with wolf-looking ears—a photographic experience that nearly led to our being trampled by an over-enthusiastic young stallion.

It's been a *long* ride.

Thank you all!

WILD HORSE GROUPS IN CANADA

Zoocheck (nation-wide)
Box 1389
Gravenhurst, Ontario
P1P 1V5
www.zoocheck.com

Canadian Horse Defence Coalition (nation-wide)
150 First Street
P.O. Box 21079
Orangeville, Ontario
L9W 4S7
www.canadianhorsedefence coalition.org

Horse Protection Society of BC
1395 242 Street
Langley Township., BC
V2Z 1L2
www.horseprotectionsociety ofbc.com

For the Ferals Society
(Health and well-being of the horses and the Syilx Okanagan people through herd management)
www.fortheferals.com

Wild Horses of Alberta Society (WHOAS)
Box 4154
Olds, Alberta
T4H 1P7
www.wildhorsesofalberta.com

Help Alberta Wildies Society (HAWS)
Box 3826
Olds, Alberta
T4H 1P5
www.helpalbertawildiessociety .com

Free Spirit Sanctuary
PO Box 1562
Cochrane, Alberta
T4C 1B5
www.freespiritsanctuary.ca

Sable Island Green Horse Society (Nova Scotia)
www.sableislandinstitute.org

ENDNOTES

Preface

1 C. Tate, *Cayuse Indians*, historylink.org/file/10365, posted 2013.

2 R.H. Ruby, J.A. Brown, and C.C. Collins, *A Guide to the Indian Tribes of the Pacific Northwest* (Norman, OK: University of Oklahoma Press, 2013).

3 W. Taylor, P. Ibrador, Y. Running Horse Collin ((Tašunke Iyanke Wiŋ), Carlton Shield Chief Gover, Jimmy Arterberry, Mani Šni (Joseph American Horse), Anpetu Luta Wiŋ (Antonia Loretta Afraid of Bear-Cook), Akil Nujipi (Harold Left Heron), Tanka Omniya (Robert Milo Yellow Hair), Mario Gonzalez (Nantan Hinapan), Bill Means, Sam High Crane, Mažasu (Wendell W. Yellow Bull), Barbara Dull Knife (Mapiya Ki Yake Wiŋ), Wakiŋyala Wiŋ (Anita Afraid of Bear), Cruz Tecumseh Collin (Wanka'tuya Kiya) . . . Alice William, Wayne McCrory et al., "Early dispersal of domestic horses into the Great Plains and Northern Rockies," *Science*, vol. 379, 2023: 1,316–1,322.

4 Linda R. Smith, Beghad Jigwedetaghel?anx, *A Yunesit'in and Xeni Gwet'in Project* (First Choice Books, 2011).

Introduction

1 J. Frank Dobie, *The Mustangs* (Lincoln: University of Nebraska Press, 2005), p. 61

2 Dobie, *The Mustangs*.

Chapter 1

1 J. Edward Chamberlin, *Horse: How the Horse Has Shaped Civilization* (Toronto: Alfred A. Knopf Canada, 2006).

Chapter 2

1 Linda R. Smith, Nabas oral literature documentation, a collaboration research study with the Yuneŝit'in government (Stone Band) and the Xeni Gwet'in government (Nemiah Band), final report to Terralingua, 2012.

2 Transcript of December 2012 interview with Martin and Margaret Quilt at Nemiah Valley for Xeni Gwet'in Aboriginal Funds for Species at Risk (AFSAR) study by Alice and Norman William, McCrory Wildlife Services, in-house project files.

3 Justice David Vickers, *Tŝilhqot'in Nation v. British Columbia*, 2007 BCSC 1700, Registry No. 90-0913, British Columbia Supreme Court, Transcripts: Testimony October 21, 2003; Cross-examination October 18, 2004. www.courts.gov.bc.ca/jdb-txt/sc/07/17/2007bcsc1700.pdf

4 David Williams, personal communications: "The homestead and beyond," personal memoir notes.

5 Email from Alice William to Wayne McCrory dated October 25, 2022.

6 References for the logging history were drawn from the following sources:

Harlan Campbell, *The Nemiah Valley: Title land, sacred land.* harlanhappydog.github.io/files/NemiahValley.pdf, accessed October 28, 2022.

Richard Littlemore, *Nemiah: Home of the Xeni Gwet'in: Pacific Salmon Forests Project* (David Suzuki Foundation and partners, 2000).

Terry Glavin and the People of the Nemiah Valley, *Nemiah: The Unconquered Country* (Vancouver, BC: New Star Books, 1992).

Justice David Vickers, *Tŝilhqot'in Nation v. British Columbia*, 2007 BCSC 1700. Exhibit 0464, Expert Report of David M. Carson, August 12, 2005. In 1999, the Ministry of Forests reported that licensees had nearly 1 million cubic metres of timber identified in forest development plans within the Brittany Triangle area.

Woodward & Company Lawyers, LLP, *Blazing a Trail for Reconciliation, Self Determination & Decolonization: Tŝilhqot'in Nation v. British Columbia and Canada*, www.woodwardandcompany.com/tsilhqotin, accessed January 2022.

7 British Columbia Commission on Resources and Environment, Cariboo–Chilcotin Land Use Plan, 1994.

8 R.M. Jeo, M.A. Sanjayan, and D. Sizemore, *A conservation area design for the central coast region of British Columbia, Canada*, Round River Conservation Studies, 1999.

9 C. Rumsey, J. Adron, K. Ciruna, T. Curtis, Z. Ferdana, T.D. Hamilton, K. Heinemeyer, P. Iachetti, R.M. Jeo, G. Kaiser, D. Narver, R. Noss, D. Sizemore, A. Tautz, R. Tingey, and K. Vance-Borland, *An ecosystem spatial analysis for Haida Gwaii, Central Coast and North Coast British Columbia* (Victoria: Coast Information Team, 2004). McCrory Wildlife Services files.

Chapter 3

1 Hope Ryden, *Mustangs: A Return to the Wild* (New York: Penguin Books, 1978).

Chapter 5

1 J.A. Storrar, R.J. Hudson, and R.E. Salter, *Habitat use behaviour of feral horses and spatial relationships with moose in central British Columbia*, Sye 10: 39–44, 1977.

2 Terry Glavin and the People of the Nemiah Valley, *Nemiah: The Unconquered Country*, pp. 11, 125.

Chapter 6

1 Norma Bearcroft, *Wild Horses of Canada* (England: J.A. Allen & Co., 1966, reprinted in 1974 by the Canadian Wild Horse Society), pp. 58–59.

Chapter 7

1 L. Wilcox, B. Robinson, and A. Harvey, *A Sense of Place: Issues, Attitudes, and Resources in the Yellowstone-to-Yukon Ecoregion*, prepared for Yellowstone-to-Yukon Conservation Initiative, 1998.

2 Centennial Project 1958, various authors, *History and Legends of the Chilcotin* (Williams Lake, BC: Cariboo Press Ltd., 1965).

3 W.P. McCrory, *Preliminary conservation assessment of the Rainshadow Wild Horse Ecosystem, Brittany Triangle, British Columbia, Canada*, a review of grizzly and black bears, other wildlife, feral horses, and wild salmon, Report to Friends of Nemaiah Valley (FONV), Victoria, BC, 2002.

Chapter 8

1 Littlemore, *Nemiah: Home of the Xeni Gwet'in: Pacific Salmon Forests Project.*

2 McCrory Wildlife Services internal files.

3 P. St. Paul, *Williams Lake Tribune*, October 21, 2003.

Chapter 9

1 www.fonv.ca/nemaiahvalley/thecourtcase

2 Supreme Court of Canada, *Tŝilhqot'in Nation v. British Columbia* (SCC 2014), scc-csc.lexum.com/scc-csc/scc-csc/en/item /14246/index.do

3 W.P. McCrory, A. William, L. Smith, B. Cross, and L. Craighead, *Inventory of wildlife, ecological, and landscape connectivity values, Tŝilhqot'in First Nations cultural/heritage values, and resource conflicts in the Dasiqox-Taseko watershed, BC*

Chilcotin, Report to Xeni Gwet'in and Yuneŝit'in First Nations, 2014.

4 Vickers, *Tŝilhqot'in Nation v. British Columbia.*

5 S. Williams, Reports of surveyors of Cariboo District, 1908.

6 Terry Glavin and the People of the Nemiah Valley, *Nemiah: The Unconquered Country* (Vancouver, BC: New Star Books, 1992).

7 V. Smith, A. Patterson, S. Elwell, and C. Mackay, 2019 Chilcotin Free Range Horse Survey.

8 Supreme Court of Canada, *Tŝilhqot'in Nation v. British Columbia* (SCC 2014), http://scc-csc.lexum.com/scc-csc/scc-csc/en /item/14246/index.do

9 Justice David Vickers, *Tsilhqot'in Nation v. British Columbia*, 2007 BCSC 1700. http://www.courts.gov.bc.ca/idb-txt/sc/07/17 /2007bcscl700.pdf.

10 W.P. McCrory, A. Williams, L. Smith, B. Cross, and L. Craighead, *Inventory of wildlife, ecological, and landscape connectivity values, Tŝilhqot'in First Nations cultural/heritage values, and resource conflicts in the Dasiqox-Taseko watershed, BC Chilcotin*, Report to Xeni Gwet'in and Yuneŝit'in First Nations, 2014.

Chapter 10

1 Environment Canada website, McCrory Wildlife Services files.

2 P. Daigle, "Fire in the Dry Interior of British Columbia," *Extension Note 8*, British Columbia Ministry of Forests (BCMOF) Research Program, Victoria, BC, 1996.

3 W.P. McCrory, *Roads to Nowhere: Technical review of ecological damage and proposed restoration related to BC Ministry of Forests control actions—2003 Chilko Wildfire, re: bulldozed fireguards and access roads and peat meadow damage*, Report to Friends of Nemaiah Valley, Victoria, BC, 2005.

4 G. Filmon, *British Columbia Firestorm 2003*, Provincial Review, Report to BC Government, 2004, accessed July 7, 2020, https://

www2.gov.bc.ca/assets/gov/public-safety-and-emergency-services/wildfire-status/governance/bcws_firestormreport_2003.pdf.

Chapter 11

1 K. Card, *Assessing Stakeholder Interests: A strategy for best management practices of free-roaming horses, Chilcotin, British Columbia*, Masters of Natural Resources Management (MNRM) thesis, University of Manitoba, 2010.

2 The Pleistocene was the last Ice Age; an earlier definition estimated it lasted from two million years to 10,000 years ago and had four glacial and interglacial periods. Continental glaciers pushed as far south as the 40th parallel. "Pleistocene," Wikipedia, 2023, https://en.wikipedia.org/wiki/Pleistocene.

3 C.R. Harington and M. Eggleston-Scott, "Partial carcass of a small Pleistocene horse from Last Chance Creek near Dawson City, Yukon," *Current Research in the Pleistocene* 13:105-107, 1996.

4 T.J. Murchie, A.J. Monteath, M.E. Mahony et al., "Collapse of the mammoth-steppe in central Yukon as revealed by ancient environmental DNA," *Nature Communications* 12, 7120 (2021). doi.org/10.1038/s41467-021-27439-6

5 M. Donovan, "Ancient DNA found in soil samples reveals mammoths, Yukon wild horses survived thousands of years longer than believed," *Brighter World*, McMaster University, 2021.

6 Sadie Parr email, January 24, 2019. Research notes from interview with Roger William.

7 Alice William, personal communication to Wayne McCrory, re-verified November 2021.

8 R.B. Lane, "Chilcotin," *Handbook of North American Indians*, Vol. 6, *Subarctic* (Washington, DC: Smithsonian Institution Scholarly Press, 1981), series ed. William C. Sturtevant, volume ed. June Helm.

9 Anonymous Nemiah Valley outfitter, notes from 2009 interview.

10 S. Parr and W. McCrory, "Gray wolves (*Canis lupus*) consume free-ranging horses (*Equus ferus caballus*) on the Chilcotin Plateau, British Columbia," *Canadian Field-Naturalist* Vol. 136. No. 3 (2022): 237–246. www.canadianfieldnaturalist.ca/index.php/cfn/issue/current

11 S. Parr, "Investigating gray wolf (*Nun*) foraging ecology in the Brittany Triangle (Tachelach'ed) region of the ʔElegesi Qiyus (Nemiah) Wild Horse (Naŝlhiny) Preserve of British Columbia 2013–2017." A 2018 report prepared for Valhalla Wilderness Society, Xeni Gwet'in Nation, Friends of Nemaiah Valley and Wolf Awareness Inc.

12 N. Webb, E. Merrill and J. Allen, *Density, demography, and functional response of a harvested wolf population in West-Central Alberta*, management summary, 2009.

13 W.P. McCrory, *Preliminary technical review of management of free-roaming ("feral") horses (*Equus ferus caballus*) in Alberta's six foothills equine zones*, report for Zoocheck, 2015.

Chapter 12

1 K.H. Knopff, *Cougar predation in a multi-prey system in West-Central Alberta*, PhD thesis, University of Alberta, 2010.

2 K.H. Knopff, A.A. Knopff, A. Kortello, and M.S. Boyce, "Cougar kill rate and prey composition in a multiprey system," *The Journal of Wildlife Management*, 74:1435–1447, 2010.

3 S. White and C. Shores, *Cougar-Caribou Dynamics in the Chilcotin, Caribou Recovery Program Quarterly Update to Stakeholders and Indigenous Nations*, 2023.

4 J.W. Turner, M.L. Wolfe, and J.F. Kirkpatrick, "Seasonal predation on a feral horse population," *Canadian Journal of Zoology* 70:929–934, 1992.

5 *Casper Star Tribune*, "Mountain lions blamed for death of wild horse foals," August 13, 2004. trib.com/news/state-and-regional

/mountain-lions-blamed-for-death-of-wild horse-foals/article_29c83cbe-c9a7-56c2-9b07-d5f2254e16b2.html

6 L.W. Blake and E.M. Gese, *Cougar predation rates and prey composition in the Pryor Mountains of Wyoming and Montana*, USDA National Wildlife Research Center Staff Publications, #1891, 2016.

7 https://wildhorsesofalberta.com/2014/01/31/our-alternatives-to-wild-horse-capture/

8 S. White and C. Shores, Cougar-Caribou Dynamics in the Chilcotin, Caribou Recovery Program Quarterly Update to Stakeholders and Indigenous Nations, 2023.

9 W.P. McCrory, *Preliminary conservation assessment of the Rainshadow Wild Horse Ecosystem, Brittany Triangle, British Columbia, Canada*, a review of grizzly and black bears, other wildlife, feral horses, and wild salmon, Report to Friends of Nemaiah Valley (FONV), Victoria, BC, 2002.

Chapter 13

1 P. Librado, C. Der Sarkissian, L. Erminia, M. Schuberta et al. "Tracking the origins of Yakut horses and the genetic basis for their fast adaptation to subarctic environments," *Proceeedings of the National Academy of Sciences of the United States of America* (PNAS), 112:50, 2015. www.pnas.org/content/112/50/E6889.abstract. Accessed January 10, 2016.

2 A.G. Morice, *The History of the Northern Interior of British Columbia, formerly New Caledonia, 1660 to 1880* (Toronto, 1904).

3 R.E. Salter and R.J. Hudson. "Feeding ecology of feral horses in western Alberta," *Journal of Range Management*, 32: 221–225.

4 R.A. Garrott and L. Taylor, "Dynamics of a feral horse population in Montana," *Journal of Wildlife Management*, 54: 603–612, 1990.

5 R.A. Garrott, D.B. Siniff, and L.L. Eberhardt, "Growth rates of feral horse populations," *Journal of Wildlife Management*, 55: 641–648, 1991.

Chapter 14

1 M.L. Morrison, L.S. Hall, S.K. Robinson, S.I. Rothstein, D.C. Hahn, and TD Rich. Conference Proceedings. "Research and Management of the Brown-headed Cowbird in Western Landscapes," *Studies in Avian Biology* 18:1–312 (Camarillo, CA: Cooper Ornithological Society, 1999). Also Vincent Muehter, web.archive.org/web/20081130205441/http://www.audubon.org/bird/research.

Chapter 15

1 T.J. Bruzda, Z. Jaworski, M. Sobczyńska, J. Ensminger, and A. Górecka-Bruzda, "Do olfactory behaviour and marking responses of Konik polski stallions to faeces from conspecifics of either sex differ?" *Behavioural Processes*, Vol. 155, October 2018, pp. 38–42.

2 A. Lemasson, A. Boutin, S. Boivin, C. Blois-Heulin, and M. Hausberger, "Horse (*Equus caballus*) whinnies: A source of social information," *Animal Cognition*, 12(5), 2009, 693–704.

3 Karen Bakker, *The Sounds of Life: How Digital Technology Is Bringing Us Closer to the Worlds of Animals and Plants* (Princeton, NJ: Princeton University Press, 2022).

4 K. Krueger, B. Flauger, K. Farmer, and C. Hemelrijk, "Movement initiation in groups of feral horses," *Behavioural Processes*, Vol. 103, 2014, pp. 91–101.

Chapter 16

1 BC Ministry of Forests, Internal Grazing Memo, Range files, Horse Control Program, Alexis Creek, Chilcotin, BC, 1988, McCrory Wildlife Services internal files.

2 John Thistle, *Range wars: ranching and pest eradication on British Columbia's interior plateau*, PhD thesis, University of British Columbia, 2009.
3 John Thistle, *Resettling the Range: Animals, Ecologies, and Human Communities in Early British Columbia* (Vancouver, BC: University of British Columbia Press, 2014).
4 Thistle, *Range Wars.*
5 Thistle, *Range wars.*
6 Ken Mather, see p. 185 citing Laing, "Some Pioneers," 259. Table compiled from the data that Laing collected, 2018.
7 Ken Mather, *Trail North: The Okanagan Trail of 1858–68 and Its Origins in British Columbia and Washington* (Victoria, BC: Heritage House Publishing Company, 2018).
8 Ken Mather, citing Laing.
9 E.P. Thompson, *Customs in Common: Studies in Traditional Popular Culture* (New York: W.W. Norton, 1993).
10 Thistle, *Range wars.*
11 Thistle, *Range wars.*
12 Thistle, *Range wars.*
13 Thistle, *Range wars.*
14 Thistle, *Range wars.*
15 Thistle, *Range wars.*
16 Thistle, *Range wars.*
17 *History and Legends of the Chilcotin.*
18 Louis LeBourdais, "Wild Horses in B.C," typewritten manuscript, December 1, 1946, Quesnel, BC, pp. 27–30, BC Provincial Archives.
19 Thistle, *Range wars.*
20 S. Williams, Reports of Surveyors of Cariboo District, 1908.
21 Thistle, *Range wars.*
22 Thistle, *Range wars.*
23 Bearcroft, *Wild Horses of Canada.*
24 Charles Lugrin Shaw, "Cayuse Hazers of the Cariboo," *Maclean's*, August 15, 1927.

25 Bearcroft, *Wild Horses of Canada.*

26 Eric Collier, "Wild Horses Roamed Chilcotin and Still the Deer Fared Well," *Williams Lake Tribune*, 1965.

27 Collier, "Wild Horses Roamed Chilcotin."

28 Thistle, *Range wars.*

29 Joanna Reid, *Grassland Debates: Conservation and social change in the Cariboo–Chilcotin, British Columbia*, PhD thesis, University of British Columbia, 2010.

30 Thistle, *Range wars.*

31 L. McFadden, "Let's Stop Slaughtering Our Wild Horses," *British Columbia Digest*, May–June 1965.

32 Thistle, *Range wars.*

33 McFadden, "Let's Stop Slaughtering."

34 Thistle, *Range wars.*

35 McFadden, "Let's Stop Slaughtering."

36 Bearcroft, *Wild Horses of Canada.*

37 Card, Katherine. *Assessing Stakeholder Interests: A strategy for best management practices of free-roaming horses, Chilcotin, British Columbia*, Master of Natural Resource Management thesis University of Manitoba, 2010.

38 Terry Glavin, "The Killing of Wild Horses: Problem Worsens in Chilcotin," *Vancouver Sun*, March 1988.

39 BC Ministry of Forests, Internal Grazing Memo, Range files, Horse Control Program, Alexis Creek, Chilcotin, BC, 1988, McCrory Wildlife Services internal files.

40 Integrated Resource Branch of Forests and Lands, strictly confidential interim briefing memo to Steve Demelt re Terry Glavin *Vancouver Sun* article, March 18, 1988, McCrory Wildlife Services internal files.

41 S.K. Preston, *A habitat-use and dietary analysis of a monogastric versus a ruminant herbivore, on forested range*, Master of Science thesis, University of British Columbia, 1984.

42 R. Grieve, Integrated Resources Branch, memo to M. Carlson, regional manager, Cariboo Region, re: Chilcotin Wild Horse Roundup, September 12, 1990. McCrory Wildlife Services internal file.

43 "Snares Threaten Horses and Wildlife," *Williams Lake Advocate*, March 29, 1995, McCrory Wildlife Services files.

44 Paul St. Pierre, *Chilcotin Holiday* (Vancouver, BC: Douglas & McIntyre, 1984), pp. 66 and 72.

45 "Mange on the Range," *BC Report*, April 1995.

46 V. Smith, A. Patterson, S. Elwell, and C. Mackay, 2019 Chilcotin Free Range Horse Survey.

47 "Wild Horses of the Chilcotin: Trouble on the Range," Vancouver *Province*, June 18, 1995.

48 Thistle, *Resettling the Range*.

49 L. McFadden, "Let's Stop Slaughtering Our Wild Horses," *British Columbia Digest*, May–June 1965.

Chapter 17

1 M. Graydon, "BC wild-horse country, 1920 to early 1930," handwritten letter, transcribed, Friends of Nemaiah Valley, 2000.

2 Charles Shaw, "Cayuse Hazers of the Cariboo." *Maclean's*, 1927.

3 R.D. Symons, *Where the Wagon Led: One Man's Memories of the Cowboy's Life in the Old West* (Toronto: Doubleday Canada, 1973).

Chapter 18

1 T.D. Hooper and M. Pitt, *Problem analysis for Chilcotin–Cariboo grassland biodiversity*, report to Ministry of Environment, Lands and Parks, Wildlife Branch, Williams Lake, BC, 1993. (Also published as Wildlife Bulletin No. B-52, 1995).

2 W.P. McCrory, *Environmental impacts of military training on an endangered grassland, Chilcotin Military Block, D.L. 7741,*

report for the Tl'esqox (Toosey) Indian Band, Riske Creek, BC, 1995.

3 BC government, *Coordinated Resource Plan for the Becher Prairie: A Guide to Development, Rehabilitation and Management*, 1977, Toosey (Tl'esqox) Band and W.P. McCrory files.

Chapter 19

1 LeBourdais, "Wild horses in BC."

2 Canadian Press article, June 18, 1995, statement on Chilcotin wild horses by Jodie Kekula, BC Ministry of Forests rangeland specialist.

3 D. Shackleton, *Hoofed Animals of British Columbia*, UBC Press and Royal British Columbia Museum handbook, 1999.

Chapter 20

1 According to 2007 BC Supreme Court documents, "close to Chilko Lake is 'Canoe Crossing," or Biny Gwechugh, place name #146, on both sides of the river. It is a site of ancient and continuing Tŝilhqot'in occupation. This was probably the large Tŝilhqot'in village close to Chilko Lake seen by McDougall, Connolly, and Nobili . . . [I]t is apparently where Nobili visited the 'great round lodge' in 1845 . . . This is certainly one of the places where Father Nobili placed a cross in 1845."

2 According to Alice William, Xeni Gwet'in consultant to this book project, some elders debate the accuracy of some of the Tŝilhqot'in names for ancestors at Biny Gwechugh as recorded in the 2007 court document. Additionally, Alice also checked out the English meaning of Biny Gwechugh by consulting with other Xeni Gwet'in knowledge keepers and found several Tŝilhqot'in interpretations. One is Big Lake and another is Big River. This is in reference to the widening of the Chilko River just below its outlet from Chilko Lake. Canoe Crossing is the

place name that locals generally use today; it refers to part of this landmark where the Tŝilhqot'in were able to easily cross the river by canoe or on horseback. For simplicity, I have used the locally accepted name Canoe Crossing as the common name. Big Lake is the more commonly accepted name for another lake in Xeni Gwet'in territory.

3 I am making the assumption that Biny Gwechugh was already a village at this time and inhabited by the Tŝilhqot'in, though there is anthropological information with respect to other tribal groups apparently being present before the Tŝilhqot'in moved into the area.

4 I found very little descriptive reference to the type(s) of dogs the Tŝilhqot'in had in pre-colonial times. This would make a valuable study, including a genetic study of carbon-14 dated bones from earlier times to see how related their dogs were to the gray wolf, as some evidence suggests. Before the horse, dogs were used as the main pack animals for the Tŝilhqot'in. They must have been large and had heavy fur to survive the cold winters. The best reference I could find was in one of the Nobili 1845 letters, where he described dogs at Fort Alexandria as "exactly like wolves." They were a much preferred food item for the voyageurs. In 1808, Simon Fraser reported a type of dog in the Fraser Canyon whose fur was used for wool by the Canyon First People.

5 Nobili's 1845 letters pp. 76–77 described the burning of the dead as ". . . a universal custom of all tribes until these last few years. Going through villages one can see the memorials of this custom; they are wooden poles planted in the ground, ordinarily along a riverbank or a lakeshore, with a small painted box on top, not more than two pans long, containing the ashes of the cremated bodies." I could find no reference to what measurement a "pan" is, other than perhaps a baking pan.

6 James Alexander Teit, *Mythology of the Thompson Indians*, 1912, *Memoirs of the American Museum of Natural History 12*, Franz Boaz, ed., publications of the Jesup North Pacific Expedition 8(2) (New York: G.E. Stechert & Co., reprinted by AMS Press, 1975), p. 399.

7 Deanne Stillman, *Mustang: The Saga of the Wild Horse in the American West* (Boston, New York: Mariner Books, Houghton Mifflin Harcourt, 2009) see p. 5 for Montezuma's dream.

8 Bernal Diaz del Castillo, *The Discovery and Conquest of Mexico 1517–1521* (New York: Farrar, Straus and Cudahy, 1956). Edited from the only exact copy of the original manuscript. [See p. 35 of softcover edition for prophesy.]

Chapter 21

1 R.B. Cunninghame Graham, *The Horses of the Conquest* (London: William Heinemann Ltd., 1930), p. 112.

2 Vega, *Manejo real.*

3 del Castillo, *The Discovery and Conquest of Mexico.*

4 Cunninghame Graham, *Horses of the Conquest.*

Chapter 22

1 Jessica Setah-Alphonse, Yuneŝit'in First Nation, interview transcript YFN02, June 16, 2017, *In Tribal Parks and Indigenous Protected and Conserved Area: Lessons Learned from BC Examples* (David Suzuki Foundation, 2018), p. 27.

2 Anthony Carter, *Somewhere Between* (Saanichton BC: Hancock House Publishing, 1966).

3 Smith, Beghad Jigwedetaghel?anx, *A Yunesit'in and Xeni Gwet'in Project.*

4 Smith, Beghad Jigwedetaghel?anx.

5 Francis Setah, "Testimony of Francis Setah" (2003a, 16, 31), translated from Tŝilhqot'in to English by Orrie Charleyboy, in Vickers, *Tŝilhqot'in Nation v. British Columbia.*

6 Teit, *Mythology of the Thompson Indians.*
7 Alice William interview with Orry Hance, email to Wayne McCrory.
8 Vickers, *Tŝilhqot'in Nation v. British Columbia.*

Chapter 23

1 Teit, *Mythology of the Thompson Indians.*
2 W.C. Wickwire, "To see ourselves as the other's other: Nlaka'pamux contact narratives," 1994, reprinted from *The Canadian Historical Review*, Vol. LXXV, No. 1, pp.1–20.
3 Alexander Mackenzie, *Voyages from Montreal on the River St. Laurence through the Continent of North America to the Frozen and Pacific Oceans in the Years 1789 and 1793 with a Preliminary Account of the Rise, Progress, and Present State of the Fur Trade in That Country* (London: Cadell & Davies, 1801; reprinted Toronto: Radisson Society, 1927).
4 Wickwire, "To see ourselves."
5 W. Kaye Lamb, ed., *Simon Fraser: Letters and Journals, 1806–1808* (Toronto: The Macmillan Company of Canada Ltd., 1966).
6 Wickwire, "To see ourselves."
7 Wickwire, "To see ourselves."
8 Wickwire, "To see ourselves."
9 June 3, 1808: "They seem to run and move about much, and some of them have been across the mountains, as they seem acquainted with the Buffalo, for on seeing our powder horns they immediately observed that they were of that animal, and a wounded Buffalo being painted on the stern of D . . ." He was likely referring to the name of one of the canoes, perhaps the *Determination.*

June 19, 1808: At a lower Nlaka'pamux village, he wrote: "We observed several European articles amongst them, viz. a copper Tea Kettle, a brass camp kettle, a strip of common blanket, and cloathing such as the Cree women wear. These things, we supposed, were brought from our settlements beyond the Mountains. Indeed the Indians made us understand as much."

10 June 16, 1808: "Here we met some of the neighbouring nation called Hakamaugh [the Thompson Indians] . . . with these two of another tribe called Suihoni [Shoshone?]; all were exceedingly well dressed in leather, and were on horseback . . . They were kind to us, and assisted us at the carrying place with their horses."

Chapter 24

1 William E. Jones and Ralph Bogart, *Genetics of the Horse*, second edition revised (Fort Collins, CO: Caballus Publishers, 1973).

2 Grant MacEwan, *Blazing the Old Cattle Trail*, revised edition (Toronto: Fifth House, 2000). interestingcanadianhistory.files .wordpress.com/2014/06/fireaway-in-canoe.jpg

3 MacEwan, *Blazing the Old Cattle Trail.*

4 Card, "Assessing Stakeholder Interests," p.71.

Chapter 25

1 A genome is the complete set of DNA of an organism. It includes all of its genes; that is, it has all of the information necessary to build and maintain that organism. For example, in people, all cells that have a nucleus have a copy of the entire human genome, which is comprised of more than three billion DNA base pairs. Genome sequencing is the process of determining the entirety, or nearly the entirety, of the DNA sequence of an organism's genome at a single time. "Genome," Wikipedia, 2023, https://en.wikipedia.org/wiki/Genome.

2 E.G. Cothran, *Preliminary analysis of the Brittany Triangle feral horse population*, 2006.

3 Y. Plante, J.L. Vega-Pla, Z. Lucas, D. Colling, B. De March, and F. Buchanan, "Genetic diversity in a feral horse population from Sable Island, Canada," *Journal of Heredity* 98:594: 602, 2007.

4 In terms of Barb ancestry, in an email to W.P. McCrory on April 11, 2022, Dr. Cothran explained: "It is unlikely that actual Barbs are part of the ancestry. The horses certainly show Iberian ancestry, but the 'genetics' has been changed by the history of the horses since they came to the New World. There are many ways that the genetics can be changed, including crossing with other types of horses or other Iberian horses, genetic drift, selection, and so on. When (how long ago) the horses came into Native American hands and then into this region of Canada is important. The longer ago it was the more the Spanish horses dominated the genetic makeup of horses in the west. Iberian-derived horses is what I would call them."

5 An Iberian is an ancient domestic horse breed that originated from the Iberian Peninsula of Spain and Portugal. They were the first warhorse and, apparently, the first horses brought to the Americas by the conquistadores. In Spain, the heritage of the Iberian horse produced the world-famed Andalusian. Iberian horse breeds with Spanish and Portuguese blood have led to many other horse breeds besides the Andalusian since they came to the New World.

6 E.G. Cothran and W.P. McCrory, *A preliminary genetic study of the wild horse (*Equus caballus*) in the Brittany Triangle (Tachelach'ed) region of the ʔElegesi Qiyus (Nemiah) Wild-horse preserve of British Columbia*, a study for Valhalla Wilderness Society (VWS), Friends of Nemaiah Valley (FONV), and Xeni Gwet'in First Nation, 2014.

7 E.G. Cothran, results of genotyping of 16 horsehair samples from the East Taseko and 43 from the Bidwell–North Tatla areas, 2018.

8 E.G. Cothran and W.P. McCrory, *Genetic evaluation of the wild horse (*Equus ferus caballus*) in the West Chilcotin (Tŝilhqot'in) region of British Columbia*, in press, 2021.

Chapter 26

1 I.V. Ovchinnikov, T. Dahms, B. Herauf, B. McCann, R. Juras, C. Castaneda, and G. Cothran, "Genetic diversity and origin of the feral horses in Theodore Roosevelt National Park," *PLoS One* 13 (8): e0200795, 2018. doi.org/10.1371/journal.pone.0200795
2 Shan Thomas, *Myth and Mystery: The Curly Horse in America* (1989), with special assistance from David Gaier and Dr. Ann Bowling, a report for the CS Fund, Freestone, California.
3 www.curlyhorsecountry.com/history_curlyhorses.htm
4 Laura McGinnis, "Feral Cattle Isolated and Distinct," AgResearch, US Department of Agriculture, Agricultural Research Service, online magazine, 2008.
5 P. Libradoa et al., *Tracking the origins of Yakut horses.*
6 en.wikipedia.org/wiki/Yakutsk
7 bcwildfire.ca/aboutus/organization/cariboo/climate.htm
8 Jack Palmantier, personal communication to Wayne McCrory, Riske Creek, BC, 1995.
9 Richmond P. Hobson Jr., *Nothing Too Good for a Cowboy* (Toronto: McClelland & Stewart Ltd., 1955).

Chapter 27

1 Dobie, *The Mustangs*, p. 61.
2 en.wikipedia.org/wiki/Mustang.

Chapter 28

1 W.P. Taylor et al., "Early dispersal of domestic horses into the Great Plains and Northern Rockies," *Science*, vol. 379, 2023: 1,316–1,322.
2 Mackenzie, *Voyages from Montreal on the River St. Laurence.*
3 Colin G. Calloway, *One Vast Winter Count: The Native American West before Lewis and Clark* (Lincoln: University of Nebraska Press, 2006).

4 Jack Nisbet, *Mapmaker's Eye: David Thompson and the Columbia Plateau* (Pullman, WA: Washington State University Press, 2005).
5 Dobie, *The Mustangs.*
6 Nisbet, *Mapmaker's Eye.*
7 Clara Graham, *Furs and Gold in the Kootenay* (Vancouver, BC: Wrigley Printing Co. Ltd., 1945).
8 Meriwether Lewis and William Clark, *Original Journals of the Lewis and Clark Expedition 1804–1806*, 8 volumes, R.G. Thwaites, ed. (New York: Dodd-Mead Company, 1904–1905, reprint. New York: Antiquarian Press, 1959).
9 Meriwether Lewis and William Clark, *The Definitive Journals of Lewis and Clark*, 13 volumes, G.E. Moulton, ed. (Lincoln: University of Nebraska Press, 1983–1993).
10 Lamb, *Simon Fraser: Letters and Journals.*
11 Mike Cowdrey, Ned Martin, and Jody Martin, *Horses and Bridles of the American Indians* (Nicasio, CA: Hawk Hill Press, 2012).
12 Cothran, *Genetic analysis of the Alberta "Wildie" horse.*
13 Smith and Jigwedetaghel7anx, *A Yunesit'in and Xeni Gwet'in Project.*

Chapter 29

1 Alice William, personal communication, 2022. One of Norman Setah's sons, who is fluent in Chilcotin, told Alice that his father, Norman Setah, an elder now passed on, relayed to him that a group of Spanish conquistadores came to the Big Creek area in the West Chilcotin and were killed by the Tŝilhqot'in.
2 Steve Arstad, "Similkameen legend challenges notion fur traders were first Europeans to set foot in south-central BC," *Penticton INFO news.ca*, April 23, 2016. infotel.ca/newsitem/similkameen-legend-challenges-notion-fur-traders-were-first-europeans-to-set-foot-in-south-central-bc/it29759. Accessed April 2022.

3 N.L. Barlee, *Similkameen: The Pictograph Country* (Big Country Books, 1978).

Chapter 30

1 Taylor et al., "Early dispersal."
2 E.G. Cothran, email to W.P. McCrory, May 10, 2022.
3 Taylor et al., "Early dispersal."
4 Tim Stephens, "A horse is a horse, of course, of course—except when it isn't," *UC Santa Cruz Newscenter*, November 28, 2017. news.ucsc.edu/2017/11/ancient-horse.html
5 P.D. Heintzman, G.D. Zazula, R.D. MacPhee, E. Scott, J.A. Cahill, B.K. McHorse, J.D. Kapp, M. Stiller, M. J. Wooller, L. Orlando, J. Southon, D.G. Froese and B. Shapiro, "A new genus of horse from Pleistocene North America," *eLife* 6:e29944, 2017. doi.org/10.7554/eLife.29944
6 L. Bourgeon, A. Burke and T. Higham, "Earliest human presence in North America dated to last glacial maximum. New radiocarbon dates from Bluefish Caves, Canada." *PLoS One* 12(1): e00169486, 2017. journals.plos.org/plosone/article?id=10.1371/journal.pone.0169486
7 C. Bidal, "Investigating Ice Age America's Ancient Abattoir," *Hakai magazine*, March 2, 2022. hakaimagazine.com/news/investigating-ice-age-americans-ancient-abattoir/
8 Smith, Nabas oral literature documentation.
9 Teit, *Mythology of the Thompson Indians.*
10 C. Richard Harington, "Vertebrates of the last interglaciation in Canada: A review, with new data," *Géographie physique et Quaternaire*, vol. 44, no. 3, 1990, pp. 375–387. www.erudit.org/revue/GPQ/1990/v44/n3/032837ar.pdf. Accessed January 1, 2016.
11 Tŝilhqot'in knowledge keepers Alice and Norman William found what they believe to be a horse hoof-print preserved in bedrock near a road towards Little Fish Lake. Another Tŝilhqot'in elder, who wished to remain anonymous, told Alice William of

another place where there are horse-hoof prints preserved in stone. Alice William, personal communication.

12 Vickers, *Tŝilhqot'in Nation v. British Columbia*, 2007 BCSC 1700.

Chapter 31

1 Buffalo Bill Centre of the West, *Unbroken Spirit: The Wild Horse in the American Landscape* (Boulder, CO: Roberts Rinehart, 1999).
Also www.bbhc.org/unbrokenSpirit/evolution_1.cfm

2 Donovan, "Ancient DNA found."

3 J.F. Kirkpatrick and P.M. Fazio, "Wild Horses as Native North American Wildlife," the Science and Conservation Center, ZooMontana, Billings, MT, 2010. www.scribd.com/document/108754124/Wild-Horses-As-Native-North-American-Wildlife#. Accessed May 22, 2015.

4 C.C. Downer, "The horse and burro as positively contributing returned natives in North America," *American Journal of Life Sciences*, Vol. 2, No. 1, 2014: pp. 5–23.

5 US National Park Service, Hagerman Fossil Beds, National Monument, Idaho. nps.gov/hafo/learn/nature/fossils.htm. Accessed July 14, 2022.

6 Ruth Gruhn, *The Archaeology of Wilson Butte Cave, South-Central Idaho*, Pocatello: Idaho State College Museum Occasional Papers No. 6, 1961.

7 Ruth Gruhn, "Two Early Radiocarbon Dates from the Lower Levels of Wilson Butte Cave, South-Central Idaho," *Tebiwa* 8:57, 1965.

8 K.A. Murphey, "The Price of a Horse: Hoof Prints on and near the Snake River Plains (AD 1690–AD 2008)," *Bruneau Desert Yacht Club Report* #2, 2008, Castleford, Idaho.

9 R. Ludvigsen, *Deep Time and Ancient Life in the Columbia Basin*, copyright 1999, Royal British Columbia Museum.

10 Ludvigsen, *Deep Time and Ancient Life.*

11 Harington, "Vertebrates of the last interglaciation."

12 Heintzman, "A new genus of horse."

13 John J. Clague and Brent C. Ward, "Pleistocene Glaciation of British Columbia," *Developments in Quaternary Science*, December 2011. Illustration adapted from Figure 44.4, with permission.

Chapter 32

1 Beringian Research Notes, No. 21, "Legend to Reality: The Story of the Whitestone Mammoth," Yukon Tourism and Culture, 2008. yukon.ca/sites/yukon.ca/files/tc/tc-research-note-whitestone-mammoth-2008.pdf

2 The woolly mammoth was a relatively small, compact elephant only 3 to 4 metres tall, with a massive head, long tusks and short legs with cushioned feet that were well adapted to living in Arctic habitats of snow and ice. Thick hair, covering their entire body, helped them survive harsh conditions. The legend of the Whitestone mammoth relayed by Charlie Peter Charlie and permission to use his story in this book were approved by the Vuntut Gwitchin Heritage Committee in February 2023.

Chapter 33

1 Dan Flores, *American Serengeti: The Last Big Animals of the Great Plains* (Lawrence, KS: University Press of Kansas, 2017).

2 Rick Hildebrand, project coordinator, Highland Valley Feral Horse Management Plan, email communications, 2021.

3 McCrory, *Preliminary technical review of management of free-roaming ("feral") horses.*

4 A.W. Bailey, D. McCartney, and M. Schellenberg, *Management of Canadian Prairie Rangeland*, 2010.

5 Cothran, *Genetic analysis of the Alberta "Wildie" horse.*

6 McCrory, *Preliminary technical review.*

7 M.M. Kaweck, J.P. Severson, and K.L. Launchbaugh, "Impacts of wild horses, cattle, and wildlife on riparian areas in Idaho," *Rangeland*, 45–52, 2018.

8 C.S. Boyd, K.W. Davies, and G.H. Collins, "Impacts of feral horse use on herbaceous riparian vegetation within a Sagebrush Steppe Ecosystem," *Rangeland Ecology & Management*, Volume 70, Issue 4, 2017, pp. 411–417.

9 R.E. Salter and R.J. Hudson, "Range relationships of feral horses with wild ungulates and cattle in Western Alberta," *Journal of Range Management* 33(4), 1980: 266–271.

10 B. De Kock, email to Wayne McCrory re: 2015 estimates from province, February 4, 2023

11 McCrory, *Preliminary technical review.*

12 McCrory, *Preliminary technical review.*

13 De Kock, email February 4, 2023.

14 McCrory, *Preliminary technical review.*

15 C. Notzke, *The Wild Horse—Alberta's Heritage Animal*, position paper in support of a bill declaring Alberta's wild horses a provincial heritage animal with associated protection, 2012.

16 C. Downer, report on wild horses and ecosystem in Rocky Mountain Foothills east of Banff National Park and west of Sundre, Alberta (Red Deer River, James River and vicinity), 2015.

17 Maureen Enns, *Wild Horses, Wild Wolves: Legends at Risk at the Foot of the Canadian Rockies* (Victoria, BC: RMB Rocky Mountain Books, 2013).

18 Dawn Dickinson, *Caught in the Spin: The Wild Horses of CFB Suffield* (Calgary, AB: Rain Cloud Publishing, 2009).

19 B.G. Weerstra and K.E. Wilkinson, *Range Assessment of the Northeast Quadrant of the Canadian Forces Base Suffield*, prepared for Department of National Defence, 1993.

20 Dickinson, *Caught in the Spin.*

21 edmonton.ctvnews.ca/herd-of-8-000-wild-elk-too-far-gone-to-control-rancher-demands-mass-cull-1.2052516/comments-7.567447/comments-7.567447
22 Dickinson, *Caught in the Spin.*
23 McLoughlin Lab in Population Ecology, Sable Island Horse Project. mcloughlinlab.ca/lab/research-2/research. Accessed April 20, 2022.
24 The "reserve" status is related to an unresolved land claim by the Mi'kmaq Nation, which, until settled, means Sable Island cannot be considered a full national park.
25 B. Freedman, *An ecological and biodiversity assessment of Sable Island*, final report to Parks Canada, 2014.
26 horse-canada.com/magazine/miscellaneous/wild-horses-of-canada-update. Accessed April 20, 2022.
27 Freedman, *An ecological and biodiversity assessment of Sable Island.*
28 "Ecology, Evolution, and Conservation of Sable Island Horses." www.sableislandfriends.ca/ecology-evolution-and-conservation-of-the-sable-island-horses. Accessed April 20, 2022.

Chapter 34

1 Kirkpatrick and Fazio, "Wild Horses as Native North American Wildlife."
2 Patrick Duncan, ed, IUCN/SSC Equid Specialist Group, *Zebras, Asses, and Horses: An Action Plan for the Conservation of Wild Equids* (Gland, Switzerland, and Cambridge, UK: International Union for Conservation of Nature, 1992).
3 Anonymous, Legal Status of Feral Horses in Canada, 2017 (British Columbia, Alberta, Saskatchewan, and Nova Scotia), in file.
4 Anonymous, BC Feral Horses Legal Memo, 2022, in file.
5 Anonymous, Alberta Feral Horses Legal Memo, 2017, in file.

INDEX

Note: Page numbers in **bold** refer to photographs or illustrations.